# THE SUSTAINMENT BATTLE STAFF
# & MILITARY DECISION MAKING PROCESS (MDMP) GUIDE

For Brigade Support Battalions,
Sustainment Brigades,
and Combat Sustainment Support Battalions

Version
**2.0**

Dr. John M. Menter, COL (RET)

ISBN: 0615697933
ISBN-13: 9780615697932

# TABLE OF CONTENTS

✩✩✩

## BRIEFING FORMATS

## OTHER GUIDANCE, TERMS, & PLANNING CONSIDERATIONS

This Guide is designed to assist the logistics planner at any level from the newly transformed Brigade Support Battalions to the Sustainment Brigade, to move through the Military Decision Making Process (MDMP) from receipt of a Higher Headquarters mission, analysis of the mission, development of courses of action, completion of operations orders/plans, preparation and execution of briefings to decision-makers, and continuous planning through current and into future operations.

The techniques adopted in this guide and used throughout the process have been developed through several years of experience working the MDMP. They have been adjusted and tweaked over time and are in use with various sustainment organizations as well as the emerging guidance published with ATTP 5-0.1, ADP/FM 3-0, and the newly revised FM 5-0 with Change 1. It is expected that this guide is a living document, subject to frequent, necessary changes as doctrine, techniques, and experiences change.

As a final note, when the term "Brigade Support Battalion" is used, it also applicable to the Aviation Support Battalion (ASB) – the sustainment structure associated with Combat Aviation Brigades.

- Editor

*This Book is dedicated to*
*The Logistician's Logistician*
*My Wife "Jeanette" who*
*without which this work*
*would not have been possible*

*The Author would also like to express his sincerest appreciation and thanks to the following units whose assistance made the orginal work possible: LTC Jody Dew and the Staff of the 751st CSSB. LTC Jim Moscarello and the staff of the 158th CSSB. CSM George Holland and Staff of the 230th Sustainment Brigade, and LTC Gregory Cornell and the Staff of the 1050th Transportation Battalion. Last and by no means least, my sincerest thanks and appreciation to Ben Terrell, whose inputs at the "dead of night" keep the Author on course and the replenishment mission on track.*

*"The more I see war, the more I realize how it all depends on administration and supply... It takes little skill or imagination to see where you would like your army to be and when; it takes much knowledge and hard work to know where you can place your forces and whether you can maintain them. A real knowledge of supply and movement factors must be the basis of every leader's plan; only then can he know how and when to take risks with those factors, and battles are won only by taking risks."*

*Napoleon Bonaparte*

A.C.P Wavell <u>Speaking Generally</u>, (London, 1946), page 78-9.

# WHY DO WE NEED A CSS MDMP GUIDE?

★ ★ ★

*"If Logistics were easy – It would be called Tactics"*
Famous Fort Leavenworth Saying

*"Forget Logistics and you lose."*
LTG Frederick M. Franks

Although the military decision making process (MDMP) is at times a cumbersome and time consuming process, the benefits of performing MDMP to standard far outweigh the time and energy consumed participating in the process. Planning success at the Brigade and higher staff level requires sufficient time to perform MDMP, having the right personnel involved in the process, and coming to the table with the necessary tools to effectively integrate the war fighting functional areas (WFFA) into the overall plan. This is especially important for the combat service support (CSS) "Sustainment warfighting functional area", specifically for the Brigade Combat Team (BCT) and its organic Brigade Support Battalions, which now under transformation has a robust Support Plans Officer logistics "planning staff". How well the Sustainment WFFA is integrated into the MDMP is a direct function of having the right personnel with the appropriate tools participating throughout the process, or at a minimum, during key events. This guide will assist the sustainment planner whether the Brigade S-4, Support Operations

Officer (SOO)/Support Plans Officer (SPO), or the Battalion S-2/3. In any event, integration of the Sustainment/CSS WFFA in the Brigade/CSSB or Sustainment Brigade MDMP is essential to ensuring current, mission specific, and future support requirements are identified. In addition it is crucial to allocating resources to accomplish the specified and implied tasks, and synchronizing key logistics events with the brigade's course of action.

"Sustainers" as logisticians are now referred to as, accomplish this planning in several ways, but they must come to the MDMP with the available tools. These tools include (but are limited to) personnel and logistics estimates (using the Logistics Estimate Worksheet, OPLOG Planner, or historical data), a draft Para 4, Annex F, and a Brigade/Division Concept of Support (CoS), and sustainment (aka CSS) synchronization matrix. With these tools, participants have the capability to understand the brigade's current situation and to analyze/adjust future requirements based on a complete picture of the logistics battlefield. Sustainers must ensure that the MDMP methodology includes a discussion of sustainment operations throughout the depth of the battlespace.

The MDMP timeline is one of the biggest challenges sustainment planners must overcome because of the possibility of multiple key events happening simultaneously. Here, the Brigade XO must deconflict critical events to maximize participation by his sustainment planning staff. Such events include sustainment rehearsals (if conducted), Sustainment/Movement Control Work Group Battle Rhythm meetings, daily operational meetings, and future planning cycles. Either of these conducted without a "Sustainer" will only spell disaster, usually at a key event or time. Remember, under modularity, your "margin of error" is now razor thin.

Finally, let's address some of the misconceptions Sustainers might have regarding the MDMP process. Most BSB/CSSB or Sustainment Brigade Commanders, SPOs and BCT S-4s argue that it is just too hard to accomplish current operations as well as plan future missions. Most believe having an assistant S4 planner at the brigade Main Command Post (MCP) is sufficient to plan and synchronize logistics support. The belief is that these planners have a rudimentary understanding of modular sustainment functions and their roles in COA development and analysis. There is also a common belief by many brigade sustainers that a brigade plan is merely a guide for how the BSB will support the BCT. Once the BSB receives the BCT order, they will perform their own MDMP and determine how they will "really" support the mission. In addition, most logisticians believe that their ability to improvise mitigates the risk of not participating in the MDMP. Finally, in the absence of active participation in MDMP, sustainers always have the "CSS rehearsal" to put the plan together. But what happens if the rehearsal isn't conducted (as we all know is what usually occurs....)

Conducting the Sustainment MDMP is essential in integrating the Sustainment War Fighting Functional Area (WFFA) into the organizations plan and for ensuring a synchronized and supportable course of action. Successful integration is a result of having the right personnel, available tools, correct MDMP doctrine & methodology, and synchronized timeline throughout the process. If this guide can assist sustainment planners in accomplishing this process, then it has accomplished its intent and mission.

*– Dr. John M. Menter, CPL, Nov 2008*

## CHAPTER 1

# ARMY TRANSFORMATION & THE BIRTH OF MODULARITY

★ ★ ★

**1. Background**. Beginning shortly after the advent of September 11th, 2001, the US Army began a complete reorganization of its structure in light of the changes to the world brought about by the end of the Cold War to create a force that was *light enough* in order to be rapidly transported to any part of the world, *yet heavy enough* to withstand enemy armor heavy counterattack operations. Army Transformation initially started in the mid 1990's as "*Force XXI*", these changes and reorganizations gained momentum as the US Army began offensive operations within Afghanistan (Operation "*Enduring Freedom*" – or *OEF*) and Iraq (Operation "*Iraqi Freedom*").

*"When the army is landed, the business is half done"*
- Maj. Gen James Wolf at the Battle of Quebec, 1759

**a. The Strategic Army Corps**. Ever since the late 1950's, Army planners (in conjunctions with their US Air Forces counterparts) envisioned the creation of a "*Strategic Army Corps or STRAC*" comprised of a Corps like structure that could be transported to hotspots anywhere in the world within a week. In time STRAC was a designation given to the <u>XVIII Airborne</u>

<u>Corps</u> at Fort Bragg, North Carolina. The designation was, in reality, the assignment of an additional mission rather than a true designation. The additional mission was to provide a flexible strike capability that could deploy worldwide on short notice without declaration of an emergency. The 4th Infantry Division (Mech) (then stationed at Fort Lewis, WA), and the 101st Airborne Division at Fort Campbell, Kentucky, were designated as STRAC's first-line divisions, while the 1st Infantry Division (Mech) at Fort Riley, Kansas, and the 82nd Airborne Division at Fort Bragg were to provide backup in the event of general war. The 5th Logistical Command (later inactivated), also at Fort Bragg, would provide the corps with logistics support, while Fort Bragg's XVIII Airborne Corps Artillery would control artillery units.

Although STRAC's mission was to provide an easily deployable force for use in a limited war or other emergency, its ability to deploy overseas was limited by airlift constraints. Without the declaration of a national emergency allowing DoD unconstrained use of the US flagged airlines of the Civil Reserve Air Fleet (CRAF), the required lift assets would not be released to support a STRAC deployment. The concept of STRAC was tested to a limited basis during the Berlin Crisis (1961) with the deployment of the 3rd Armored Cavalry Regiment to Germany within 30 days, and was ready for full implementation during the Cuban Missile Crisis (1962). Ultimately STRAC died a quiet death in the late 1960's with the XVIII Airborne Corps continuing to assume the role of a rapid response force for the duration of the 20th Century.

**b. Exercise REFORGER** (from REturn of FORces to GERmany). The REFORGER exercises were designed to prove U.S. Army's ability to move large conventional military forces rapidly from the continental United States to Central Europe in the event of a conflict with the Soviet Union. The first exercise was conducted in 1967, when due to the increasing pressures and cost of the Vietnam War, the United States Army announced plans to withdraw 28,000 troops (roughly two divisions) from Europe in 1968. To demonstrate its continued commitment to NATO, the US agreed to a large scale force deployment of not less than three brigades of a single division to Europe in an annual exercise. Thus was born REFORGER, which both tested the ability of conventional forces to fight in a conventional war scenario and demonstrated American determination.

REFORGER was not merely for show—in the event of a conflict, it would be the actual plan to strengthen the NATO presence in Europe. In the instance of armed conflict within central Europe, it would have been referred to as **Operation REFORGER**. Important components in REFORGER included the Military Airlift Command, the Military Sealift Command, and the Civil Reserve Air Fleet.

While REFORGER clearly demonstrated American resolve and support for NATO, it wasn't until REFORGER '83 that an American Division (1st Cavalry Division) became the "First unit to train as a 9,000 man division-size element in Northern Europe." This was the first U.S. unit deployment to Holland and Northern Germany since World War II. By April 1993, the last REFORGER was undertaken (a mere shadow of the original), conducted largely as computer-driven logistical exercise. This last exercise included only a portion of one unit from the United States.

For REFORGERs training value, it became clear that extensive preparation of pre-positioned equipment and stocks within Europe was required before the arrival of any rapidly deployable US force. The US Navy's Military Sealift Command's (and to a lesser extent the US Air Force's Military Airlift Command) ability to rapidly move large (and heavy) forces from the United States to Europe (or any where within the world for that matter) remained largely untested until August 1990 with the commencement of *Operation "Desert Shield."*

*A US M60A1 tank moves through a village in West Germany,*
*as part of REFORGER '82 Exercise*

**c. Army Division 86, Army of Excellence (AOE), and** *"Force*
*XXI"*. At the conclusion of the Vietnam War and shortly after
the Arab-Israeli "Yom Kippur War", then Chief of Staff of the
Army, General Creighton Abrams, chaired a board of senior
officials to focus on the next series of key weapons systems
that the Army would require to fight future foes. Out of
this was born the M1 *"Abrams"* Main Battle Tank, the M2/3
*"Bradley"* Infantry Fighting Vehicle, the AH-64 *"Apache"* Attack
Helicopter, and the MIM-104 *"Patriot"* Air Defense System,
and the M270 Multiple Launched Rocket System (MLRS),
with all being fielded with the decade of the late 1970's and
early 1980's. With the fielding of new systems coupled with
a revised doctrine dismissing the former embraced "Active
Defense" which had been the cornerstone of tactical operations within NATO, change was in the air and was coined
"Army (or Division) '86.

In short, within the Division 86 heavy divisions, much of the
structure of which survived into the early 1980s Army, numbered approximately 20,000 men. Divisions were organized as
6 tank battalions and 4 mechanized infantry battalions in its

armor version, 5 and 5 in its mechanized infantry form. It added a significant new component in an air cavalry attack brigade (complete with the division's aviation assets and cavalry squadron), and it expanded the division artillery into batteries of 8 howitzers. It departed the World War II and ROAD triangular principle by strengthening each maneuver battalion from 3 line companies to 4 and adding TOW missile companies and other changes. Within the Division Support Commands (DISCOM), the Maintenance, Transportation, Quartermaster, and Medical Battalions were reconfigured into three Forward Support Battalions (each with Supply & Transport, Maintenance, and Medical Company) and a Main Support Battalion. These organizational changes could only work by adding additional combat service support structure to the organization. Before long, tactical units became "too fat" for use in a global contingency outside the plains of Germany.

By the early to mid 1980's, it also became apparent that pre Army Division 86 existing unit Tables of Equipment (commonly referred to as a "TOE") were insufficient to accommodate the logistical requirements needed to sustain readiness. Typical of this insufficiency were US armor battalions and cavalry squadrons equipped with the new M-1 tank. Fuel consumption quadrupled and soon overwhelmed the capacity of the unit's support platoon. Newer (and more complex) systems required more extensive maintenance organizations and sophisticated mechanics. Changes were not simply of a logistical nature – newer systems had an impact on doctrine as well as the Army began adaptation of its just release *Airland Battle* concept. These newly fielded systems scheduled for production and fielding in the 1980s presented an even greater leap ahead in combat power as demonstrated during Brigade Combat Team rotations at the Army's National Training Center, Fort Irwin, California.

The Army of Excellence (or "*AOE*") model followed shortly after as the US Army's effort to remedy this situation by the design and creation of a new, strategically deployable light infantry division limited in strength to approximately 10,000 personnel, globally deployable in approximately 500 airlift sorties.

Creation of the AOE light infantry division embodied a noteworthy turn in the history of Army tactical organization. With it, the Army fashioned a division for use primarily in the contingency world, with only a collateral mission for reinforcement of heavy forces and only then where terrain and circumstance called for it. Ordinarily it would fight in components as part of an integrated heavy/light or light/heavy force. The light infantry division gave the Army a new and necessary flexibility. Force structure decisions followed which converted two non-mechanized infantry divisions to the new type and added two more in the Active Army and one in the reserve components for a total of five light infantry divisions. Army division totals in the AOE reorganization went from 16 Active Army and 8 Army National Guard to 18 and 10, respectively.

This organization, while functional for the time being, did have its problems. Primary criticisms of the light infantry division were that it was too light, lacked tactical mobility, long range artillery, a roust anti-armor capability, and that its likely adversaries in the increasingly heavily armed third world would out gun, outmaneuver, and defeat it. This was clearly demonstrated at the Fort Irwin high desert training area in March 1983 during an exercise when the 40th Infantry Division (Mech) (California Army National Guard) overran a newly deployed brigade of the 82nd Airborne Division. But in the context of the more powerful corps to which it belonged, the AOE heavy division found general acceptance. There was recognition that the corps together with its divisions retained, as a unit, very strong combat power and that it constituted the right doctrinal answer.

Accompanying the debate of the light division was evolving support for the utility of heavy/light or light/heavy mixes of forces. Such mixes made good tactical sense where mission, enemy, terrain, troops, and time available - the "METT-T" considerations of doctrine - dictated the need and the wisdom of mixed forces. From the logistician's point of view, it was a nightmare, with CSS units insufficiently equipped to hand non-routine unit attachments. Heavy units lacked transport support for attached light infantry, while light infantry units could not substantially maintain attached armor/mech units. It was often said within the light infantry community that AOE was "nothing more than the Army's turning a soldier into a pack mule."

In August 1990, Iraq invaded its neighbor Kuwait. This aggression prompted an immediate response from the United Nations of which the United States took the lead in assembling coalition forces in Saudi Arabia to defend the Saudi's and eject Iraqi forces from Kuwait. Within a short time, it became readily clear that the concept of rapidly moving US forces from the continental United States to the Middle East "ala REFORGER" was broken beyond repair. Instead of a rapid response of heavy forces beyond deployment of the XVIII Airborne Corps (*Operation Desert Shield*), it would take almost six months to generate sufficient combat power to begin *Operation Desert Storm.* The weight problem of these heavy forces envisioned to fight in central Europe had come home to roost.

In 1993, the US Army's Training and Doctrine Command (TRADOC) had written a new, more versatile, fundamental operational doctrine to fit the new strategic circumstances of a smaller, primarily U.S. based force projection Army to reflect the redraw of forces from Germany and the overall draw down of the US Army in the wake of the Cold War ending . That design project, titled Force XXI, began on 8 March 1994 when Chief of Staff of the Army, General Gordon R. Sullivan, directed the start of a major campaign effort to create a new and highly effective fighting force for the 21st century. Progressing toward incremental realization at the year 2000, the Force XXI redesign was the last of the major operational Army reorganizations of the 20th century and would supersede the Army of Excellence which had been implemented in the mid-1980s. It was the first force redesign effort in which a full panoply of newly-emergent, computer-driven constructive and virtual simulation methods, equipment, and software were joined to actual live field simulation to test and analyze new military unit designs. In addition, the multi-year Force XXI design effort was the first to invent and embody for those fighting units a linked, instantaneous common operating picture and situational awareness of the close and distant events of the unfolding battle. "Digitization" was the rubric given this revolutionary emerging capability.

One of the key structure changes of Force XXI was the creation of "*Forward Support Companies*" out of the combat arms maneuver battalions and attaching them to the Brigade's Forward Support Battalions. Here, the battalion's Support and Maintenance Platoons were pulled out of the unit and combined into a separate structure acting as a single unit. Combat Arms battalions shrank from four companies to three, along with the removal of a corresponding service support slice from the Headquarters Company.

FORCE XXI was the structural organization largely in place throughout most of the US Army as it entered the 21$^{st}$ Century. For all it's innovations in digital Command and Control (C$^2$), leveraged automation systems, and logistics support restructuring, FORCE XXI was still a large, heavy division-centric force that still lacked strategic deploy ability.

**d. Army Transformation & Modularity**. Two major but entirely separate actions occurred at the close of the 20$^{th}$ Century that would ultimately intertwine to undermine the FORCE XXI structure. The first was the publication of a book in 1996 by Colonel Douglas MacGregor named "*Breaking the Phalanx: A New Design for Landpower in the 21st Century1.*" Here, MacGregor basically wrote that with tech-

---

1    Breaking the Phalanx: A New Design for Landpower in the 21st Century by Douglas A. Macgregor, Center for Strategic and International Studies (Washington, D.C.) Published by Greenwood Publishing Group, 1997, ISBN 0275957942, 9780275957940

nology and resourcing, today's maneuver brigades would dominate the battlefield with division's reduced to simple Command and Control (C[2]) Centers (after all, this is how the Israeli Army fights with their brigades). Massive divisional structures would give way to smaller, more agile (and easily transportable) Brigade Combat Teams. Needless to say, MacGregor's thesis was met with mixed reviews within the Army community, much of which still dominated by the Cold War Generals in charge. But in 2000, George Bush was elected President and with him came a new Secretary of Defense - Donald Rumsfeld. One of Rumsfeld's first orders of business was the restructuring of the US Army to a more agile, easier deployable, brigade-centric force to distant theaters within the world (the lessons of the ill fated 55 day deployment an Apache[2] Attack Helicopter battalion from the 11th Aviation Brigade in Germany to Albania in

---

2    Planning for Task Force Hawk didn't start until March 30th 1999; even though, the planning for Operation Allied Force had begun in the winter of 1998. Gen Clark and Admiral James O. Ellis, discussed how to utilize the Apaches to augment the Air Force assets posed to strike in 4 days. The Army's planners would be strapped for time to put together a plan to deploy a mission that had never been employed by an AH-64 Apache unit Instead of supporting ground troops the Apaches would be supporting Air Force missions. Gen. Clark's vision for the unit was to destroy the Yugoslavian units stationed in Kosovo supporting the Serbian police force. The Yugoslavian units were not formed in their typical company or battalion sized formations but rather spread out through the countryside. This made acquiring the targets and relaying the information to bomber units who couldn't spot them easily. It was projected that the Apache units would be able to identify and eliminate these targets more efficiently, due to their effectiveness during Operation Desert Storm. By March 22, 1999, Army planners finished with the initial plans for operation. These plans projected that the forces would be deployed to Macedonia, but the Macedonian government refused to allow offensive NATO operations to be speared from their country. "Army planners in Germany learned the mission would probably be cancelled on the Friday before Easter." Many soldiers would be given their first day off in weeks; however, on April 3rd, Gen. Clark decided to deploy the task force. It was announced on April 4th, by the Department of Defense that Task Force Hawk would be deployed to Albania to assist in Operation Allied Force. The original size of the task force was estimated at 2000 but had to be increased due to the lack of force protection that was present in Macedonia.

support of Operation *"Allied Force"* in Kosovo, April 1999 bore this out). It was fate that these two personalities would meet as philosophical equals in regards to Army reorganization. Transformation gained additional momentum in Oct 2001 when Army Planners in planning Operation *Enduring Freedom,* struggled to find a suitable, yet adequate (hence modular) structure to support US – SOF operations in Afghanistan in the wake of the September 11th World Trading Center bombing by Al Qaeda. By 2004, a new (and radical) unit organizational structure was at last developed and released that would use the best of FORCE XXI, but focus at the Brigade-centric level, thus giving arise to what is today referred to as "Army Transformation."

Under Army Transformation, traditional divisional brigades are reorganized into Brigade Combat Teams[3], designed to operate without outside support for three days with only supplies and fuel aboard their vehicles when they roll away from the aircraft delivering them to an area of operations.

Key to the success of transformed Brigade Combat teams required their deployment capability to go anywhere within the world within 96 hours, a full division within 120 hours, and five divisions on the ground within 30 days. Every piece of equipment belonging to the newly formed Brigade Combat Team had to be transportable within either a C-130 or C-17 aircraft, and required minimal RSO (Reception, Staging, & Onward Movement) support. From this point, the Brigade Combat Team would leave the Aerial Point of Embarkation (APOE) to operate without any further support for a minimum

---

3    The idea of a Brigade-centric force was not uncommon – most divisional brigades undergoing a combat training rotation at the National Training Center, Fort Irwin, would add addition transport & maintenance (from the base division's Main Support Battalion), a military intelligence company (for the division's MI Battalion), signal assets (from the division's Signal Battalion), and so on, often swelling up from a base strength of 1,700 to 4,000 soldiers per rotation.

of three days. Additionally, BCTs are designed for field-level maintenance self-sufficiency with no reliance on EAB field maintenance support.

Along with the reorganization of Active/Reserve Component divisional combat brigades, the ARNG Separate Enhanced Brigades (eSBs) were also transformed into modular Brigade Combat Teams (See Fig 1 below). As of this writing, there are fielded:

AC: 33 Div Bdes organizing into *42 BCTs (19 Heavy, 17 Inf/ Light, 6 Stryker)

ARNG: 23 Div Bdes + 15 eSBs into 28 BCTs (6 Heavy, 21 Inf/ Light, 1 Stryker)

* 6 More BCTs are scheduled for fielding TY09 – 13.

# Standard Brigade Combat Teams

*Figure 1. Brigade Combat Team Organization and Structure*

## 2. What has changed under "Transformation" for the Logistician?

Over the past decade since the inception of Army Transformation and Modularity, many organizational structural designs and naming conventions (UEx, UEy to name a few) have taken place. While the Operational side (Army, Corps and Divisions) remain in hierarchy similar to their past counterparts, the logistics redesign is revised, largely to reduce layering, redundancy, while expanding capability. (See Figure 2).

*Figure 2. The New Look of Sustainment Support*

First item to note is the elimination of the Corps/Area Support Groups, and the Corps/Division Support Commands (COSCOM/DISCOM), transferring and realigning these unit capabilities into the new "Sustainment Brigade" (More on the

Sustainment Brigade capabilities below). Per Para 1-8, ATP 4-93[4], the role of the Sustainment Brigade is defined as follows:

> *"The sustainment brigades are extremely flexible headquarters elements, capable of providing mission command to a wide variety of subordinate organizations during unified land operations. The sustainment brigade is designed to provide mission 5command of theater opening, theater distribution, and sustainment within an assigned area of operation. The sustainment brigade is task organized with a mix of functional and multifunctional battalions based on their location and assigned missions. It can provide support to any Army formation and can also, under certain circumstances, operate as a joint logistics command."*

Additionally, the old AOE Theater-Army Command (TAACOM) is replaced with a more streamline Theater Sustainment Command (TSC)[5]. To assist the TSC Commander, the Expeditionary Support Command (ESC) is created to assist in the coordination and conduct of distribution operations within the theater/area of responsibly.

Breaking this down further, Figure 3 & 4 depicts roles and responsibility migration of material management functions from AOE to Modular structures.

---

4    Feb 2012 Final Draft

5    TSCs may also be known as SC(T), while ESCs are sometimes referred to as SC(E)., however neither nomenclature are in use today.

*Figure 3. Migration of Logistics Functions AOE to Modular*

The total migration of material management sustainment functions from AOE to transformed – modular sustainment structures is outlined below in Figure 3.

## Materiel Management Functions
### From the Army of Excellence (AOE) to the Modular Force

| AOE | Category | Modular Force |
|---|---|---|
| • Property Book Management<br>  – Division: DMMC<br>  – Non-Division: Embedded PBO at Brigade<br>• Asset Visibility: DMMC/CMMC/TMMC | Class VII<br>Property<br>Accountability<br>Asset Visibility | • Property Accountability: BDEs (BCTs and SPT BDEs) with embedded PBOs<br>• Asset Visibility: Division/Corps/Army Service Component Command (ASCC) G–4 |
| • DMMC, CMMC, TMMC<br>  – Overlapping redundancy | General Supplies<br>Class I, Water,<br>Class IIIB | • TSC, ESC (if utilized), SUST BDE DMC manages stocks<br>• BCT requirements sent to TSC/ESC DMC through supporting SUS BDE |
| • DMMC (DAO): Coordinates and controls Class V use within the Division<br>• CMMC: Managed Corps CSAs/ASPs<br>• TMMC: Managed Theater TSA/ASPs<br>• TMMC ICW ASCC G–3: Establish CSRs | Class V | • BSB BAO: Coord BCT requirements<br>• Div/Corps G–4: Planning and oversight<br>• TSC/ESC/SUST BDE: Manage stocks, issues MROs to CSSBs ASAs<br>• TSC ICW ASCC G–3: Establishes CSRs/Stockage Obj/NICP requisitions |
| • DMMC/CMMC/TMMC with duplication at Division/Corps/Theater G–4 | Maintenance/<br>Readiness<br>Management | • BSB: maint mgmt/readiness for its BCT<br>• Division/Corps G–4: Monitors readiness information for CDR, establishes priorities, write plans/orders |
| • Managed by hierarchal MMCs (DMMC, CMMC, TMMC)<br>• Each level conducted manager reviews with SARSS–2 boxes<br>• SARSS data communicated to hierarchal boxes (SARSS–1 to SARSS–2A/D to SARSS–2A/C) | Demand<br>Supported<br>Class II, IIIP,<br>IV, IX | • SUST BDE single face to the customer<br>• Overall centralized management at the TSC/ASC or ESC (if utilized)<br>• Time sensitive RIC GEO functions pushed to SUST BDEs as required<br>• SARSS–1 data communicated to CTASC directly |

*Figure 4. Migration of Material Management Functions*

Combat Sustainment Support Battalions (CSSBs) are an inherent new structure functioning as the workhorse of the Sustainment Brigade. Developed as an outgrowth of the AOE Corps Support Battalions, CSSB are multifunctional in nature with no two CSSB tasked organized alike. Per Para 4-10, FM 4-93.2 (Sustainment Brigade):

> "*CSSB is a tailored, multifunctional logistics organization. It is a flexible and responsive team that executes logistics throughout the depth of their assigned AO. The CSSB subordinate elements may consist of functional companies providing supplies, ammunition, fuel, water, transportation, cargo transfer, MA, maintenance, field services, and HR management. This framework enables*

*the employment of a tailored logistics unit capable of adapting quickly to changing tactical conditions. The CSSB works through the sustainment brigade in concert with the TSC for logistics operations to effectively support the maneuver commander.*

The sustainment support structure found within the transformed – modular brigade is the Brigade Support Battalion (BSB). One of the single greatest impacts on the transformed brigade size organizations was the placement of both a network support (i.e. signal) unit within the Brigade's Special Troops Battalion and a dedicated logistical support structure – the Brigade Support Battalion (BSB). While remarkable that this capability is now found within these newly transformed Brigade structures – not all BSBs are alike. (see Chapter 2 on BSBs)

The creation of the BSB addresses an issue plaguing divisional Brigade Commander's since the creation of the Forward Support Battalions in the mid 1980's; who owns the unit and who is the Brigade Logistician? Followers of the FM 63 series will tell you the FSB is owned by the DISCOM Commander and that the FSB Cdr is the Brigade Logistician. Maneuver Commanders will cite the FM 71-123, counter claiming that the Brigade Commander owns the FSB and the Brigade S-4 is the Brigade Logistician. Under transformation, the BSB is established as an integral component of the Brigade with its commander as the Brigade's Sustainment Operator. Like it's FORCE XXI predecessor, BCT & Support Brigade BSBs come with a Forward Support Company for each of the Brigade's organic battalions

On a final note regarding transformed sustainment and support to organizations, it is important to note that:

1) There is one TSC assigned per theater AOR. All TSCs are aligned with a corresponding Army Service Component Command (ASCC).

2) Sustainment Brigades work for either the TSC or the ESC (or SC(E)) Commander. They are not assigned to Corps or Divisions (hence why they own their own Distinctive Unit Insignia – DUI). There are insufficient Sustainment Brigades to dedicate one per Division; further it would be a highly inefficient use of the distribution assets within them and would overall disrupt the Sustainment Command's *supply distribution chain.*

3) There is no rule of allocation of Sustainment Brigades required to support a Corps or Division. Allocation is based on requirements and workload. Concurrently, subordinate support battalions are organized with any combination of subordinate units form the force pool.

4) Medical organizations are designed and tailored to support the force. They are not subordinate to the Sustainment Brigade, but rather to the Medical Deployment Support Command (MDSC) via the locally assigned Medical Brigade. Human Resource – HR (Personnel and Finance) units are also modular configured and scalable based on METT-TC.

5) All modular transformed brigades possess a Brigade Support Battalion[6]. The same cannot be said for "functional" (i.e. Engineer, Military Police, Chemical, Ordnance/EOD, & ADA) brigades. Support relations will need to be established for these structures. Most if not all sustainment (formerly known as "Combat Service Support") battalions work for a Sustainment Brigade. The only exception is the Brigade Support Battalion.

---

6    The exception here is the Battlefield Surveillance Brigade which possesses a Brigade Support Company (BSC) in lieu of a Brigade Support Battalion. Within the Combat Aviation Brigade, the BSB is referred to as the Aviation Support Brigade or "ASB".

7) Most maneuver (formerly known as "Combat Arms") and maneuver support (formerly known as "Combat Support) battalions have attached Forward Support Companies. Military Police, EOD, Civil Affairs/Psyops & SOF battalions do not. Like functional brigades, support relations need to be established for these structures.

**3. Changes in Latitudes, Changes in Attitudes – the revision of Combat Service Support into the new Sustainment Doctrine.**

As CSS structure transformed from the rapidly obsolete AOE into modular formations (see Figure 3 above), it was inevitable that CSS doctrine would need to change as well to reflect the leveraged capabilities inherent with the creation of the new distribution-based units/nodes and the employment of logistics automation.

*Figure 5 – Evolution of Military Logistics*

One goal of a transformed logistics[7] system is to eliminate reliance on stockpiles located at each echelon from the Brigade to the Theater level (the so called massed based "Iron Mountains"). These stockpiles are vulnerable to enemy attack, difficult to move, and reduce the tactical commander's flexibility.

*Operation Shield/Desert Storm* typified the difficulties associated with the length of time required to assemble the required amount of supplies to support 3rd US Army's offensive operations into Kuwait[8]. Support to the Persian Gulf provided an example of the problems facing the defense distribution system throughout the 1990s. Although combat performance had been justifiably esteemed across the board, there were significant problems in logistics support. Distribution times were long, variable, and unpredictable, due largely to inefficient processes, clogged ports, and a myriad of other problems. The result was materiel often took more than 35 days to get out of the United States.

The answer would evitable would be found within the civilian sector which had undergone a revolution throughout the late 1980's, creating in distribution based systems, slimming down warehousing operations and replacing it with "velocity management." Thus was born *"Supply-chain" Management* logistics.

What is *Supply-Chain Management?* It is the system relationship among transportation, inventory requirements, warehousing, exterior packaging, materials handling, and some activities or cost centers involved. More important, technological improvements

---

7   A general definition of logistics is "the process of anticipating customer needs and wants; acquiring the capital, material, people, technologies, and information necessary to meet those needs and wants; optimizing the goods-or service-producing network to fulfill customer requests; and utilizing the network to fulfill customer requests in a timely way."

8   As documented in "Moving Mountains – Lessons in Leadership and Logistics from the Gulf War" by LTG (R) William G. Pagonis (Boston, Harvard Business School Press, 1992) ISBN 0-87584-508-8

in inventory management, bar coding, transport tracking allowed for cost saving by reducing warehouse inventory and giving customers the ability to track in bound shipments, allowing for "just-in-time" deliveries.

Put another way, *Supply-Chain Management* can be viewed as a pipeline or conduit for the efficient and effective flow of products, materials, services, information, and financials from the supplier's suppliers through the various intermediate organizations/companies out to the customer's customers or the system of connected logistics networks between the original vendors and the ultimate final customer. By the time the US Armed Forces began to adapt these practices in the late 90's and the beginning of the 21$^{st}$ century, they had been honed to a fine (and efficient) science by such companies as General Motors, Target Stores, nearly all major grocery store chains, and the master practitioner of the supply-chain management concept – Wal-Mart!

How does this apply within the military environment? Distribution in the new logistics system substitutes speed for mass. This transformed logistics system combines situational understanding by way of the Common Operational Picture (COP) and capabilities with efficient delivery systems to form a seamless distribution pipeline. The supply pipeline becomes the warehouse and represents inventory in motion. (Figure 6)

The logistics imperative of increased velocity reduces both organizational and material layering (thus the elimination of the Division and Corps Material Management Centers or "MMCs"). Logisticians control the destination, speed, and volume of the distribution system. With In-Transit Visibility (ITV), Total Asset Visibility (TAV), advanced materiel management, and advanced decision support system technology, logisticians will have access and visibility over all items within the distribution pipeline.

It is this technology that allows logisticians to divert, cross-level, and mass logistics assets anywhere, anytime to support the maneuver commander. Logisticians maintain situational awareness of the battlefield via the Logistics Common Operating Picture, otherwise known as the *"LCOP"*, which greatly facilitates logistics planning and execution.

# Military Distribution Simplified

| **Sustainment** | + | **Movement** | + | **Force Protection** | = | **Distribution** |
|---|---|---|---|---|---|---|
| LOG REPORTING | | TMR/STMR | | Convoy Security Process | | |
| Distro Matrix | | Distro Matrix | | Distro Matrix | | |
| Critical Reports | | Critical Reports | | Critical Reports | | |
| Manifesting | | Manifesting | | | | |
| STAMIS | | MSR/ASR Status | | MSR/ASR Status | | |

*Figure 6 – Military Distribution Simplified9*

On a final note, with the recent 22 February 2011 publication of FM 3-0 (Operations), the US Army's longstanding love affair with the term "Combat Service Support" as an oversimplified definition of logistics has come to an end. The new term

---

9    LTC James H. "Cotton" Henderson, *The Process of Military Distribution Management,* (Bloomington, Authorhouse, 2006) p. 6.

used to denote the Army's replenishment process of her units is "*Sustainment*". Per Para 4-47, FM 3-0, Sustainment is defined as:

> *"The sustainment warfighting function is the related tasks and systems that provide support and services to ensure freedom of action, extend operational reach, and prolong endurance. The endurance of Army forces is primarily a function of their sustainment. <u>Sustainment determines the depth and duration of Army operations.</u> It is essential to retaining and exploiting the initiative. Sustainment provides the support for logistics, personnel services, and health service (excluding force health protection, which is a component of the protection warfighting function) necessary to maintain operations until mission accomplishment. Internment, resettlement, and detainee operations fall under the sustainment warfighting function and include elements of all three major subfunctions. FM 4-0 describes the sustainment warfighting function, and FM 4-02 discusses the Army Health System."*

Such is the magnitude of this change that FM 4-0 "Combat Service Support" was in rewritten in 2009 to reflect this change and was released as FM 4-0 "Sustainment". In 2011, the U.S. Army Combined Arms Support Command (CASCOM) published Army Doctrinal Publication (ADP) 4-0 "Sustainment" in order to further define and refine this emerging concept, targeting this publication towards middle and senior leadership of the Army, officers in the rank of major and above who command Army forces in major operations and campaigns or serve on the staff's that support those commanders.

A comparison of the old "Combat Service Support" FM with the new "Sustainment" FM is provided below.

## COMPARISON OF OLD TO THE NEW

Topics of relevance in the current version will migrate to the draft

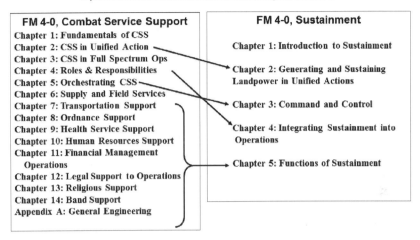

*Figure 7 – FM 4-0 "CSS" versus the new FM 4-0 "Sustainment"*

Since its inception in late 2009, FM 4-0 continued to be modified along with its newly published sister publication ADRP 4-0 'Sustainment' in order to bring it in line with the evolution of contemporary military operations as the U.S. Army has moved from the concept of *'Full Spectrum Operations'* to its newly conceived 'Unified *Land Operations'* as defined within the doctrine supporting ADP 3-0 and ADRP 3-0.

## SUSTAINMENT COMPARISON BETWEEN FM 4-0 (2009) and ADP 4-0 (2011)

| FM 4-0, Sustainment (2009) | ADP 4-0, Sustainment (2011) |
|---|---|
| Chapter 1: Introduction to Sustainment | Chapter 1: Sustainment Warfighting Function |
| Chapter 2: Generating and Sustaining Landpower in Unified Actions | Chapter 2: Sustainment Principles |
| Chapter 3: Command and Control | Chapter 3: Sustainment in Support of Unified Land Operations |
| Chapter 4: Integrating Sustainment into Operations | Chapter 4: Sustainment of Decisive Action |
| Chapter 5: Functions of Sustainment | Conclusion |

*Figure 2. The New Look of Sustainment Support*

It is not inconceivable that within the near future, perhaps within the decade, U.S. Army (as well as joint Service components) sustainment operations will mirror those performed by their civilian counterparts. However it is now defined in light of new technology and the completion of Army Modularity transition, the old time tested adage still rings true today:

***Famous Saying:***
***Amateurs talk Tactics; Professionals talk Logistics***
***(now Sustainment)***

## CHAPTER 2

# THE SUSTAINMENT BRIGADE, COMBAT SUSTAINMENT SUPPORT BATTALION (CSSB), & THE BRIGADE SUPPORT BATTALION (BSB)

*"We can get along without anything but food and ammo.
The road to glory cannot be followed with much baggage."*
- Maj. Gen Richard Ewell, 1862

**1. Background**. With the Army undergoing reorganization from the AOE/FORCE XXI based TOEs into a modular "plug & play" based organization, sustainers were presented a series of new structures, ideally suited to support the emerging Brigade Combat Teams and the newly created Support Brigades (Maneuver Enhancement, Combat Aviation, Battlefield Surveillance, and Fires Brigades). Each sustainment structure tasked organized in support of the combatant's mission, equipment, troops, terrain, time and civilian (METT-TC) considerations. These are the Sustainment Brigade, Combat Sustainment Support Battalion, and the Brigade Support Battalion[10].

---

10  For Combat Aviation Brigades, the BSB is referred to as the Aviation Support Battalion (ASB).

## 2. The Key Sustainment Organizations

**a. The Sustainment Brigade.** Sustainment Brigade's are created as a logistical structure to bridge the gap between Brigade Combat Teams (BCTs)/Support Brigades and the Theater Sustainment Command/Expeditionary Sustainment Command in the wake of the elimination of the DISCOMs/COSCOMs and their affiliated Corps/Area Support Groups in order to create a more efficient and streamline distribution operation. Sustainment Brigades possess only one assigned organic unit – a Special Troops Battalion (STB), with all other subordinate units assigned per METT-TC. Sustainment Brigade's provide:

Mission: Plans, synchronizes, monitors, and executes sustainment operations. Conducts distribution operations within assigned AO. Conducts Theater Opening and/or Theater Distribution operations when directed. Provide support to joint, interagency, and multinational forces as directed.

Capabilities
- Scalable tailorable brigade providing full spectrum support
- Configures for, distributes to, and retrogrades to and from maneuver BCTs, other Support Brigades, and to joint forces as directed
- Supports Theater opening or Theater distribution operations with augmentation
- Provides postal, replacement operations, strength management, casualty operations and essential personnel services as directed.

*Figure 2-1 – Generic Sustainment Brigade Mission and Capabilities.*

\* Distribution and distribution management of material to BCTs/Spt Bdes as part of a theater-wide distribution process. Sustainment Brigades were designed to be part of a single, distribution-based logistics system within the AOR.

\* Area (GS) customer support to units within an assigned Area of Responsibility (AOR), C² by either the TSC[11] or affiliated ESC.

\* Command and Control HQ's with a functioning Distribution Management Center to manage the flow of logistics to the BCTs or assigned force.

**Sustainment Brigade Missions**. (See Figure 2-1) Sustainment Brigades, when task organized with CSSBs, Transportation Battalions, Movement Control Battalions, POL Supply Battalions and on occasion, a Transportation Theater Opening Element (TTOE), are capable of conducting the flowing missions:

---

11   When in garrison, AC Sustainment Brigades are OPCON to the Corps/Division HQ's on whose installation they are stationed. For ARNG, they are TRA to a Division HQ's. USAR Sustainment Brigades are assigned against Regional Readiness Commands (RRCs).

* **Theater Opening (TO)** (Figure 2-2) consist of $C^2$ of theater opening, Theater RSO[12] initial theater sustainment contracting, establish rapid & effective port clearance, and provide physical security and force protection. Depicted below is a typical Sustainment Brigade organized for a Theater Opening (TO) mission:

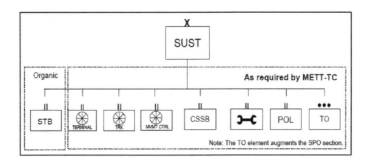

*Figure 2-2 Sustainment Brigade assigned with a Theater Opening mission.*

* **Theater Distribution (TD)** (Figure 2-3) consists configuring/ reconfiguring loads, storage of bulk supplies and ASL items, direction of the distribution of all supplies and services, provision of airdrop assistance, SOF operations, and theater ground distribution network maintenance. The TD also provides Total Asset Visibility (TAV)/In-Transit Visibility (ITV) over assets within the pipeline, operates regional hubs, movement control operations, and on order (O/O) deploys an EEE to establish a robust distribution operations beyond the theater base. Depicted below is a typical Sustainment Brigade organized for a Theater Distribution (TD) mission:

---

12  RSO defined is **Reception** (unloading, marshalling, and transporting), **Staging** (assembling, holding, and organizing), and **Onward Movement** (movement and delivery)

## THEATER DISTRIBUTION ELEMENTS

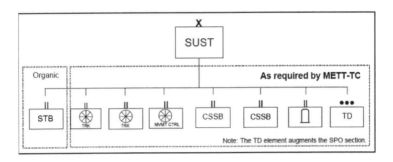

*Figure 2-3 Sustainment Brigade assigned with a Theater Distribution mission.*

\* **Operational & Tactical Sustainment Operations**. (Figure 2-4) The workhorse mission for the majority of Sustainment Brigades, Operational/Tactical Sustainment operations provide; supplies field service, field and selected sustainment level maintenance, recovery, and field feeding. Additionally, Sustainment Brigades missioned with operational/tactical sustainment may plan and conduct LSA (base) & base cluster self-defense, provide sustainment management information and advice to commanders and staff within its AOR, exercise technical supervision over operations for all sustainment units, and provide logistics systems management, plans, policies, and procedures for logistics automation systems. Sustainment Brigades assigned this mission are highly involved in providing local/regional contractual support. Other sustainment operations may include operations as part of an Army, Joint, Interagency, and Multinational (JIM) forces. Depicted below is a typical Sustainment Brigade organized for a basic tactical sustainment missions:

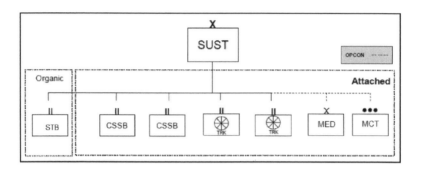

*Figure 2-4 Generic Sustainment Brigade assigned with an Operational/ Tactical sustainment mission.*

**b. Combat Sustainment Support Battalion (CSSB).** (See Figure 2-5) An integral component of the Sustainment Brigade, CSSBs, are also organized and configured per METT-TC conditions. In many regards, they may be thought of as a cross blending of the robustness of the Divisional Main Support Battalion coupled with the multifunctional capability of the Corps Support Battalion.

# Combat Sustainment Support Battalion

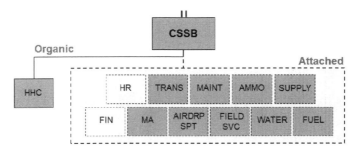

*Figure 2-5 Generic Combat Sustainment Support Battalion.*

Overall, the CSSB is a flexible, responsive, modular sustainment organization that is tailored to execute logistics sustainment throughout the depth of its assigned AO. Under the C2 of the Sustainment Brigade, a CSSB may consist of some or all of the functional companies shown: supply, ammunition, fuel, water, transportation, cargo transfer, aerial delivery, mortuary affairs, maintenance, and field services. CSSBs are capable of receiving and C² HR and Finance management units, but these functions are typically assigned to the Brigade's Special Troops Battalion (STB). The organic structure contains a command group and staff sections consisting of a S1 Section, S2/3 Section, S4 Section, Property Book/Class VII Section, S6 Section, Unit Ministry Team (UTM), and a Support Operations Team. This tailored sustainment framework enables the employment of a unit capable of quickly adapting to changing tactical conditions.

The CSSB is structured to optimize the use of sustainment resources (through situational understanding the LCOP) and therefore, minimizes the sustainment footprint in the AO.

Supported units rely heavily on CSSBs to meet sustainment requirements beyond their internal capabilities. It is important to note that CSSBs are tasked to support one to three, brigade sized maneuver or non-maneuver elements. The CSSB is the Sustainment Brigade element that provides the distribution link between the theater base, APOD, SPOD and the supported units. Its structure includes cargo transfer and movement control assets, fused with supply functions based on mission of assignment. The CSSB performs the function of transporting commodities to and from the maneuver BCTs/ maneuver support brigade BSBs, and to/from theater repair or storage facilities. It maintains the flow of replenishment using Expeditionary Support Packages (ESP), to include retrograde of unserviceable components, end items and supplies. It also monitors distribution of sustainment replenishment that is throughput directly from the theater base by assets of the Corps Sustainment Brigade tasked with the theater distribution mission and, assisting with transportation coordination and delivery if necessary. Additionally, the CSSB augments/supplements supported units during the normal replenishment cycle, delivering sustainment that is not being throughput directly to units. The CSSB has organic maintenance capabilities for self-sustainment.

A typical CSSB mission statement reads:

> *"To provide command and control of assigned and attached units providing area support sustainment operations and limited distribution operations within its assigned area of operations."*

To accomplish this, CSSBs usually possess the following capabilities:
- Provide equipment maintenance support, tailorable to units assigned in its area of support.
- Provide Class I support.
- Provide transportation support within the area for local haul.
- Provide multiple SSA capability with Class II, III(P), IV, VII and IX.
- Distribution operations within an assigned AO.
- Establish and operate a Convoy Support Center (CSC).
- Provide field services including shower, laundry and clothing repair.
- Pack/Unpack containers during container operations.

CSSBs may be configured for heavy, light, or area support operations.

In heavy operations, CSSB are configured with mostly heavy lift transportation elements (MDM, PLS,) heavy POL haul (M969 5K or M1062 7.5K tankers) and heavy equipment transporter (HET M1070s) systems. This configuration was typical of CSSBs employed in Iraq during the period 2005 until the cessation of combat operations in mid-late 2010.

In light operations, CSSB are configured with mostly to support troop lift transportation elements (LT/MDM) limited POL/Water haul and airdrop operations. This was typical of CSSBs employed in Afghanistan during the early years of Operation Enduring Freedom (OEF).

In area support operations, CSSB are configured with a balanced support mix for both light and limited heavy units as well as any aviation elements operating within the AO. This configuration was typical during the drawdown of Operation Iraqi Freedom (OEF) and Operation New Dawn (OND), and is also found in CSSBs employed in Afghanistan during the surge period of 2010.

Regardless of the configuration of the CSSB, in all cases these organizations may be further augmented with contractor/ LOGCAP support, depending on the level of security and maturity of the area of operations. During the OEF drawdown and into OND, it was fairly common to have a CSSB HQ's over seeing pure 'white' contractor operations with no attached 'green' sustainment units.

To accomplish their respective support missions, CSSBs are task organized with a number of functional company sized sustainment organizations. The following is a listing of the various company, platoon, and section units that might be found with the battalion:

* **Transportation Units/Truck Companies**. Transportation elements of the CSSB provide mobility of personnel ad all classes of supply (less Class VIII which is handled through medical channels). They are designed, equipped, and trained to meet Army sustainment needs by performing integrated transportation operations in support of full spectrum operations (per FM 3-0, *Operations*). Based on mission requirements, transportation units may include: Combat Heavy Equipment Transporter (M1070) Company, Light or Light/ Medium Truck Company, Medium Truck Company, Palletized Load System (PLS) Truck Company, Movement Control Battalion (MCB) or subordinate Movement Control Team (MCT). Truck Companies essentially provide transportation for movement of break bulk cargo, containers, bulk water/POL, heavy lift combat systems, reconfigured loads on flatracks, and of course, personnel.

* **Quartermaster Support Company (QSC).** Aside from the transportation elements, the QSC is the workhorse organization of the CSSB. QSC's provide $C^2$ for two to four subsistence or area support platoons, providing food service and supervision/ common tools for unit level maintenance. The QSC when typi-

cally task organized with one subsistence platoon and three area support platoon can provide the following support:

- Receive, store and issue a cumulative 94 STONs of CL I/day
- Provide refrigeration for perishable rations and augment subsistence personnel at CL I issue point.
- Deliver perishable subsistence to CL supply points
- Receive, store, issue and account for 208 STONs of CL II, III (P), IV, and IX supplies.
- Each area support platoon can operate in two different locations.
- Provide limited configuration loads support.

**\* Petroleum, Oil and Lubricant (POL) Supply Company (PSC).** The mission of the POL Supply Company (PSC) is to receive, store, issue, and distribute bulk POL products in support of Theater, Corps or Division operations. Based on task organization, PSCs provide the following support:

In tactical sustainment support, the PSC is authorized three (3) 50,000 gallon platoons with the capability to:

- Store 1.8M gallons of fuel.
- Receive/issue 600K gallons daily.
- Area Support Sections stores/receives/issues 360K gallons
- Distribution Sections transports 146,250 gallons daily.
- Establish and operate six hot refueling sites.

In operational sustainment support, the PSC is authorized three (3) 210,000 gallon platoons with the capability to:

- Store 5M gallons of fuel.
- Receive/issue 900K gallons daily.
- Area Support Sections stores/receives/issues 360K gallons.

- Distribution Sections transports 146,250 gallons daily.
- Establishes and operates six hot refueling sites.

CSSB's responsible for large POL storage and distribution may have a **POL Quality Analysis (QA) Team** attached. This team operates a local petroleum laboratory that performs complete specification and procurement acceptance testing of petroleum products received from supported units. The POL QA team capabilities include:

- Technical assistance for the storage, handling, identifying, sampling and quality evaluation of POL products & containers, for all US and Allied forces within the unit area of operations.
- Petroleum quality surveillance testing outside FOB conditions.
- "B-Level" quality surveillance testing on ground and aviation fuels, with limited "B-level" testing of packaged POL products using information to make recommendations for correct use, recycle and discard of product.

\* **Quartermaster Field Service Company (FSC)**. The Quartermaster Field Service Company (also known as the SLCR Co) provides direct support (DS) shower, laundry, and clothing repair support for approximately 21,000 soldiers on an area basis. During mid-heavy combat operations, military personnel provide most if not all field service support in forward areas, while contractors/Host Nation Support (HNS) and LOGCAP providing much of the support in low combat/stability operations. Quartermaster Field Service Companies are capable of providing:

- Laundry services totaling 315K lbs of laundry/week based on 15 lbs/soldier per week in support of 21,000 troops.
- Each SLCR section can support 500 troops per day/3500 troops per week.

- Distribution for individual laundry with organic distribution assets providing 24-hour laundry service.
- Limited light textile repair.
- Unit level maintenance on organic equipment.
- Food service for assigned and attached personnel.
- Delousing service when deemed necessary by medical authority.

   * **Support Maintenance Company/Component Repair Company**. The US Army's two level maintenance system uses modular designed field level maintenance units called *Support Maintenance Companies* (SMCs) and sustainment level maintenance units called *Component Repair Companies* (CRCs). These units are often supported by *Collection and Classification* (C&C) *Companies* that have the capability to attach classification teams forward, at the direction of the Distribution Management Center (DMC), to expedite component and end item repair & salvage into the distribution system. Each type of maintenance organization is built from a company HQs that is capable of commanding platoon/team level units. All of these maintenance units are found within CSSBs within a Sustainment Brigade.

   First unit is the Support Maintenance Company (SMC) whose mission is to provide area support to all units within the Sustainment Brigade area of operations. It provides Corps & Division area support field maintenance, supports field level theater opening packages, and is capable of accepting modules (platoon, sections, and teams) from CRCs and C&Cs. Its mission is to command and control cellular platoons, modules, and teams performing field maintenance (on system repair and replacement) and return to user operations. SMC capabilities include:

- Co HQs element that normally does not exceed 250 personnel
- Unit can integrate civilian augmentation (approx 10% of the overall unit strength) from the Logistics Support Element) as required.
- Provide mission staging operations.
- Conduct tactical and operational area field maintenance support.

The second maintenance support type unit is the Component Repair Company (CRC). Its mission is to provide sustainment level support to the theater supply system. CRCs are employed in any location within the distribution system beginning at the national source of repair. CRCs provide component repair capability and return the repaired item to the supply system, normally operating in conjunction with a Supply Support Activity (SSA). A CRC may attach platoons, sections, teams to an SMC or other sustainment units.

The last maintenance support type unit is the Collection & Classification Company. C&C Cos establish and operate collection and classification facilities for the receipt, inspection, segregation, disassembly, preservation, and disposition of serviceable/ unserviceable Class VII & IX material (except items unique to cryptographic material, missile systems, aircraft, airdrop equipment, unmanned aerial vehicles, and medical equipment) and similar foreign material.

* **Quartermaster Collection Company – Mortuary Affairs (MA)** provides $C^2$, administrative, logistical, field feeding support, and unit level maintenance management to the company. These units are task organized with two (2) Forward Collection Platoons (FCPs) and one (1) Main Collection Platoon (MCP) capable of:

- Processing 240 remains and personal effects/day from up to twelve locations. This includes evacuation of remains to the MCP.
- MCP can process 400 remains daily.
- Coordinate evacuation of remains and personal effects to the Theater Mortuary Evacuation Point (TMEP).
- Operate a Mortuary Affairs Decontamination Control Point (MADCP) when supported by a chemical decontamination company.

\* **Quartermaster Mortuary Affairs Company (MAC)**. The MAC provides $C^2$, administrative, logistical, and field feeding support and consolidated unit level maintenance for organic units. These units are organized with two personal effects platoons, two evacuation/mortuary platoons, and one collection platoon. This unit's capabilities are:

- Receiving, storing, safeguarding, inventorying, processing, and ensuring proper disposition of personal effects for approximately 500 remains.
- Standing up and operating a Theater Mortuary Evacuation Point (TMEP), which can process and evacuate up to 500 remains per day.
- Standing up and operating an in-theater mortuary when augmented with civilian personnel.
- Setting up and operating five Mortuary Affairs Collection Points (MACP) to receive, process, and coordinate 100 remains and personal effects per day from five separate locations. This includes the evacuation of remains to CONUS/OCONUS military mortuaries.

\* **Quartermaster Water Purification and Distribution Company (WPDC)**. The WPDC provides C2 for two to four platoons for company level administration, unit supply, food service and unit maintenance. These units are typically task organized with two water purification platoons (using 6 3K/day ROWPU systems) and two water storage and distribution platoons. In this configuration, the WPDC is capable of:

- Producing 360K gallons of potable water using a fresh water source per day. (6 systems operating 20hrs/day) or 240K gallons of potable water using a salt water source per day.
- Water storage for 168K gallons of water.
- Static storage of 160K gallons of potable water at one location or 80K gallons at two locations.
- Distribution of up to 66K gallons of water per day based on 75 percent availability of equipment and two trips per day.

CSSB's assigned to Sustainment Brigades responsible for supporting airborne operations or airborne delivery support may be assigned the following quartermaster companies:

**\* Quartermaster Heavy Airdrop Supply Company (QHASC).** The mission of the QHASC is to pack parachutes & temporarily store and/or rig supplies and equipment for airdrop operations conducted by Joint (Army, Air Force, USMC, etc) Services. The QHASC is capable of:

- Airdrop of 200 short tons (STONs) of the following classes of supply on a daily basis: Class (including water) – 20 STONs, Class II – 10 STONs, Class III (P) – 10 STONs, Class IV – 20 STONs, Class V – 110 STONs, Class VII – 10 STONs, Class VIII – 10 STONs, and Class IX – 10 STONs.
- Personnel parachute support to include packing and unit maintenance for up to 450 soldiers during a 45 day period.
- Assists aircraft loadmaster in loading of supplies and equipment into aircraft and in release of supplies and equipment from aircraft in flight.

- Providing technical advice and assistance in recovery and evacuation of airdrop equipment.
- Provide technical/rigger inspection of airdrop equipment upon initial receipt from supply source.
- Can perform the Army portion of the joint inspection of airdrop loads.

\* **Aerial Delivery Support Company (ADSC)**. The ADS Company's mission is to provide $C^2$, company level administration, and logistics support, for two to four Aerial Delivery Support Platoons. This company is task organized with three (3) Aerial Delivery Support platoons to provide the following services:

- 1200 personnel parachutes per day/High altitude low opening (HALO) 39 parachutes/cargo and small extraction parachute pack.
- 225 ST per day (containerized delivery system or type V heavy drop platforms).
- Field level maintenance of airdrop equipment/limited receipt, storage, and issue of air items.

All phases of the company's mission are directed through the unit's aerial delivery office. This office plans, coordinates, and supervises aerial delivery operations and directs company missions.

Often times, smaller aerial delivery units are required, especially in the event company size aerial delivery support units are unavailable. In this event, the **Aerial Delivery Support Platoon** is used. This platoon has the mission of packing parachutes and temporary storage and rigging of equipment and supplies for airdrop by the Army, Air Force, or other services. It provides personnel and cargo parachute supply, parachute packing, and field level maintenance of airdrop equipment. It is assigned to an Aerial Delivery Support Co (ADSC) HQ or an Aerial Delivery Office, and is capable of:

- 400 personnel parachutes per day/HALO 13 parachutes/ cargo and small extraction parachute pack.
- 75 ST per day (Containerized delivery system or type V heavy drop platforms.
- Field level maintenance of airdrop equipment/limited receipt, storage, and issue of air items.

Finally, CSSB's assigned to a Sustainment Brigade responsible for a Theater Opening (TO) mission, may be assigned the following quartermaster companies:

* **Quartermaster Force Provider Company**. The Force Provider Company HQ's provides the necessary command and control for one to six Force Provider Platoons operating in up to six (6) independent Force Provider Modules, with each modular capable of supporting 550 soldiers. With modules combined, it supports a brigade size force of 3300 personnel. The Force Provider Company may be assigned to either a TSC or CSSB, and may be detached to operate separately in an austere environment. The Force Provider Platoon provides one Force Provider module, supporting 550 soldiers, with climate controlled billeting, food service support, shower and latrine facilities, laundry service, and MWR facilities.

* **Quartermaster Heavy Material Support Company (HMSC)**. The mission of the Quartermaster Heavy Materiel Support Company (HMSC) is to receive, store, maintain, deprocesses (as required), and issue Class VII items of equipment, (excluding aircraft and medical, marine, and railway mission-oriented equipment). It may also receive, store, issue, and classify Class VII that results from theater two-level maintenance and retrograde actions. The HMSC's capabilities encompass the following:

- Receives, warehouse, and issue approximately 1,400 tons of Class VII material per day. Initially, these items may be a part of the PWRMS.

- Deprocess approximately 300 tons of Class VII equipment to ready-for-issue status per day. The unit's deprocessing platoon is staffed for a single 12 hour shift since approximately 80% of the Class VII items received into the theater are already been deprocessed. The supply operation office and supply platoon are capable of operating 24 hrs/day.
- Provide in storage maintenance (not to exceed the unit maintenance) on all material warehoused by the supply platoon.

**c. The Brigade Support Battalion (BSB).** As mentioned earlier, Brigade Combat Teams (BCTs) must be self contained, ready-to-fight structures capable of world-wide deployment in 96 hours. To enable self-sustainment, BCTs have a Brigade Support Battalion (BSB) as an organic part of the unit structure to accomplish internal sustainment. The BSB provides the brigade with the self-sustainment capability to support internal needs for fuel, ammunition, Force Health Protection (FHP), maintenance, water production and common supplies, thus reducing the need for reliance on higher logistics organizations for anything other than replenishment operations for up to 72 hours (3 DOS) of high intensity combat. The overall ratio of combat soldier to support is 3:1

Sustainment operations are founded on a distribution-based, centrally managed, force-projected concept of support that is fully integrated in the brigade concept of operations and scheme of maneuver. To meet the challenge of supporting the warfighting mission and meet time objectives, the brigade (either BCT or Spt Bde) employs a sustainment force (in the form of the BSB) that possess a self-sustainment capability to support internal needs for fuel, ammunition, FHP, maintenance, water production, and common supplies.

The BSB consists of a Headquarters and Headquarters Company (HHC), a Distribution Company, a Field Maintenance

Company (FMC), a Medical Company[13], and three (3) or four (4) Forward Support Companies (FSC), with the exception of the Stryker BCT, which at present does not possess FSCs[14]. The BSB combines situational understanding with efficient delivery systems to form a distribution pipeline, reducing most stockpiles. Supplies are tailored and packaged for specific supported units based on a specific time and location. Total asset visibility, including in-transit visibility, through sustainment $C^2$ systems, gives sustainment personnel visibility over all assets and infrastructure capacity in the Area of Operations (AO). Reliance upon distribution-based sustainment operations allows the BSB to place a smaller footprint on the battlefield. (See Figure 2-6)

# BSB ORGANIZATION

*Figure 2-6 Organization of the Brigade Support Battalion.*

13 The Medical Company is not allocated to BSB supporting Combat Aviation Brigades (CAB), Maneuver Enhancement Brigades (MEB), Fires Brigades, of Battlefield Surveillance Brigades (BsfB).

14 Staffing is currently occurring to determine whether FSCs will be included within future Stryker Brigades MTOEs.

Success in battle is dependent upon the unity of effort between the maneuver brigade and the BSB. The combat commander succeeds or fails by how well the sustainment operators within the BSB understand the sustainment characteristics of responsiveness, simplicity, flexibility, attainability, sustainability, survivability, economy, and integration, and their applicability to the mission of the Brigade Combat Team.

**The modular Brigade Support Battalion versus the AOE Forward Support Battalion.** The FSB has been in the Army's force structure since the early 1980's They are somewhat similar in that they are both multifunctional units that provide dedicated logistics and FHP to a brigade. (See Figure 2-7)

The FSB, a subordinate element of the Division Support Command (DISCOM), provides Direct Support (DS) to brigade and division units operating in the brigade area. It provided all logistical support, and ties together the entire spectrum of supplies, maintenance, and services for the maneuver brigade. The FSB is organized with a Headquarters and Headquarters Detachment (HHD), Supply Company, Maintenance Company, and Medical Company.

By contrast, the BSB, organic to the brigade it supports, provides support to a brigade level combat team. The BSB is organized with an HHC, Distribution Company, Field Maintenance Company (FMC), Brigade Support Medical Company (BSMC), and a Forward Support Company (FSC) for each of the brigade's maneuver battalions. The FSCs perform the functions previously performed by the maneuver battalion support platoon and maintenance platoon, both of which no longer exist.

*Figure 2-7 The Brigade Support Battalion vs
The Forward Support Battalion*

The FSB and BSB are similar in that they both are fixed multifunctional units that support brigade-size units. However, there are some distinct differences. The most significant difference is in the relationship between the battalion and the brigade it supports. The FSB was assigned to a DISCOM and provided DS to the brigade it supported, essentially being in the awkward position of having to serve two masters (per the old FM 63 series Manuals). On the other hand, the BSB is organic to the brigade it supports. Organizationally, the BSB is more robust and has more organic capability than the FSB (*See Figure 2-7 above and 2-8 below*). An example is the addition of the FSCs to support the brigade's maneuver battalions. Additionally, the BSB has a more robust supply and distribution capability in its Distribution Company, than the FSB's Supply Company, with organic transportation assets in addition to separate platoons for supply and fuel and water. The FSB Supply Company did not have a distribution capability for supplies other than Class III(B). The company had to rely on the DISCOM's Main Support Battalion's (MSB) Co B (Transportation Motor Transport Company) to deliver supplies to the BSA for transloading to supported unit vehicles. Additionally, the Distribution Company has the capability to purify and distribute water, while the FSB had no organic water supply or production capability, often times having to receive a ROWPU support team from the MSB.

For maintenance operations, the two battalions provide support in the same manner, but have slightly different organizations. In addition to the Company Headquarters, the FSB's Maintenance Company has three sections (Maintenance Control, Service/Recovery, Class IX Support), two platoons (Automotive/Armament and Ground Support Equipment), and a number of System Support Teams (SSTs) that support tank and mechanized infantry units. On the other hand, the BSB's Field Maintenance Company is organized with a Company Headquarters, Maintenance Control Section, and two platoons (Area and Base). The Area Support Platoon contains the company's recovery and mechanical maintenance (automotive and track) capability, while the Base Support Platoon contains the electronics and missile, ground support equipment, and armament repair capability. The BSB's Field Maintenance Company does not have the SSTs like the FSB because of the presence of the FSCs in the battalion; the FSCs have Field Maintenance Teams similar to SSTs. Additionally, when workload exceeds its organic capability, the FSB Maintenance Company may receive augmentation from a Sustainment Brigade Support Maintenance Company.

Force health protection between the two battalions is provided essentially the same, but with organizational variations.

The major difference is in the BCT BSB's BSMC, which has a Preventive Medicine Section, a Behavioral Health Section, and a Brigade Medical Supply Office to manage Class VIII resupply and medical equipment; the FSB's Medical Company does not have these capabilities. Additionally, unlike the FSB Maintenance Company, the Medical Company does not receive augmentation from the MSB's medical company (it no longer exists), when patient load exceeds its organic capability, instead, must transport casualty overflow to the nearest practical Support Brigade Medical Company (SBMC) or Combat Support Hospital (CSH).

# Increased Sustainment Capability w/I BCT

*Figure 2-8 BSB Increased Sustainment Capabilities*

**Brigade Support Battalion Mission**. The mission of the BSB is to provide sustainment support to the brigade and is responsible for sustainment operations throughout the brigade. It distributes all supply classes; performs field maintenance and recovery; and provides health services support (HSS)[15] for force health protection. It carries the sustainment stocks that exceed the organic carrying capability of the brigades maneuver battalions of three days of requirement for high intensity operations. The BSB also provides organic field feeding to the brigade through field feeding teams in the HHC, BSB, and the FSCs, and provides area support (supply, maintenance, and medical) to FOB/BSA tenant units. The BSB may function in a highly dispersed manner, with some BSB elements close to the maneuver units and others within the support area in a non-contiguous battlefield. The BSB commander serves as the senior logistics advisor for support to the brigade. His battle staff monitors and manages sustainment operations through on-site supervision, recurring reports, and an array of digital $C^2$ information systems.

To accomplish its mission, the BSB is composed of four companies; the Headquarters Co, Distribution Co (Co A), Field Maintenance Co (Co B), and in BCT BSBs – Forward Medical Co (Co C).

* **Headquarters Company**. The role and organization of the Company Headquarters is similar throughout each company assigned to the BSB. The Company Headquarters is comprised of a Company Commander, Company Executive Officer, First Sergeant, Supply Sergeant, CBRN Specialist, Armorer, and various support personnel.

Besides the common responsibilities, the Company Commander is also responsible for commanding and controlling the company; developing the headquarters occupation plan; ensuring local headquarters security, including constructing defensive positions, arranging and moving the headquarters, training, morale, welfare and recreating (MWR) activities for the headquarters; billeting; field sanitation, supply for the headquarters, field maintenance for organic equipment; and coordinating health service support.

---

15   As noted, this function is not provided outside BCTs or within Support Brigades.

The Company Headquarters also has a field feeding section, which provides food service support to all elements of the battalion and separate companies/elements within the brigade not supported by another organization.

Due to the similarities in role and organization the Company Headquarters will not be addressed when discussing the Distribution Company and the Field Maintenance Company. The mission and organizational structure of the BSB Headquarters and Headquarters Company is essentially the same despite the composition of the brigade to which it is assigned. All HHCs are comprised of a Command Section, S1 Section, S2/S3 Section, S4 Section, S6 Section, Support Operations Section, Unit Ministry Team (UMT), and a Company Headquarters Section with a Field Feeding Section. The minor exception to this rule is the Stryker Brigade Combat Team (SBCT); the assets found in the Support Operations Section comprise a Distribution Management Cell.

* **The Distribution Company (Co A)**. The Distribution Company is fundamentally organized in the same fashion despite the composition of the BCT to which it is assigned. Each Distribution Company is comprised of a Company Headquarters Section, Transportation Platoon, Supply Platoon, and a Fuel/Water Platoon. The mission and composition of both the Supply Platoon and the Fuel/Water Platoon are the same throughout each BCT. The variance lies in the Transportation Platoon; BCTs categorized as 'light' will have a higher number of truck squads than 'heavy' BCTs due to a limited wheeled vehicle equipment density within each maneuver battalion. Likewise, as in the case of the Fires Brigade, truck squads are equipped with wheeled assets that provide the same capability/maneuverability as the maneuver battalions within the BCT.

Distribution Companies are comprised of three platoons – transportation platoon, supply platoon, and fuel/water platoon – the Distribution Company provides direct transportation support to the brigade, provides Class I, II, III(P), IV, V, VI, VII and IX receipt and distribution support, maintains limited Class II, III(P), IV, and IX ASL, purifies, stores, and distributes potable water within the brigade, and receives, stores, and issues bulk petroleum.

**Transportation Platoon**. The Transportation Platoon provides direct transportation support to the BCT. Platoon assets serve as the basis for logistics package (LOGPAC) operations between elements of the brigade and the FSCs co-located with line companies forward of the BSB within the TF Support Areas (TFSAs). The Transportation Platoon transports Class I, II, III(P), IV, V, VI, limited VII, and bottled water in configured loads during LOGPAC operations. The Supply Platoon typically transports class IX.

The platoon is comprised of a platoon headquarters and three truck sections, the Transportation Platoon is highly mobile and equipped with truck assets, such as the Heavy Expanded Mobility Tactical Truck – Load Handling System (HEMTT-LHS), Containerized Roll-In/Roll-Out Platform (CROP), and Container Handling Unit (CHU) to allow it to keep up with the maneuver elements and operate in all weather conditions and environments. The BSB Transportation Cell within the Support Operations Section is the tasking authority for the Transportation Platoon assets, and uses Movement Tracking System (MTS) and/or FBCB2 to communicate with the platoon and manage transportation assets.

**Supply Platoon**. The Supply Platoon manages the distribution of all classes of supply for the brigade, less bulk water, Class III(B), and Class VIII. The Supply Platoon is task-organized into three primary sections, each of which is responsible for the following functions:

- General Supply Section – The General Supply Section receives, stores (limited), and issues Class II, III(P), IV, and VII in support of the BCT. It receives Class I and bottled water from the Sustainment Brigade at the Field Ration Issue Point and distributes rations in conjunction with the Transportation Platoon to the FSCs. Configured loads are transferred from the incoming modes of transportation to flatracks in the supply marshalling area for distribution to units.

- Class IX Section – The Class IX Section receives, stores (limited), and issues Class IX to the BCT, maintains the brigade's Class IX authorized stockage list (ASL), and provides direct exchange for reparable items.
- ATHP Section – The Ammunition Transfer/Holding Point (ATHP) Section supports the ammunition requirements of the BCT, operating the BCT ATHP within the BSA. The ATHP serves mainly as a transload point, conveniently located to facilitate rapid issue.

The Supply Platoon also contains a Platoon Headquarters Section; co-located with the Platoon Headquarters Section is the Stock Control Section. Utilizing SARSS or GCSS-A, the Stock Control Section facilitates on-site item management. Key functions of this section include operating SARSS or GCSS-A for ordering and receiving; maintaining a current listing for all on-hand commodities; and delivering issued assets (LOGPAC) and picking-up retrograde (turn-ins to maintenance and/or for disposal).

**Fuel & Water Platoon**. The Fuel and Water Platoon is responsible for the purification, storage, and distribution of bulk water, as well as the receipt, blending, storage, and distribution of Class III(B) to the BCT, the Fuel and Water Platoon consists of two primary sections – the Class III Section and the Water Support Section.

The Class III Section provides reinforcing Class III(B) resupply to the FSCs and area support to brigade units through receipt, storage, and issue of bulk petroleum. This section also provides retail capability to individual BSB vehicles and supply point distribution to BSA tenant units. The entire section is fully mobile, with the modular tankrack fuel farm providing the ability to displace even when it contains fuel. The Class III Section is further equipped with a fuel additive injector, giving it the capability to receive commercial Jet A1 fuel and blend it to the single battlefield fuel, JP8.

The Water Support Section purifies, stores and distributes potable water to the BCT. This section is equipped with organic purification equipment - the Tactical Water Purification System (TWPS) and the Lightweight Water Purifier (LWP) - both of which can operate up to 20 hours a day (shutting down for four hours for maintenance). This equipment provides the Water Support Section the capability to purify up to 24,000 gallons of water per day from a fresh water source. Water purification does not occur at levels below the BSB; the Water Support Section is the only BCT asset for potable bulk water. Water is distributed to brigade units during LOGPAC operations.

**Distribution Company Operations – the "Concept of Support."** (See Figure 2-9) Replenishment of general supplies within the BCT is a combination of MSO, SRO, and CRO. First, let's define what is an MSO, SRO, and CRO operation.

- Mission Staging Operations (MSOs) are intense time-sensitive operations, which include all preparations for an upcoming mission – planning, troop leading, rehearsals, training, reconnaissance and surveillance, reconstitution – to ensure mission success. MSOs are planned deliberate operations that can last 1-3 days and require support from both the tasked Sustainment Brigade and the BSB.
- Sustainment Replenishment Operations (SRO) is defined as quick, in-stride sustainment operations that are conducted within a unit's battle rhythm with a duration of 3-7 hours. An SRO can be either a deliberate or hasty operations as dictated by OPTEMPO.

- Combat Replenishment Operations (CROs) are brief or pit-stop like events to rearm, refuel, provision essential supplies, and support maintenance function by cross leveling and use of on-board spares with duration of up to 3 hours.

The BCT deploys to a theater of operations with three combat loads of supplies using organic assets – one at using-unit level, one at FSC-level, and one at BSB-level stored by the Support Platoon. Each combat load is configured based on mission and supported unit composition. Within the FSC, general classes of supply configured as combat loads remain uploaded on the vehicles used to distribute them. The FSCs provide combat replenishment from these combat loads to supported units via logistics packages (LOGPACs) during CRO. The Distribution Platoon of the FSC is responsible for conducting LOGPAC operations and interfaces directly with each line company.

During SRO, the BSB Distribution Company conducts replenishment operations (ROs) via LOGPACs of the FSC's combat loads. The FSC Company Commander sends a request for replenishment of Class I, II, III, IV, V, VII, or IX through either BCS[3] or FBCB2 to the BSB S4. The request is passed through the Support Operations Office to the Distribution Company; upon receipt of the request, the Company Commander tasks the appropriate platoon to conduct the LOGPAC mission. Direct coordination occurs between the FSC and the Distribution Company for date, time, and location of delivery.

MSO operations are conducted with the support of the Quartermaster Supply Company (QSC) of the Sustainment Brigade, the FHP units of the Medical Brigade, and supported BSBs. The QSC area support platoons build configured loads from modules and bulk supplies received from both theater distribution Sustainment Brigades and CONUS. Depending upon the quantity of supplies to be replenished and the location of the supported BSBs on the battlefield, configured loads are either transported forward via LOGPACs to supported BSBs during MSO or issued during extended pauses in tactical operations from the Sustainment Brigade MSO site. The overall concept is depicted as Figure 6.

# DISTRIBUTION
# CONCEPT OF SUPPORT

*Figure 2-9 Distribution Company "Concept of Support"*

\* **Field Maintenance Company (Co B).** The BSB maintenance concept centers on the Modular Logistics Concept that replaces the AOE four-tiered system of organizational, direct support, general support, and depot-level support maintenance with a two-tiered construct that is centrally managed. The two tiers are field and sustainment maintenance; field maintenance is a combination of organizational and direct support maintenance and includes tasks that directly return a system to an operational status whereas sustainment maintenance includes tasks that support the supply system. The two-tiered system ultimately provides greater capability per maintainer and reduces the number of maintainers within an area of operations (AO), thus reducing the logistics footprint.

The Field Maintenance Company is fundamentally organized in the same fashion despite the composition of the brigade to which it is assigned. The mission of the FMC remains the same - provide field maintenance support to the brigade (either BCT or Support), to include recovery, automotive/armament, ground support, electronic maintenance, and maintenance management. However, within both the IBCT (Infantry) and the SBCT (Stryker), the FMC is comprised of a Company Headquarters Section, Maintenance Control Platoon, and Maintenance Support Platoon. The Maintenance Control Platoon functions in the same manner as the Area Support Platoon of the HBCT and is comprised of a Platoon Headquarters Section, Recovery Section, and Wheeled Vehicle Repair Section. The Maintenance Support Platoon is organized in the same manner as the HBCT Base Support Platoon. The Platoon Headquarters Section, Missile/Electronics Repair Section, Ground Support Equipment Repair Section, and the Armament Section perform consolidated maintenance on low-density equipment for the BCT, to include the BSTB, Brigade Headquarters, and FSCs. The organizational structure of the FMC assigned to the Fires Brigade is identical to that of the HBCT FMC.

The FMC provides field maintenance support to the brigade, to include recovery, automotive/armament, ground support, electronic maintenance, and maintenance management to brigade elements located in the LSA/FOB and reinforcing maintenance support to the FSCs. Comprised of a Maintenance Control Section, an Area Support Platoon, and a Base Support Platoon, the Field Maintenance Company also serves as a source for maintenance advice for the brigade and acts as the central entry and exit point into the brigade for low density equipment.

**Maintenance Control Section (MCS)**. The Maintenance Control Section (MCS) serves as the management cell for all field maintenance and recovery mission activities within the BSB, Brigade Special Troops Battalion (BSTB), the Brigade Headquarters, and as tasked for support to the FSCs. It is important to note that although the Maintenance Control Section serves as the management cell for these activities, the BSTB contains a Maintenance Section within its HHC that is responsible for providing wheeled, tracked, and generator maintenance to the BSTB and Brigade Headquarters. The BSTB Maintenance Section is not sufficiently manned to provide maintenance to attached elements and certain low-density equipment; that support is provided by the BSB.

The MCS further provides technical inspectors, monitors job orders, and maintains limited combat spares (PLL and shop stock). The technical inspectors are responsible for all aspects of quality assurance, technical inspection, and quality control maintenance activities of the company. The MCS currently utilizes SAMS-E, SAMS-1, SAMS-2 (to be replaced by GCSS-A), and FBCB2 to assist in mission accomplishment. The MSC receives missions from either supported units via call for support (CFS) messages transmitted through FBCB2 or the Support Operations Section as taskings for reinforcing support to the FSCs.

**Area Support Platoon**. The Area Support Platoon is comprised of a Platoon Headquarters Section, a Recovery Section, and a Mechanical Maintenance Section, the Area Support Platoon provides mechanical, automotive, and track field maintenance for the BSB and limited reinforcing maintenance to the FSCs. Each section of the Area Support Platoon is responsible for the following functions:

- Platoon Headquarters Section – Provides command and control of assigned and attached personnel and supervision for the administrative functions of the other sections. Through direction from higher headquarters, it coordinates all training activities for assigned personnel.

- Recovery Section – Provides welding and recovery/lift support to the BSB and other units operating within the LSA/FOB. A limited equipment density of recovery vehicles dictates the extent to which the Recovery Section can perform its mission. Self-recovery and like-vehicle recovery are emphasized as the primary means of recovery across the brigade. Maintenance Collection Points (MCP) are established throughout the brigade AOR in the event that distance recovery by the FSCs to the Field Maintenance Company is too far. After an FSC has recovered a vehicle to the UMCP, assets from the Recovery Section transport the vehicle the remaining distance to the BSA.
- Mechanical Maintenance Section – Provides automotive and track field maintenance for the BSB. As directed by the MCS, this section also provides maintenance on an area support basis to other units residing in the BSA and reinforcing maintenance to the FSCs. Area support maintenance includes reinforcing maintenance support to the BSTB Maintenance Section.

**Base Support Platoon**. The Base Support Platoon performs consolidated maintenance on low-density equipment for the brigade, to include the BSTB, Brigade Headquarters, and FSCs. It is comprised of four sections that perform distinct key functions, as follows:

- Platoon Headquarters Section – Provides command and control of assigned and attached personnel and supervision for the administrative functions of the other sections. Through direction from higher headquarters, it coordinates all training activities for assigned personnel.
- Missile/Electronics Repair Section – Provides missile, electronic equipment, and weapon systems field maintenance for those units within the brigade that do not have the capability embedded in their supporting FSCs. This

section conducts float management of communications and electronic equipment to the FSCs; float management entails 'floating' a piece of mission-capable equipment to an FSC as a temporary replacement for a non-mission capable piece of equipment. This program maintains the combat power of a line company by limiting the duration of time a unit is without a piece of equipment.

- Ground Support Equipment (GSE) Repair Section – Provides field maintenance on non-vehicular environmental control, power generation, water purification, petroleum, CBRN, and engineer equipment for the BSB, BSTB, and Brigade Headquarters and on an area basis for brigade LSA/FOB tenant units.
- Armament Section – Provides field maintenance for weapons assigned to the BSB, BSTB, and Brigade Headquarters and on an area basis for brigade LSA/FOB tenant units. This section further provides consolidated low density equipment armament support to the brigade as required.

**Brigade FMC Maintenance Concept of Support**. (*Figure 2-10*) All requests for BSB maintenance support flow through the Maintenance Control Section (MCS). The maintenance message flow begins when the MCS receives a call for support (CFS) message from a supported unit other than an FSC – requests for support from the FSCs must first go through the BSB Support Operations Section. The MCS forwards a Logistic Task Order (LTO) to the appropriate maintenance section via FBCB2. The section responds to the LTO with an acknowledgement message, which is then forwarded to the requesting crew/operator. When the LTO is accepted, the section NCOIC coordinates support with the requesting unit and dispatches a mechanic to the location identified. The mechanic will diagnose the problem and determine if the required combat spares are on-hand to complete the repair. If the parts are not on-hand, he will send a message via FBCB2 to the MCS requesting the required repair parts. When the parts are readily available, the mechanic replaces the part forward at the breakdown site or at the Unit Maintenance Collection Point (UMCP). When required parts are not on-hand, the MCS orders required parts through GCSS-A; if the Class IX Section of the Distribution Company does not have the parts available or the part has a long order ship time from the vendor, either the unit of the Recovery Section recovers the vehicle to the BSA. As necessary, the MCS coordinates with the Support Operations Section to evacuate the system to a Sustainment Brigade maintenance unit for repair.

# MAINTENANCE
# CONCEPT OF SUPPORT

*Figure 2-10 Maintenance "Concept of Support"*

**\* Brigade Support Medical Company (BSMC) (BCTs only).** The overall mission of the Brigade Support Medical Company (BSMC) is to provide Level II FHP to all BCT units operating within the BCT area of operations (AO). This includes ground ambulance evacuation, dental services, Class VIII resupply and medical equipment maintenance support, limited medical laboratory and radiology diagnostic services, limited patient holding, preventive medicine consultation and support, combat and operational stress control support, mass casualty triage and management, and patient decontamination. The company also provides Level I FHP on an area basis to BCT units that do not have organic medical assets. This includes sick call services and emergency medical treatment for wounded and non-battle injury patients.

The organizational structure and mission of the BSMC is fundamentally the same despite the composition of the BCT to which it is assigned. The medical company assigned to the SBCT is equipped with one Treatment Section consisting of three treatment teams rather than the Treatment Squad found in the HBCT and has five evacuation squads, like the HBCT. Additionally, the BMSO is located within the Company Headquarters Section as opposed to serving as its own section.

As mentioned prior, the Fires Brigade, Combat Aviation Brigade, and the Maneuver Enhancement Brigade do not have an organic medical company and should coordinate for FHP support from the FHP units force pooled managed by the theater Medical Deployable Support Command (MDSC) via their command HQ's to obtain level II FHP.

The BSMC locates and establishes its company headquarters in the BSA and establishes a Level II Medical Treatment Facility (MTF). The company is organized into a Company Headquarters Section, a Preventative Medicine Section, a Behavioral Health Section, a Treatment Platoon, an Evacuation Platoon, and a Brigade Medical Supply Office.

The **Company HQ' Section** is organized into a command element, a supply element, and an operations and communications element. The Company Headquarters Section provides command and control for assigned and attached units. It also provides unit-level administration, general and Class VIII logistics supply/re-supply and medical maintenance (SBTC only), arms maintenance, CBRN operations, and communications/ electronics support to organic and attached units. For communications, the Company Headquarters Section employs AM and FM tactical radios, unit level computers, FBCB2, MC4, and a manual switchboard.

The command element is responsible for providing billeting, security, training, administration, and discipline for assigned personnel.

The operations and communications element sets up communications equipment and establishes the net control station (NCS) for the company. This element also establishes the internal wire communications net and establishes contact with battalion headquarters and with supporting and supported units.

The supply element establishes both the unit and Class VIII supply distribution points. They ensure all supplies are secured, properly stored, and protected from the environment. The supply element also establishes the unit fuel and water points and supports the company during establishment with additional items such as sandbags, tent pegs, and other standard equipment associated with establishment.

The **Preventative Medicine Section** is OPCON to the Brigade Surgeon Section although assigned to the BSMC. This section provides advice and consultation in the areas of food, water, and arthropod-borne diseases, non-battle injuries (NBI), environmental sanitation, epidemiology, and entomology, as well as conducts occupational and environmental health (OEH) surveillance and medical surveillance. This section also provides limited sanitary engineering services and pest management.

The **Behavioral Health Section** is comprised of a behavioral science officer and a behavioral health specialist this Section provides training and advice in the control of stressors, the promotion of positive combat stress behaviors, and the early identification, handling, and management of misconduct stress behavior and battle fatigue. This section also surveys social and psychological data and counsels personnel with personal, behavioral, or psychological problems.

The Behavioral Health Section utilizes the BSMC Level II Medical Treatment Facility (MTF) as the hub of its operations but may travel to supported units as required. The section's priority functions are to promote positive stress behaviors, prevent unnecessary evacuations, and coordinate return to duty (RTD), not treat cases.

The **Treatment Platoon** is responsible for operating the Level II Medical Treatment Facility (MTF). This platoon provides professional services in the areas of sick call service, emergency medical treatment, advance trauma management, and operational dental care. In addition, the platoon provides basic diagnostic laboratory and radiological services and patient holding support. The Treatment Platoon is organized around a Platoon Headquarters, Medical Treatment Squad, Area Support Squad, Area Treatment Squad, and Patient Holding Squad.

The Platoon Headquarters directs, coordinates, and supervises platoon operations, including overseeing platoon operations, OPSEC, communications, administration, organizational training, supply transportation, patient accountability, and statistical reporting functions. This section also directs the activities of the company's Level II MTF and monitors Class VIII supplies, blood usage, and inventory levels. Additionally, the Platoon Headquarters coordinates with the Support Operations Section for patient evacuation.

The Medical Treatment Squad within the BCT, which is comprised of two treatment teams, and the Medical Treatment Section within the SBCT, which is comprised of three treatment teams, provides emergency and routine sick call to soldiers assigned or attached to supported units. This squad can perform its functions while located in the company area, or can operate independently of the BSMC for limited periods of time. The Medical Treatment Squad/Section has the capability to split and operate as separate treatment teams for limited periods of time. While operating as separate elements, both teams may operate separate treatment stations.

The Area Support Squad includes the dental and diagnostic support elements of the Level II MTF. Typically staffed with a dental officer, a dental specialist, a medical laboratory sergeant and specialist, and an x-ray sergeant and specialist, the Area Support Squad is organized into three elements with each performing specific functions:

- Dental Element – Provides operational dental care, to include emergency treatment.
- Medical Laboratory Element – Performs clinical laboratory and blood banking procedures to aid physicians and physician's assistants (PA) in the diagnostics, treatment, and prevention of diseases. This element is responsible for storing and issuing blood, performing urinalysis and occult blood procedures, collecting and processing clinical specimens for shipment, and maintaining the blood inventory status.
- Radiology Element – Performs routine clinical x-ray procedures to aid physicians and physician's assistants in the diagnosis of patients. Specific functions performed by this element include operating and maintaining fixed and portable x-ray equipment, taking x-rays of the extremities, chest, trunk, and skull, and performing manual and automatic radiographic film processing.

The Area Treatment Squad is the base medical treatment element of a Level II MTF. It provides sick call services and initial resuscitative treatment (advanced trauma management and emergency medical treatment) for supported units. This squad does not deploy from the BSMC nor reinforce/reconstitute other medical units.

The Patient-Holding Squad operates the patient-holding facility of the BSMC Level II MTF. Its primary mission is to hold patients awaiting evacuation out of the brigade AO; a secondary mission is to hold patients, who are expected to return to duty within 72 hours, and is staffed and equipped to provide care for up to 20 patients.

The **Evacuation Platoon** performs ground evacuation and en route patient care for supported units. The platoon consists of a Platoon Headquarters, three Evacuation Squads (Forward), and two Evacuations Squads (Area).

The Platoon HQs directs and coordinates ground evacuation of patients, supervises the platoon, and plans for its employment. It maintains communications to direct ground evacuation, provides ground ambulance evacuation support for the maneuver battalions of the BCT, and provides ground evacuation support to other units receiving area medical support from the BSMC.

The Evacuation Squads provide ground ambulance evacuation of patients from forward areas to the BSMC Level II MTF. Evacuation personnel perform emergency medical treatment (EMT), evacuate patients, and provide for their continued care en route. Each team carries an on-board medical equipment set (MES) designed for medical emergencies and en route patient care. Evacuation personnel obtain appropriate dispatch and road clearances and establish ambulance exchange points (AXP) as required by mission. Ambulances are usually positioned forward with the aid stations of maneuver battalions. Forward ambulances normally evacuate patients from the aid stations to AXPs where patients are placed in a ground or air ambulance for evacuation to the BSMC.

The mission of the **Brigade Medical Supply Office** is to provide Class VIII/blood resupply and unit-level medical equipment maintenance and repair. Personnel assigned to this section plan, coordinate, and manage a variety of functional areas pertaining to technical materiel, equipment, and services used in support of the FHP mission.

The BSMC possesses limited Class VIII/blood management capability. During deployment, lodgment, and early buildup phases, medical units operate from planned, prescribed loads and from existing pre-positioned stocks identified in applicable contingency plans. Initially, the Class VIII resupply effort will be via pre-configured Class VIII packages tailored to meet the needs of the BCT. These medical logistics (MEDLOG) packages are scheduled based on projected casualty estimates and are adjusted based on requirements identified by the Brigade Surgeon Section (BSS). MEDLOG packs will continue until line item requisitioning can be established. All BCT medical units will deploy with supplies to support a 72-hour self-sustainment mission within the AO.

**Brigade Medical Evacuation Concept of Support**. (*Figure 2-11*) At the point a soldier is injured, treatment is first rendered at the unit level. Depending upon the extent of the injury, the soldier may treat himself (self-aid), be treated by a fellow soldier (buddy-aid), or receive more advanced first aid by a soldier trained at the unit-level as a combat lifesaver. In the event that emergency resuscitative care or advanced trauma management is required, the soldier is first taken to the maneuver battalion aid station.

Due to OPTEMPO and relative size of the battlefield, all maneuver battalions assigned or attached to the BCT are equipped with either an organic medical platoon or medical section responsible for establishing the Battalion Aid Station (BAS). Assigned to the HHC, each medical section consists of at least one trauma specialist trained to perform Level I emergency life-saving measures and stabilization of the patient for evacuation to a higher level facility. The Battalion Aide Station may be augmented by Treatment Teams from the BSMC Treatment Platoon and/or Ambulance Squads from the Evacuation Platoon for a limited period of time.

Ground ambulances from the BSMC Evacuation Platoon evacuate the injured soldier from either the BAS or designated patient collection points to the BSMC Level II MTF. As determined by METT-TC, the Evacuation Platoon may also established ambulance exchange points (AXP) – designated locations forward of the BSA where patients are exchanged from one evacuation platform to another. AXPs are utilized by the BSMC when it is unfeasible for the Evacuation Platoon to travel as far forward as the BAS or when it is unfeasible for ambulance crews from the BAS to travel as far to the rear as the BSA.

Upon arrival at the BSMC Level II MTF, the injured soldier receives further resuscitative care and diagnostic laboratory and radiological services as required. When injuries are beyond the capability of the BSMC, the soldier is evacuated to a Level III MTF, either a combat support hospital (CSH) or other hospital with advanced clinical treatment capabilities. Depending upon the location of the Level III MTF, the patient may be evacuated by ground or air. The injured soldier can be placed in the patient-holding facility while awaiting evacuation to the next level of care.

# COMBAT HEALTH SUPPORT
# CONCEPT OF SUPPORT

*Figure 2-11 Combat Health Support "Concept of Support"*

The FHP concept of support is greatly enhanced by the use of the Medical Communications for Combat Casualty Care (MC4) digitized communications system. MC4 integrates medical information systems with contingency support to warfighters across all levels of healthcare by providing timely medical information to support $C^2$, situational understanding, and Class VIII management. It is capable of sharing data with other emerging digitized systems including Army Battle Command System (ABCS), Global Combat Support System–Army (GCSS-A), and Battle Command Sustainment Support System (BCS³). MC4 links commanders with health care providers to track casualties throughout the battlefield in order to focus FHP where it is most needed. Of the many benefits it offers, maximizing the use of limited medical assets, minimizing and focusing patient evacuation, linking health care providers in theater with the sustaining bases, and increasing the span of control of medical units are most significant.

**d. The Forward Support Company (FSC).** In Chapter 1, one of the structural components to come out of the *Force XXI* concept was the inception of the Forward Support Company. The Forward Support Company (FSC) are assigned to a BSB in order to provides field maintenance, distribution-based resupply of Classes I through VII and IX, and subsistence support for all organic and attached units of a maneuver battalion. FSCs are assigned to Brigade Support Battalions supporting Heavy, Infantry, and Airborne Brigade Combat Teams, Fires Brigade, and Maneuver Enhancement Brigade. (See Figure 2-12) As of this writing, Force Developers are staffing development of FSCs within Stryker Brigade's maneuver battalions. FSCs are not found in the following battalion-size organizations: Military Police, Civil Affairs, Chemical, ADA, and Special Forces Battalions. It should be noted that this discussion on the FSC is only an overview.

# Heavy Brigade Combat Team
## (Organic Log Support)

**Mission: The FSC is a multi-functional company assigned to the BSB and may be OPCONed to a supported battalion. The FSC provides field maintenance and all classes of supply (minus Class VIII).**

*Figure 2-12 FSC Composition and Disposition, Brigade Combat Team*

There is much discussing in the field today as to whether FSCs can be assigned or attached to maneuver battalions. Unit Commander's will direct what ever command relationship is necessary to facilitate a successful operation, but bear in mind that officially, FSCs cannot be assigned or attached to the maneuver battalions since the FSC Direct Combat Probability (DCP) Code is 2 which allows females inside such organizations, but not within combat (i.e. DCP Code 1) units. Attaching/assigning FSCs to the maneuver battalions limits the flexibility of the BSB Bn Cdr to surge capability within the BCT, such as moving a Company Repair Team (CRT) from one battalion to another to quickly improve the unit OR.

In Support Brigades (i.e. Combat Aviation, Fires or Maneuver Enhancement) the relationship between the BSB, FSC, and battalion is not as clear cut as found within the Brigade Combat Teams, especially within the Reserve Component where each piece may be located over several states. Here, FSCs have a more direct support relationship with its supported battalion than with the BSB, which has the possibility of creating problems, especially in delineating reporting responsibilities and requirements. Ultimately, it is the Brigade Commander who directs the command and reporting relationship between the FSC, the supported battalion, and the BSB.

The FSC is comprised of three core elements – a Headquarters Platoon with a Field Feeding Section, a Distribution Platoon, and a Maintenance Platoon. The organizational structure of an FSC may be augmented or reduced as necessary to meet the mission requirements of the supported maneuver battalion. In particular, the Maintenance Platoon is tailored to reflect the equipment density of the supported maneuver battalion. Maintenance sections are reorganized and equipped with mechanics and tools specific to the equipment utilized by each maneuver battalion. This modular construct allows an FSC to be self-sustaining and provides the maneuver battalion commander the flexibility to stage FSC assets far forward of the Combined Arms Battalion/Task Force Support Area.

* **FSC Company Headquarters**. The role and organization of the Company Headquarters is similar throughout each variation of the FSC. The Company Headquarters is comprised of a Company Commander, Company Executive Officer, First Sergeant, Supply Sergeant, CBRN Specialist, Armorer, and various support personnel.

The Field Feeding Section provides food service support to the maneuver battalion and all personnel assigned or attached to the FSC. The Field Feeding Section is equipped with one or two Containerized Kitchens (CK). Each CK interfaces with the company level kitchens located either forward with the line company to which they are assigned or in the TF/CABSA with the FSC. Key functions of the Field Feeding Section include food

distribution to maneuver units forward of the TF/CAB Support
Area and preparation of both heat-and-serve meals and cook-
prepared (A or B) meals. The Field Feeding Section has the
capability to prepare one heat-and-serve meal and one cook-pre-
pared (A or B) meal per day.

* **Distribution Platoon**. The Distribution Platoon is comprised of four sections – Platoon Headquarters, Class III/Water,
Class V, and General Supply – the Distribution Platoon provides
Class I (rations), II, III (P and B), IV, V, VI, and VII support to
the maneuver battalion.

Aside from providing C2 and administration support to the
Distribution Platoon, the Platoon Headquarters Section manages the distribution of supplies coming from or passing through
the FSC in support of the maneuver battalion. Co-located with
the Platoon Headquarters Section is the Stock Control Section;
utilizing SARSS or GCSS-A, the Stock Control Section facilitates
on-site item management. Key functions of this section include
operating SARSS or GCSS-A for ordering and receiving; maintaining a current listing for all on-hand commodities; processing receipts, issues, and turn-ins; establishing a limited storage,
receipt, and issue facility for all supported commodities; and
delivering issued assets (LOGPAC) and picking-up retrograde
(turn-ins to maintenance and/or for disposal).

The Class III/Water Section provides fuel and water support
to the maneuver battalion through SRO and CRO. During SRO,
bulk fuel is received from the Distribution Company of the BSB
and stored in HEMTT tankers located in the FSC AO. The fuel
is then distributed to maneuver units located forward of the TF/
CAB Support Area via LOGPAC through CRO.

Within a BCT, water purification, storage, and distribution
occurs within the Distribution Company of a BSB. The BSB
delivers water forward to an FSC during SRO; an FSC in turn
delivers water to maneuver units located forward of the CABSA
via LOGPAC during CRO. It is important to note that bulk water
purification is not conducted forward of the BSB.

The Class V Section provides ammunition re-supply support to the maneuver battalion through SRO and CRO. The General Supply Section transports Class I, II, III (P), IV, and VII to maneuver units located forward of the CABSA through SRO and CRO.

* **Maintenance Platoon**. The Maintenance Platoon is comprised of a headquarters section, maintenance control section, recovery section, maintenance service section, and field maintenance teams (FMT) specific to the equipment density of the supported unit. The platoon's mission is to provide field maintenance (organizational and DS level) to both the maneuver battalion and all equipment assigned or attached to the FSC.

The Headquarters Section provides C2 and administrative support to the Maintenance Platoon. Co-located with the Headquarters Section, the Supply Section possesses the capability of providing Class IX support (combat spares) to each maneuver company, the engineer company, and the HHC. The Supply Section also maintains the FSC's combat spares (PLL, shop and bench stock) and provides exchange of repairable items.

The Maintenance Control Section (MCS) is the primary manager for all field maintenance in both the FSC and the supported maneuver battalion, and establishes the maintenance platoon's priorities based on command guidance. The MCS performs all TAMMS functions and dispatching operations and tracks scheduled services using the Standard Army Maintenance System – Enhanced (SAMS-E) for the maneuver battalion and the FSC. Although services are not a responsibility of the HBCT, they are still recorded in order to ensure compliance with service schedules. All maneuver company SAMS-E boxes are consolidated at the MCS and it is the responsibility of the MCS to supervise all SAMS-E operators.

The Recovery Section provides direct recovery support to elements of the FSC and limited reinforcing recovery support to the FMTs. Reinforcing recovery support becomes necessary when a vehicle cannot be repaired on-site and the FMT does not have the required assets to transport the vehicle to the Unit Maintenance Collection Point (UMCP).

The Maintenance Section provides field maintenance to the FSC and maneuver Battalion HHC. Field maintenance is the combination of organizational maintenance and direct-support maintenance. Mechanics assigned to the FSC have the capability to perform both organizational and direct-support repairs. This capability enhances the flexibility of the maneuver battalion in that vehicles requiring direct-support repairs do not have to be evacuated to the BSB. This section also provides maintenance support to elements attached to the battalion and reinforcing maintenance to the FMTs.

The Maintenance Section is also responsible for assisting with organizational services on selected pieces of equipment organic to the FSC and the maneuver battalion HHC, and assists the FMTs in completing services for the maneuver companies. Services, however, are not performed by the FSC on its vehicles. This requirement is supported by the sustainment brigade through its maintenance units or through contracted services.

The maneuver battalion's first level of support is provided by the Field Maintenance Teams (FMTs). The FMTs are organized to provide field maintenance for all combat platforms organic to maneuver companies/troops/batteries. The type of maneuver battalion supported by the FSC determines the number and composition of FMTs.

The scope and level of repairs completed by the FMTs are METT-TC dependent. Repairs are performed as far forward as possible in order to limit the duration of time a piece of equipment is removed from the battle. During combat, FMTs will perform battle damage assessment and repair (BDAR), diagnostics, and on-system replacement of line replaceable units. Emphasis is placed on trouble-shooting, diagnosing malfunctions and fixing the equipment by component replacement. If the tactical situation permits, FMTs focus on completing jobs on site. The FMTs carry limited Class IX repair parts; if inoperable equipment is not repairable due either to METT-TC or a lack of repair parts, the team uses recovery assets to assist the maneuver company and may, as necessary, recover inoperable equipment to the UMCP or designated linkup point.

## 3. Summary and Conclusion.

How do these newly transformed structures work together in achieving material and service distribution across the operating environment? An overview of the roles and responsibilities between the above sustainment organizations is depicted in Figure 2-13 below.

Outside the TSC and ESC, Sustainment Brigades command all CSSBs and all other sustainment forces inside their task organization. The Sustainment Brigade issues distribution directives to the CSSBs, which in turn issue orders to transportation companies for execution. The Sustainment Brigade needs to attend the various Logistics Distribution Boards to understand the overall theater situation.

To maintain situational awareness of the operating environment distribution network, Sustainment Brigades collect and analyzes In-Transit Visibility (ITV) distribution information to monitor routes and provide location of its convoys. This assists in movement control for convoy force protection through a unit's battlespace. Sustainment Brigades also uses ITV to establish delivery schedules to its CSSBs in support of the TSC and/or its supported command's priority of supply and effort.

The Sustainment Brigade and subordinate CSSBs track and maintain visibility of its assets (known as Total Asset Visibility or "TAV" – ground and aerial platforms) that are available for distribution. The CSSB maintains visibility of its capacity to store commodities as another aspect of physical distribution.

# Sustainment Brigade and Brigade Support Battalion Distribution Operations Roles

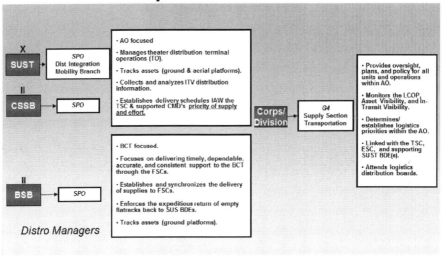

*Figure 2-13 Distribution Operations Roles*

The Brigade Support Battalion (BSB) is not under the command of the TSC but rather is its respective brigade customer. The BSB commands the FSCs and the Distribution Company. The BSB SPO issues distribution directives to the Distribution Company to replenish the FSCs.

The BSB focuses on delivering timely, dependable, accurate, and consistent support to the BCT through the FSCs. It monitors and tracks inbound Sustainment Brigade convoys to synchronize force protection plans. The SPO synchronizes and establishes delivery schedules to the FSCs through its Distribution Company.

The BSB's role for physical distribution is to enforce the expeditious return of empty flatracks back to Sustainment Brigades. Like the CSSB, it tracks its capability to distribute commodities to FSCs in addition to maintaining visibility of its ability to store various commodities.

The Forward Support Company does not have a distribution management mission but rather a distribution *execution mission.* This unit provides habitual support to a designated battalion.

Distribution operations in the modular force are more dynamic than in the past. The competition for scarce resources and the reduction of large piles of commodities have forced the Army to go to a distribution system. With current enablers such as RFID, BCS3, MTS, and eventually GCSS-A, distribution managers are now able to track commodities as they traverse the battlefield.

## Blast from the Past

# "I don't know what this *logistics* stuff is, all I know is I want some"

**Admiral William "Bull" Halsey, 1941**

## CHAPTER 3

# THE SUSTAINERS MILITARY DECISION MAKING PROCESS (MDMP)

*"A good staff has the advantage of being more lasting
than the genius of a single man"*
—Baron Henry De Jomini, The Art of War, 1862

**1. Background**. The most fundamental planning activity a Sustainment unit must achieve is how it organizes itself to fulfill its portion of the overall Theater Supply Chain management and accomplish distribution operations in an effective and cost efficient manner without endangering the very soldiers its supports. This is the process of Sustainment MDMP, the process of which is covered in greater detail in the Chapter 4 – 18 of this guide.

At this point, I should comment that it is not the intent of this Battlestaff Guide to supplant any prior published commercial MDMP guides, Chapter 4, ATTP 5-0.1 (Commander and Staff Officer Guide), or Appendix B, FM 5-0 (Army Planning and Orders Production), but rather to supplement and provide guidance from a Sustainment operations perspective. Far too many times, Sustainment (aka *"Combat Service Support"* or *"CSS"*) soldiers are trained in the Military Decision Making Process from the maneuver (*combat arms*) stand point, completely missing those critical aspects sustainers need to identify and plan for outside what "*the trigger pullers*" look for.

The Military Decision Making Process is not new. The applied process of solving tactical situations and problems can be traced back at least 2,000 years, but began to gain prominence in the early 19th century post-Napoleonic Europe. Following the writings Baron Henri De Jomini, the Prussians took the lead with the creation of a "*Generalstab*" or General Staff under the direction of General Helmuth von Moltke. Using the process of "staff studies" (the forerunner of the MDMP), the German General Staff was able to create various operations (then known as "War") plans in the event of general war within Europe, most notably the infamous "*Von Schlieffen Plan*"[16] of World War I fame. By the turn of the century, this process was adapted by the world's leading powers to include the United States. Throughout the First and Second World War, the process slowly evolved. It was in the late 1980's and early 90's that the decision process used today by Army staffs from battalion to Army level took shape.

**2. The Process Itself**. Per Appendix B, FM 5-0 (Mar 2010), the Military Decision Making Process is defined as:

> '*An iterative planning methodology that integrates the activities of the commander, staff, subordinate headquarters, and other partners to understand the situation and mission; develop and compare courses of action; decide on a course of action that best accomplishes the mission; and produce an operation plan or order for execution.*'

---

16  Contrary to popular brief, the "*Von SchlIefflen Plan*" was less a warplan and more an operational "concept". The plan, as designed in 1905, theorized a massive offensive operation into France based on a projected force structure that was anticipated to be in place within five – ten years of the plan's development. Unfortunately for the German Army, the Reichstag (Parliament) never allocated funding for their creation – instead diverting money to the Kaiser's pet project – creation of the Imperial German Navy.

In concept, MDMP is a blending of the Commander's guidance, intuition, experience, (coined as an understanding of "*The Art of War*") coupled with the Staff's knowledge of doctrine, tactics, techniques, and methodology (otherwise known as "*The Science of War*") (See Figure 3-1). Strong Commander's can compensate for weak staffs by articulating clear planning guidance and establishing definitive course of action criteria. Conversely, strong staffs can accommodate weak commanders but only up to a point. Balancing this process is the all encompassing factor of "time" availability. The less time available, the greater the direct command involvement in the process (See Figure 3-2 – The Planning Continuum). Ultimately, it is the organizational commander who must assume responsibility for what the unit does or fails to accomplish.

As stated in FM 5-0 and Army Tactics, Techniques and Procedures (ATTP) Manual 5–0.1, *Commander and Staff Officer Guide*[17], the strength of the MDMP process is that it is "*an established and proven analytical planning process.*" The total process consists of seven major steps, from receipt of mission to orders production, with over 40 substeps involved. The MDMP entails deliberate planning and development of multiple courses of action in order to determine the best course of action for a given situation or circumstance.

---

17   For this guide, the ATTP 5-0.1 used is the September 2011 model.

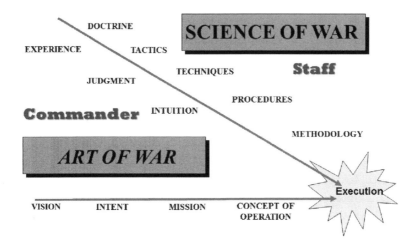

*Figure 3-1 The MDMP Conceptual Framework*

**MDMP's Advantages**: The main advantages to using the MDMP process is that it analyzes and compares multiple friendly and enemy Course of Action (COA) in order to identify the most effective possible friendly COA. The process also allows for extensive coordination and synchronization in plans and orders. With total staff involvement in the process, it minimizes the chance of overlooking critical aspects of the operation. Finally, it helps identify possible contingencies for branch and sequel development.

**MDMP's Weakness**. The MDMP's greatest weakness is the large amount of time required to conduct a detailed mission analysis. Time is usually the one asset there is never enough of, making a complete MDMP ineffective. Whether in the training environment of NTC/JTRC or the present world COE, unit commanders often do not have sufficient time to conduct deliberate planning because of the rapidly changing situation and mission.

Although B-182 through B-186 of FM 5–0 provide guidelines for conducting planning in a time-constrained environment, it still focuses on a very structured decision making process. Current operations often cannot support a structured decision making process that takes a significant amount of time to conduct.

### 3. Sustainment MDMP Focus and Overview.

The focus of any MDMP planning process is to quickly develop a flexible, tactically sound, fully integrated, synchronized and effective distribution plan that: compliments the existing theater distribution plan, and increases the likelihood of the customer's mission success with the fewest casualties possible.

The MDMP is a sound and proven process that required modification with slightly different techniques to ensure effectiveness when time is limited. Although there is still only one process, omitting steps of the MDMP is not the solution. Anticipation, organization, and prior preparation are the keys to success in a time-constrained environment.

The commander decides how to shorten the process (See Figure 3-2 The Planning Continuum). There are four primary techniques to save time.

The first is for the commander to limit the number of COAs developed and war gamed. This is normal for Sustainment units since the number of different COAs (FLE, CSC, CRSP, etc) is generally smaller than for maneuver/maneuver support units.

The second is to increase the unit commander's involvement, allowing him to make decisions during the process without waiting for a detailed briefing after each step.

The third is for the commander to become more directive in his guidance and limiting options. This focuses the staff on what the commander feels is the most important.

The fourth is maximizing parallel planning. Some portions of the planning sequence can be conducted at the same time or carried out in more detail to assist later in the process (i.e. identifying tasks for subordinate units for use in the OPORD while in the COA process). Any involvement by either the unit's organic/attached organizations (and in the case of the BSB: FSCs) will greatly facilitate this action.

While the steps used in a time-constrained environment are the same, many of them may be done mentally by the commander or with less staff involvement than during the full process. The products developed when the process is abbreviated may be the same as those developed for the full process; however, they may be much less detailed or some omitted altogether. This is entirely the unit commander's or XO's call.

For Sustainment Brigades and CSSBs, the SPO & S-3 are the key players in the MDMP process. For a BSB, the SPO, S-3 and BSMO are key players in the Brigade Combat Team MDMP process. In all three organizations, the SPO is the most critical part of the unit's mission analysis and COA steps. In BSB's, the BSMO will stay with the Brigade planners throughout the MDMP process.

*Figure 3-2 The MDMP Planning Continuum*

## 4. Sustainment MDMP and Design.

Recent changes to FM 5-0 introduced staffs to the concept of 'Design' and its applicability to the overall MDMP process. Without the need of going into intricate detail, the first question a sustainer needs to ask: "Is this a complex problem or situation?" If not, then Design is not required (but a problem statement still is). Overall, all sustainment operations (and thus the Unit's problem statement) needs to focus on *"How to efficiently and effectively conduct distribution operations to my customers"* (i.e. – the tactical supported units)

Of a personal note, not only do I believe that design is applicable at the tactical level of sustainment; I believe that most sustainers should incorporate Design into MDMP for planning. Commanders, or staff, should organize their thoughts along functional lines focused to location or customer. Of course, the "steps" remain the same: identify the current situation, describe the end state, identify the problem(s) (or difference between the current situation and desired end state), then define the tasks required to address the problem. The end product, matrixed against time, is essentially a Gantt Chart. For the CSSB or BSB commander/staff, a sample of this matrix is depicted in Figure 3-3 below.

| Customer or Location: | | | |
|---|---|---|---|
| **Functional Area (Lines of Effort)** | **What is the current sustainment situation?** | **What is the desired objective?** | **What is the real issue(s)?** |
| Automation | | | |
| Contracting | | | |
| Distribution | | | |
| Human Resources | | | |
| Material Readiness | | | |
| Mobility | | | |
| Munitions | | | |
| Supply & Services | | | |

*Figure 3-3 Functional areas shown equate to the SPO branches, but others are just as applicable: fixing, fueling, manning, arming, sustaining; or simply: sustainment, distribution, Human Resource (HR), and contracting*

Once the commander or staff has identified what the issues are in each functional area, then the staff identifies tasks, or courses of action, required to address each issue. A COA that addresses multiple issues or functional areas, or addresses the same functional area for multiple customers would be a high-payoff task. Developed COAs are then laid out in a synchronization matrix type format (Pert Chart).

I believe that using design in conjunction with MDMP would be more appealing to sustainers is due to the number of times I have observed sustainers complain that '*there is only one way to accomplish the commander's desired endstate for sustainment so we can only develop one COA and there is nothing to wargame'*. Design assists the SPO in looking at the sustainment situation from a different angle and possibly seeing multiple COAs. If they still only see one COA, it also helps analyze the single course of action by laying the multiple tasks on a single time chart and determining how to complete each.

**5. Sustainment MDMP Steps**. (See Figure 3-4 below) As mentioned prior, the MDMP consists of seven (7) steps along with the appropriate chapter each step (inputs and outputs) is addressed in detail:

1.  **Receive warning order from higher (Chapter 4)**
    - Alert the Staff and other Key Participants
    - Gather the tools and other documents related to the mission
    - Begin Intelligence Preparation of the Battlefield (IPB)
    - Situation update briefings by staff
    - Commander provides initial guidance
    - Issue Warning Order #1 (Identify change of mission and initial guidance to commanders)
    - Update staff (running) estimates/Commander's Estimate

Receive OPORD from higher (followed by confirmation brief to higher)

2.  **Mission Analysis (Chapter 5)**

Mission Analysis Brief (Chapter 14)
    - Commander's guidance and intent
    - Issue Warning Order #2 (Refined guidance and approved mission statement)

3.  **Course of Action Development**—criteria approved for course of action comparison **(Chapter 6, with Briefing format found in Chapter 15)**

4.  **Course of Action analysis and "wargaming" (Chapter 7)**
    - Initial wargame
    - Course of action analysis
    - Update staff estimates

5.  **Course of Action comparison (Chapter 8)**

6.  **Decision brief to commander (Chapter 16)**
    - Commander decision
    - Issue Warning Order #3 (Scheme of Support, Scheme of Defense)

Gather tools
    - Detailed graphics
    - Detailed concept (support and defense)

Finalize plan—detailed support matrix

7.  **Order Preparation & Production (Chapter 9)**
    - Order approved for issue
    - Rehearse operations order brief

Issue operation order (followed by confirmation brief or 'back brief')

| Key inputs | Steps | Key outputs |
|---|---|---|
| • Higher headquarters' plan or order or a new mission anticipated by the commander | Step 1: Receipt of Mission | • Commander's initial guidance<br>• Initial allocation of time |
| | Warning order | |
| • Higher headquarters' plan or order<br>• Higher headquarters' knowledge and intelligence products<br>• Knowledge products from other organizations<br>• Design concept (if developed) | Step 2: Mission Analysis | • Problem statement<br>• Mission statement<br>• Initial commander's intent<br>• Initial planning guidance<br>• Initial CCIRs and EEFIs<br>• Updated IPB and running estimates<br>• Assumptions |
| | Warning order | |
| • Mission statement<br>• Initial commander's intent, planning guidance, CCIRs, and EEFIs<br>• Updated IPB and running estimates<br>• Assumptions | Step 3: Course of Action (COA) Development | • COA statements and sketches<br>  - Tentative task organization<br>  - Broad concept of operations<br>• Revised planning guidance<br>• Updated assumptions |
| • Updated running estimates<br>• Revised planning guidance<br>• COA statements and sketches<br>• Updated assumptions | Step 4: COA Analysis (War Game) | • Refined COAs<br>• Potential decision points<br>• War-game results<br>• Initial assessment measures<br>• Updated assumptions |
| • Updated running estimates<br>• Refined COAs<br>• Evaluation criteria<br>• War-game results<br>• Updated assumptions | Step 5: COA Comparison | • Evaluated COAs<br>• Recommended COAs<br>• Updated running estimates<br>• Updated assumptions |
| • Updated running estimates<br>• Evaluated COAs<br>• Recommended COA<br>• Updated assumptions | Step 6: COA Approval | • Commander-selected COA and any modifications<br>• Refined commander's intent, CCIRs, and EEFIs<br>• Updated assumptions |
| | Warning order | |
| • Commander-selected COA with any modifications<br>• Refined commander's intent, CCIRs, and EEFIs<br>• Updated assumptions | Step 7: Orders Production | • Approved operation plan or order |
| CCIR — commander's critical information requirement<br>COA — course of action | | EEFI — essential element of friendly information<br>IPB — intelligence preparation of the battlefield |

*Figure 3-4 The steps of the MDMP as depicted in ATTP 5-0.1*

## Blast from the Past

# "No battle plan survives first contact with the enemy."

**Field Marshal Helmuth Von Moltke,
Chief of the Prussian General Staff**

## CHAPTER 4

# RECEIPT OF MISSION

### RECEIPT OF MISSION

The MDMP always begin with the receipt of a mission, whether that is in the form of a hard copy or digital OPORD/OPLAN, Warning Order, or Fragmentary Order. Commanders are expected to make informed decisions based on the best and most thorough information at hand. This decision-making process can be deliberate, using an extended period of time prior to execution; or it can be constrained by time or circumstances; or in anticipation of a new mission and conducted under combat conditions.

### ACTIONS UPON RECEIPT OF MISSION

1. S-3 issues a warning order to staff alerting them of the pending planning process.

2. One order is broken into the basic order and annexes, which are distributed to the necessary staff sections for immediate reading. Ten (10) copies of the basic order must be produced along with Annex A (TASKO) and should be given immediately to CDR, XO, S-1, S-4, S-2, S-3, OPS NCOIC, S-6, and the SPO (Spt Ops Off). The Plans Officer also receives a copy (Sus Bde/CSSB). See Chapter 18 for specific Orders Breakdown.

3. S-2/3 & SPO meet with the CDR and XO to receive initial guidance. Planning guidance considerations (See Chapter 12)

4. The XO calls the staff together for initiation of the MDMP. Other staff officers can be present for planning as needed.

5. A current situation update is called for, as necessary, from the OPS NCOIC. An S-2 section rep briefs the staff on current enemy situation, based on the new mission.

6. The following tools are gathered: OPORDS, appropriate maps, standard drops, graphics overlays, own and higher SOPs, appropriate FMs/ADPs/ATTPs, and any existing staff (henceforth known as 'running') estimates. A COP (Common Operating Picture) workstation is set aside for any graphics requirements. SPOs should also obtain a copy of the HHQ's and supported customer unit Concept of Support.

7. The XO, based on current time and execution time, establishes planning guidance and timeline for planning milestones based on a 1/3 - 2/3 time analysis (See Chapter 7).

8. The S-6 off posts an updated POC listing with key personnel and phone numbers

   a. For the Sus Bde, key personnel are ESC Cdr/SPO, Supported Corps/Div S-4s, attached CSSB Cdrs/SPOs.
   b. For CSSBs, key personnel are the HHQs Sus Bde Cdr, S-3, SPO, habitual supported BCT/Spt Bde S-4's, BSB SPOs, and CSSB Co Cdrs/1SGs.
   c. For BSBs, key personnel are the supporting Sus Bde Cdr/SPO, habitual supporting CSSB Cdr/SPO, BCT/Bn S-4s, and FSC Co Cdrs.

9. Staff members read the mission and intent statement one and two levels up and begin their mission analysis and staff estimates. Staff estimate guidelines are found in Chapter 11.

10. Staff Officers should develop a generic list of requirements for particular types of missions (See Para 4.1, Chapter 4).

11. The S – 3 issues Warning Order #1 to all subordinate units.

12. At the Sustainment Bde level, XO dispatches LNOs to the supported Div G-4 or other critical supported organization (if not co-located) and co-ordinates with respective CSSB LNOs for integration with Sustainment Bde Plans Staff. BSBs may opt to dispatch LNOs to supporting Sus Bde/CSSBs (either or).

13. Staff members return at a given time to review their estimates and begin the process of gathering information for the Mission Analysis Briefing (See Chapter 13). As a TTP – if it takes longer than 15 minutes to update a staff estimate, it is not considered a current 'running' estimate.

14. The S – 3 (or designated Plans Off) completes a current Situation Template prior to Mission Analysis.

15. At the Sustainment Bde level, the SPO receives any (available) Div or supported BDE Spt Concept overlays from the Div G-4/BDE SPO per suspense in WO #1.

## 4.1 RECEIPT OF A MISSION CHECKLIST & DRILL

### STEP 1 ALERT THE BATTLE STAFF

| TASK DESCRIPTION | PERSONNEL |
|---|---|
| Upon receipt of the mission (or WARNO), alert & assemble the Staff | OPS NCOIC |
| Prepare initial planning timeline – post time schedules | CDR, XO |

### STEP 2 RECEIVE OPLAN/OPORD

| TASK DESCRIPTION | PERSONNEL |
|---|---|
| Acknowledge receipt of OPLAN/OPORD | S3/OPS NCOIC |
| Inventory/Confirm components of OPLAN/OPORD/record list of TBPs | S3/OPS NCOIC |
| Reproduce OPLAN/OPORD, ANNEXES and appropriate OVERLAYs | OPS NCOIC |
| Distribute OPLAN/OPORD | OPS NCOIC |
| Receive Situational Update Brief | CDR, STAFF, APPROPRIATE UNIT PSNL |

## STEP 3 PREPARE PLANS, AREAS, AND SYSTEMS

| TASK DESCRIPTION | PERSONNEL |
|---|---|
| Establish/Open Request for Information (RFI) Log | OPS NCOIC |
| Set up the TOC/Plans Area for mission analysis | S-3/Plans Off, OPS NCOIC |
| Determine map boxes for 1:50,000, 1:100,000 and 1:250,000 scale maps. Set appropriate BCS system raster map series as required | S-2, S-3, OPS NCOIC |
| Prepare map boards (1: 50,000, 1:100,000 and 1:250,000 scale maps). Post any doctrinal templates on appropriate (digital) map/COP. Post appropriate Div/Bde Opns and Sustainment graphics. | Plans Off, S-2 & OPS NCOIC |
| Determine naming & numbering conventions for this mission/operation | S-3/Plans Off |
| Update Subordinate Unit Status (Personnel, Intelligence, Sustainment, SPT Opns, Staff Estimates) | STAFF |

## STEP 4 ISSUE WARNING ORDER #1

| TASK DESCRIPTION | PERSONNEL |
|---|---|
| Receive initial Cdr's planning guidance | STAFF |
| Prepare Warning Order #1 | S-3/Plans Off |
| S-3 reviews warning order | S-3 |
| CDR signs warning order | CDR |
| Issue Warning Order #1 to all subordinate and supporting units | S-3, OPS NCOIC |
| Confirm receipt by all addressees | OPS NCOIC |

## 4.2 WARNING ORDER #1 CHECKLIST

1. Reproduce the following parts of higher order for inclusion in WO #1:

   a. All heading data including classification, issuing HQ data, order number and code name, references and time zone data.
   b. Situation, including enemy, friendly attachments/ detachments and assumptions (if OPLAN). Attach ANNEX A (TASK ORGANIZATION) and ANNEX B (INTELLIGENCE) if available.
   c. Mission of higher commands one and two levels up.
   d. Execution, including concept of operations, tasks to subordinate units and coordinating instructions.
   e. Sustainment paragraph (Paragraph 4).
   f. Command and Signal (Paragraph 5).
   g. All overlays.
   h. Other ANNEXES as appropriate.

2. Cover sheet specifying:

   a. Type of Operation
   b. Location of operations
   c. Initial planning guidance of CDR including planning timeline.
   d. Subordinates movement requirements.
   e. LNO dispatch instructions.
   f. *Suspense for submission of initial BDE Spt Concept overlays from BDE Spt Ops Off's to Sustainment Bde Spt Ops.*
   g. Requirement for submission of updated PERSTAT/ LOGSTAT and other required status reports by subordinate units within one (1) hours of WO #1 receipt.
   h. Distribution to all staff elements and all subordinate and supporting units.

## 4.3 WARNING ORDER (WARNO) FORMAT.

_____

(Classification)
(Change from oral orders, if any) (Optional)

Copy ____ of ____ copies
300th CSSB
(Place of issue)
(Date-time-group of signature)
(Message reference number)

WARNING ORDER _____

References: (Refer to higher headquarters OPLAN/OPORD, and identify map sheet for operation).

Time Zone Used Throughout the Order: (Optional)

1. SITUATION.
    a. Enemy forces. (S-2)
    b. Friendly forces. (S-3)
        (1) Higher commander's mission.
        (2) Higher commander's intent.
    c. Attachments and detachments. (S-3 NCO)
    d. Assumptions (OPLAN only).

2. MISSION. (S-3, XO) (Higher headquarters restated mission)

3. EXECUTION.
    a. Intent. (Cdr)
    b. Concept of Support. (SPO)
        (1) Sub-unit tasks.
        (2) Sub-unit tasks.

    c. Concept of Maneuver. (S-3)

        (1) Sub-unit tasks.

        (2) Sub-unit tasks.

    d. Sub-unit tasks (for all).

    e. Coordinating instructions. (S-3)

        (1) CCIR.

        (2) Risk guidance.

        (3) Time line.

        (4) Guidance of orders and rehearsals.

        (5) Orders group meeting (attendees, location, and time).

        (6) Earliest movement time and degree of notice.

4. SUSTAINMENT. (S-1 / S-4) (Optional)

    a. Special equipment. (Identify requirements and coordinate transfers)

    b. Transportation. (Identify requirements and coordination for pre-position of assets)

5. COMMAND AND SIGNAL. (XO / S-3) (Optional)

    a. Command. (XO)

        (1) Location of the Commander (State where the Commander plans to locate him/herself. If the operation is phased, state the location of the commander by phase).

        (2) Succession of command (State the succession of command if different from unit SOP).

        (3) Special Instructions for XOs (Specify responsibilities of XOs and associated CPs, by phase if necessary).

    b. Control

        (1) Scheme of CP employment (State the scheme of CP employment, including each CP location and how the CP is used. State which CP is the primary controlling CP for the operation). *(Note – a Forward*

*Logistics Element (FLE) or CRSP must have a C2 node for effective operations).*

(2) Special Instructions for CPs (State tasks or additional instructions for each CP not detailed elsewhere. This might include movement of key staff officers between CPs and movement of functional cells. List by phase if necessary).

(3) Liaison requirements (Provide instruction for liaison to higher, lower, and adjacent commands).

c. Signal. (S-3)

(1) Network operations (Include network control procedures for network administration and management).

(2) Signal Operating Instructions (Identify current SOI edition in effect).

(3) Recognition and identification instructions (Special instructions not included in the SOP, friendly recognition signals, vehicle markings, etc).

ACKNOWLEDGE:

MENTER
LTC

OFFICIAL:
COLE

ANNEXES:

———————
(Classification)

## 4.4 CDR's INITIAL GUIDANCE CHECKLIST

1. Upon initial review of a new mission, the CDR will issue initial guidance to the XO and S-3 to guide the planning process. Periodic review and update of this guidance will be done by the CDR as planning progresses.

2. CDR's guidance will focus on the CDR's purpose, method and desired end state of any event.

3. CDRs estimate will review available data including:

   a. CDR's assessment of staff experience, cohesiveness and level of rest or stress.
   b. Weather and light requirements for planning, rehearsals and movement.
   c. Presence or absence of needed staff estimates.
   d. Time requirements, specifically time available for mission receipt to mission execution, time requirements to plan, coordinate, issue OPORD, and prepare/execute mission.

4. Initial CDR's guidance will contain the following as a minimum:

   a. Whether full or abbreviated MDMP is to be conducted.
   b. Abbreviations to the MDMP, if any.
   c. Scope of IPB to be prepared.
   d. Guidance on timeline for planning, preparation and execution of mission.
   e. CCIR guidance, especially FFIR instructions.
   f. Special LNO instructions and whether to dispatch.
   g. Initial recon to begin.
   h. Any authorized movement required
   i. Any additional tasks.
   j. Any Decision Points.

**As a minimum, basic Sustainment Commander's Guidance should include:**

1. Does the distribution mission involve long hauls? (Preference for Line Haul or Local Haul distribution operations). If Line Haul, is a FLE or CRSP required? Have the commander define his/her 'operational reach'.

2. For Sustainment Brigade: Use of a Ring Route or 'Hub and Spoke' distribution operation.

3. For Sus Bde/CSSBs: Cross leveling of transportation units to create a 'multi-functional' capability)

4. Guidance on the unit of Host Nation Trucking or 'White' contractor assets.

5. Guidance on 'Red Line' (i.e. when available assets dip below a particular level of availability of 'Red Line'. Example: M1075 PLS availability dips below 50%).

## 4.5 COMMANDER'S GUIDANCE WORKSHEET.

### Commander's Guidance Worksheet

| OPORD # | Unit HQs | DTG | Cdr's Signature |
|---------|----------|-----|-----------------|
|         |          |     |                 |

1. **Commander's Intent**
   **a. Broader purpose**



   **b. Key tasks**

    **c. Endstate**

2.   **Decisive points/ actions:**

3.   **COAs to consider (where/ when/ how to mass to accomplish mission and intent)**
    **a. Friendly**

    **b. Enemy**

4.   **How we must posture for next phase (logistically/ geographically)**

5.   **Recon and Surveillance (formerly ISR) guidance**

6.   **Deception guidance**

7. **Priorities for:**
   a. **Man**

   b. **Arm**

   c. **Fuel**

   d. **Fix**

   e. **Move**

   f. **Sustain**

   g. **Force protection/ security measures to be implemented**

   h. **Intelligence**

8. **Risk (areas acceptable)**


9. **CCIR**
   a. **PIR**

   b. **FFIR**

   c. **EEFI**

10. **Decisions I see myself making:**


11. **Time plan (confirm/ readjust proposed timeline)**


12. **Type order**


13. **Type Rehearsal**

## Para 4.6 REQUEST FOR INFORMATION (RFI) LOG

### Request for Information (RFI) Log    Page ____ of _____

| FROM | TO | SUBJECT | ACTION TAKEN | DATE/ TIME | REC BY |
|---|---|---|---|---|---|
|  |  |  |  |  |  |
|  |  |  |  |  |  |
|  |  |  |  |  |  |
|  |  |  |  |  |  |
|  |  |  |  |  |  |
|  |  |  |  |  |  |
|  |  |  |  |  |  |
|  |  |  |  |  |  |
|  |  |  |  |  |  |
|  |  |  |  |  |  |
|  |  |  |  |  |  |
|  |  |  |  |  |  |
|  |  |  |  |  |  |
|  |  |  |  |  |  |
|  |  |  |  |  |  |
|  |  |  |  |  |  |
|  |  |  |  |  |  |
|  |  |  |  |  |  |

NOTE: The S-3 NCO maintains a copy of this log in the TOC during the planning and execution of an operation. During planning, each staff section develops RFI's for the assigned units or Sus Bde/CSSB /Div/BCT which are recorded here and updated at each briefing. Sample RFI format is found in Para 4.7. The following codes are used to identify staff sections, followed by a number/and DTG. Example S14/110900 is from Support Opns, #14, on 110900. P = S-1, I = S-2, O = S-3, L = S-4, X = XO, S = SO, M = CSM, C = BC

## Para 4.7 REQUEST FOR INFORMATION (RFI) FORMAT

### XYZ<sup>th</sup> BSB Request For Information (RFI)

| 123<sup>rd</sup> BSB, 99<sup>th</sup> HBCT | | | |
|---|---|---|---|
| Request for Information (RFI) Worksheet | | | |
| Classification (circle one): | TOP SECRET CONFIDENTIAL | | SECRET UNCLASSIFIED |
| RFI #: | Urgency: | | FLASH IMMEDIATE |
| DTG: | | | PRIORITY ROUTINE |
| Info needed by: | | | |
| LTIOV: | | | |
| Subject: | | From: | |
| POC: | PH#: | FAX#: | Call Sign: |
| To: | | Unit: | |
| Question: | | | |
| Resources Consulted: | | | |

| Response to: | From: |
|---|---|
| To: | DTG: |

| Answer: | | | | |
|---|---|---|---|---|
| Method Received: FM | | FAX | HARD COPY | Other: |
| Control # | Received by: | Staff Section: | Forwarded to: | Date forwarded: |

## CHAPTER 5

# MISSION ANALYSIS

## ★★★

## MISSION ANALYSIS STEPS

1. Analyze the higher HQ's order.
2. Conduct initial Intelligence Preparation of the Battlefield (IPB)/Logistics Preparation of the Battlefield (LPB) (Terrain analysis focusing on road networks, weather analysis, enemy OB, and threat integration).
3. Determine specified, implied and essential tasks.
4. Review available assets and identify shortfalls.
5. Determine constraints. (Note – restraints and constraints are now considered one. Additionally, Constraints must be stated, but may be constrictive or prescriptive).
6. Identify critical facts and assumptions.
7. Begin Composite Risk Management.
8. Determine initial commander's critical information requirements (CCIR) and EEFIs.
9. Develop Recon and Surveillance (R&S) synch tools.
10. Develop the Recon and Surveillance Plan.
11. Update planned use of available time.
12. Develop initial themes and messages.
13. Development of a proposed Problem Statement)
14. Develop a proposed Mission Statement.
15. Present the Mission Analysis briefing.
16. Develop an initial commander's Intent.

17. Issue the commander's guidance.
18. Develop Course of Action evaluation criteria
19. Issue Warning Order #2 to all subordinate and supporting units.

## MISSION ANALYSIS PROCESS

1. XO ensures that the designated staff members work sequentially through the tasks set forth in the "Mission Analysis Checklist", Para 5.2 (Mission Analysis Checklist).

2. The S – 3 and S – 2 Off/NCO, (with input from all staff), prepares the IPB/LPB products (MCOO, Intel Estimate, Enemy SITEMP's) based on the considerations contained in Para 5.4 (IPB/LPB Considerations in the Sustainment Planning Process). Remember that Sustainment IPB/LPB focuses on the major road networks, how terrain interacts (i.e. – bridges, passes, towns and cities), and the impact/influence of forces considered hostile towards the sustainment unit conducting distribution operations.

3. Each Staff Section prepares a "Mission Analysis Work Sheet" (Para 5.6 - Mission Analysis Worksheets) for review by the S – 3 and SPO. Use the generic considerations found in Para 5.3 (Mission Analysis Guidelines) and the Sustainment Functions based considerations found in Para 5.5 (Sustainment Mission Analysis Initial Worksheet).

4. The CDR prepares his own Mission Analysis (called the *Commander's Estimate*) in parallel with the staff. He issues his initial intent and guidance following the Mission Analysis Briefing. The CDR's initial intent is based on the considerations initially addressed in Para 5.1 (Mission Analysis Products) as well as thoughts derived from his/her Commander's Estimate. The CDR's guidance is based on the considerations at that criteria

identified in Chapter 12 (Commander's Guidance Guidelines). Finally, the CDR approves the restated mission at the end of the Mission Analysis Briefing.

5. Final result is the products listed in Para 5.1 1(Mission Analysis Products).

## 5.1 MISSION ANALYSIS PRODUCTS

### MISSION ANALYSIS PRODUCTS

1. Staff Estimates. (Most critical: Intel, Logistics (Sustainment), and Personnel)

2. List of Specified, Implied, and Essential Tasks.

3. List of Facts and Planning Assumptions necessary to continue planning. **(Test for an assumption: "Would the result change if the assumption wasn't made?")**

4. MCOO, SITEMP's and Event Templates.

5. Enemy "most likely COA" and "most dangerous COA."

6. Enemy/COE operations template down to squad level, Ground Avenue of Approach Overlay down to company level, Air Avenue of Approach Overlay and artillery range fans for all templated indirect fire systems.

7. Priorities for each sustainment function (human resources, supply, maintenance, transportation, field service, Combat Health Support (CHS), EOD, Finance Management Spt, Legal, and Religious)

8. Commander's Planning Guidance used to develop COAs.

9. Commander's Intent.

 a. The Commander's Intent is a clear concise statement of what the sustainment force must do to succeed with respect to the conduct of distribution to the sustainment unit's customer's factoring in terrain (the existing distribution network), terrain, enemy and to the desired end state. It provides a link between the mission and the concept of the operation by stating key tasks that, along with the mission, are the basis for the subordinates to exercise initiative when unanticipated opportunities arise or when the original concept of the operation no longer applies. Intent is normally expressed in four to five sentences and is mandatory for all orders. The mission and the commander's intent must be understood two echelons down.

 b. Key tasks are those that must be performed by the unit, or conditions that must be met, to achieve the stated purpose of the operation (para 2 of the OPLAN/OPORD). The operation's tempo, duration, and effect on the enemy, and terrain that must be controlled, are examples of key tasks. Remember – all key tasks provided by the commander must be applicable to all COAs directed by the commander.

 c. The commander's intent does not include the "method" by which the force will get from its current state to the end state. The method is the concept of the operation. End state is the conditions that, when achieved, accomplish the mission. The conditions to attain are the "aims" set for within the operation. (FM 3-0, *Operations*). It is not another "checklist" of events or circumstances.

 d. The **commander personally prepares his intent statement (time permitting)**.

10. Approved Restated Mission.

11. Warning Order #2.

12. Time and Location for Course of Action Brief.

## 5.2 MISSION ANALYSIS CHECKLIST & DRILL

### STEP 1.1 DETERMINE HIGHER COMMANDER'S INTENT

| TASK DESCRIPTION | PERSONNEL |
|---|---|
| Review Commander's Intent (higher and next higher) | ALL |
| Extract Intents and load into Briefs (MA, COA DB, and OPLAN) | S-3, *Plans Off* |
| Post intents | Clerk |
| Determine any "language" conflicts between intents | S-3, *Plans Off* |

### STEP 1.2 DETERMINE HIGHER HEADQUARTERS' MISSION

| TASK DESCRIPTION | PERSONNEL |
|---|---|
| Review Mission Statements (higher and next higher) | ALL |
| Extract Mission Statements and load into briefs (MA, COA DB and OPLAN) | S-3, *Plans Off* |
| Post Mission Statements | Clerk |
| Review AO/AOR-check operational graphics to verify and ID Area of Interest | ALL |
| Analyze concept of operation and the higher/customer concepts of support | ALL |
| Develop standard area of operation sketch for COA development | S-3, *Plans Off* |
| Determine any "language" conflicts between missions | S-3, *Plans Off* |
| Provide staff with Mission Analysis Sheets, Asset Availability Worksheets, and RFI forms. | S-3/OPS NCO |

## STEP 2 CONDUCT INTELLIGENCE/LOGISTICAL PREP OF THE BATTLEFILED

| TASK DESCRIPTION | PERSONNEL |
|---|---|
| Complete/Brief weather effects chart | S-2/NCO |
| Complete/Brief terrain effects to include the distribution networks within the AO/AOR (MSRs and ASRs) | S-2/NCO |
| Complete/Brief situational templates | S-2/NCO |
| Review AO/AOR-check operational graphics to verify and ID Area of Interest | ALL |
| Analyze concept of operation and the higher/customer concepts of support | ALL |
| Develop standard area of operation sketch for COA development | S-3, *Plans Off* |
| Determine any "language" conflicts between missions | S-3, *Plans Off* |

## STEP 3.1 IDENTIFY SPECIFIED AND IMPLIED TASKS

| TASK DESCRIPTION | PERSONNEL |
|---|---|
| Identify specified (paragraphs 2, 3, coordinating instructions and annexes) tasks (Mission Analysis Worksheet – Para 5.3) | ALL |
| Load specified tasks in mission analysis brief | S-3, *Plans Off* |
| Identify implied tasks (Mission Analysis Worksheet – Para 5.3) | ALL |
| Load implied tasks in mission analysis brief | S-3, *Plans Off* |

## STEP 3.2 IDENTIFY ESSENTIAL TASKS

| TASK DESCRIPTION | PERSONNEL |
|---|---|
| Identify essential tasks (Mission Analysis Worksheet – Para 5.3) | ALL |
| Determine final list of essential tasks | S-3, *Plans Off* |
| Load final list of essential tasks in mission analysis brief | S-3, *Plans Off*, Clerk |
| Complete/brief Draft Operational Timeline | SPO, S-3 |

## STEP 4 REVIEW AVAILABLE ASSETS (CUSTOMER AND SUPPORTING) & ID SHORTAGES

| TASK DESCRIPTION | PERSONNEL |
|---|---|
| Review all higher forces available | ALL |
| Determine all Sus Bde/CSSB/BSB forces and sustainment related assets available | ALL |
| Complete/Brief Unit Task Organization | S-3, *Plans Off* |
| Review Customer forces available list | ALL |
| Load supporting (i.e. Sustainment ) & supported unit (i.e. customer) forces and assets available for mission analysis brief | S-3, *Plans Off*, Clerk |

## STEP 5 DETERMINE CONSTRAINTS

| TASK DESCRIPTION | PERSONNEL |
|---|---|
| Determine constraints (must do) (Mission Analysis Worksheet – Para 5.3) | ALL |
| Determine restrictions (can't do) (Mission Analysis Worksheet – Para 5.3) | ALL |
| Determine external support mission | SPO |
| Load constraints in mission analysis briefing | S-3, *Plans Off*, Clerk |

## STEP 6 DETERMINE CRITICAL FACTS AND ASSUMPTIONS

| TASK DESCRIPTION | PERSONNEL |
|---|---|
| Identify critical facts (Mission Analysis Worksheet, Para 5.3) | ALL |
| Identify assumptions (Mission Analysis Worksheet, Para 5.3) | ALL |
| Load facts and assumptions info for mission analysis brief | S-3, *Plans Off*, |

## STEP 7 BEGIN COMPOSITE RISK MANAGEMENT

| TASK DESCRIPTION | PERSONNEL |
|---|---|
| Determine higher guidance on risk | S-3, S-1, *Plans Off* |
| Risk-What fails to accomplish the mission | ALL |
| Risk-What achieves the mission, but fails to achieve the desired results | ALL |
| Risk-What achieves the mission, but at too great a cost | ALL |
| Prepare risk information for mission analysis brief. Fill in CRM Matrix | S-3, S-1, *Plans Off*, Clerk |

## STEP 8 DETERMINE INITIAL CCIR (PIR, FFIR) AND EEFI'S

| TASK DESCRIPTION | PERSONNEL |
|---|---|
| Determine Priority Intelligence Requirements (PIR) (Note – All PIRs should be tied to either a decision required of the Commander or the execution of a Battle Drill) | ALL |
| Determine Friendly Forces Intelligence Requirements (FFIR) | ALL |
| Determine Essential Elements of Friendly Information (EEFI) | ALL |

## STEP 9 DEVELOP INITIAL INTELLIGENCE COLLECTION (IC) SYNC TOOLS

| TASK DESCRIPTION | PERSONNEL |
|---|---|
| Identify requirements and intelligence gaps | S-2/S-3 |
| Evaluate available assets (int/ext) to collect information | S-2/S-3 |
| Recommend IC assets controlled by organization to collect on IRs | S-2/S-3 |
| Submit requests for information (RFIs) to adjacent/ higher collection support | S-3 |
| Begin assembling the IC Sync Matrix | S-3 |

## STEP 10 DEVELOP INTELLIGENCE COLLECTION (IC) PLAN

| TASK DESCRIPTION | PERSONNEL |
|---|---|
| Develop IC Scheme of Support | S-2/S-3 |
| Complete the IC Tasking (Sync) Matrix & Overlay | S-3 |

## STEP 11 UPDATE PLAN FOR THE USE OF AVAILABLE TIME

| TASK DESCRIPTION | PERSONNEL |
|---|---|
| Review time available for mission execution | XO |
| Review time available for collaborative planning sessions and the medium (Adobe Chat, face-to-face, teleconference, etc) over which they will take place | XO |
| Prepare time analysis info for MA brief and WARNO #2 | XO |
| Review total time from receipt of mission to execution | XO |
| Review use of 1/3 of total time as planning time | XO |
| Complete detailed planning timeline-alert battle staff | XO |

## STEP 12 DEVELOP INITIAL THEMES AND MESSAGES

| TASK DESCRIPTION | PERSONNEL |
|---|---|
| ID 'Actors' (Individuals, Organizations, Public) connected with the planned operation | XO, S-3, S-2, S-7 (if avail) |
| Develop 'Information Themes' that support the points the Commander desires to get across to the public at large about their operation. (Note – Ensure that themes tie objectives, Lines of Effort (LOE), and End State conditions). | XO, S-3, S-7 (if avail) |
| Develop 'Messages' to support appropriate Information Theme (Note – A message is verbal, written, or electronic communication that supports an Information Theme focused on a specific actor, or public. It must be in support of a specific action or task. | XO, S-3, S-7 (if avail) |

## STEP 12.1 DEVELOP A PROPOSED PROBLEM STATEMENT

| TASK DESCRIPTION | PERSONNEL |
|---|---|
| Compare current situation with the desired end state | ALL |
| Brainstorm and list issues that impede the unit from achieving the desired end state. (Note – In developing the Problem Statement for Sustainment units, the problem inevitably becomes one of establishing the most efficient and effective means to conduct distribution to the unit's customers within the assigned AO/AOR. | ALL |

## STEP 13.1 DEVELOP A PROPOSED MISSION STATEMENT

| TASK DESCRIPTION | PERSONNEL |
|---|---|
| Develop proposed mission statement - load in MA Brief and WARNO #2. As a minimum, the Mission Statement must contain 'WHO', 'WHAT', 'WHERE', 'WHEN' (either On Order O/O, or with a Date/Time/Group – DTG), 'WHERE', and 'WHY'. A Mission Statement may also contain more than one essential task. | S-3, *Plans Off & Clerk* |
| Review proposed mission statement | ALL |
| Write/Brief proposed CCIR | XO, S-3, S-2 |

## STEP 13.2 COMPLETE MISSION ANALYSIS WORKSHEETS

| TASK DESCRIPTION | PERSONNEL |
|---|---|
| Review base plan and all appropriate annexes | ALL |
| Identify and record critical tasks and assumptions | ALL |
| Identify and record forces available | ALL |
| Identify and record specified and implied tasks | ALL |
| Identify and record essential tasks | ALL |
| Identify and record draft CCIR | ALL |
| Complete header information on worksheet and turn in to XO or (S-3) | ALL |

## STEP 13.3 STAFF ESTIMATE EXCHANGE

| TASK DESCRIPTION | PERSONNEL |
|---|---|
| Update staff estimate for exchange of information with staff | ALL |
| Present critical information to staff | ALL |
| Receive terrain analysis from S-2/Intel NCOIC | ALL |
| Complete/Brief commo-logistics automation support and charts | S-6, SASMO |

## STEP 14 PRESENT THE MISSION ANALYSIS BRIEF

| TASK DESCRIPTION | PERSONNEL |
|---|---|
| Provide MA information input to S-3 (Annotate Mission Analysis Worksheet, Para 5.3) | ALL incl LNO's |
| Review forces available information | ALL (as necessary) |
| Site setup for briefing | S-3 Section |
| Prepare slides and handouts | OPS NCOs |
| Rehearse briefing | ALL |
| Conduct briefing | ALL |
| Receive & Post Cdr's guidance | ALL |
| Update/Brief RFI status | OPS NCOIC |

## STEP 15 DEVELOP AND ISSUE COMMANDER'S INTENT

| TASK DESCRIPTION | PERSONNEL |
|---|---|
| Develop and review the purpose of the mission | CDR, XO, S-3 |
| Develop and review key tasks the unit needs to accomplish in order for the mission to be successful. These are not a regurgitation of the Units 'Specified' Task. An example of a key task might be the establishment of a CRSP, or FLE, or might require the unit's OR rate must remain above 75% operational. | CDR, XO, S-3, SPO |
| Develop what constitutes the 'End State' of the mission and/or criteria of success. | CDR, XO, S-3, SPO |

## STEP 16 DEVELOP AND ISSUE INITIAL PLANNING GUIDANCE

| TASK DESCRIPTION | PERSONNEL |
|---|---|
| Cdr provides planning guidance obtained through his/her CDR's Estimate. | CDR |
| Number of Courses of Action for staff consideration are identified | CDR |
| Unit cross attachments if any/LNO dispatch locations | CDR |
| Command and Control Nodes/CPs/Echelonment of Forces (if any) | CDR, XO, S-3, S-6 |
| Modifications to time available | CDR, XO |

## STEP 17 DEVELOP COURSE OF ACTION EVALUATION CRITERIA

| TASK DESCRIPTION | PERSONNEL |
|---|---|
| Determine proposed criteria with weights based on the assessment of its relative importance and CDR's guidance. | XO |
| Criteria reviewed and presented at the MA Briefing for CDR approval | XO, STAFF |

## STEP 18 ISSUE WO#2

| TASK DESCRIPTION | PERSONNEL |
|---|---|
| Provide input for WO#2 | ALL |
| Prepare WO#2 | S-3, SPO |
| S-3 review and CDR sign | S-3, CDR |
| Issue Warning Order #2 to all subordinate and supporting units | XO, S-3 |

## 5.3 MISSION ANALYSIS SUSTAINMENT STAFF OFFICER GUIDELINES

**All Staff Officers:**
1. Specified and implied tasks
2. Mission essential tasks
3. Constraints & Restraints
4. Time considerations
5. Recommended CCIR

**S-1:**
1. Personnel status of organic and attached units.
2. Forecasted personnel status.
3. Civilian and military medical assets available (including Class VIII supply status).

**S-4:**
1. Maintenance status
2. Forecasted vehicle, weapons and equipment status
3. Supply status of Classes I, II, III, IV, V, VII and IX supplies for internal support
4. Transportation assets available
5. Availability and status of services for internal organizational support
6. Host nation and foreign nation support

**S2 & S2 NCO**
1. Initial IPB, including the following:
   (a) Define battlefield environment
   (b) Define battlefield effects
   (c) Evaluate the threat, to include:
       (1) Enemy combat power
       (2) Enemy vulnerabilities
       (3) Threat COAs (arranged in order of probability of adoption)
   (d) Determine assets available

2. COE and local criminal elements - capabilities and trend analysis.
3. Cultural, religious, historical, and high-density civilian population areas

**S-3 & S-3 NCO:**
1. Current situation of subordinate units and activities
2. Status of task organization
3. Assets available
4. Mission and intent two levels up
5. Engineer assets available in the area of operations.
6. Capabilities of available engineer assets (for example: MSR/ASR maintenance & repair, number of survivability emplacements for CL III and V facilities)

**S-6 Signal:**
1. Communications maintenance status and connectivity (JNN, VSAT, FM, MSE, etc)
2. Network Signal Company status and deployment
3. Higher headquarters' signal plan

**CBRNE:**
1. Assets available, to include reconnaissance, decontamination, smoke, and constraints
2. MOPP status
3. CBRN threat status
4. Troop safety criteria

**SPT OPS:**
1. Displaced civilian movement, routes, and assembly areas
2. Host nation and foreign nation support
3. Non-government and private volunteer organizations; independent organizations operating
4. Status of CL I, II, III, IV, V, VI, VII and IX for external support.
5. Customer (supported units) maintenance status

**BSB Co C (Med)/BSMO (Note: Sus Bde must coordinate med support for subordinate CSSBs and Trans Bns via nearest Medical Brigade)**

1. Brigade medical asset capabilities
2. CL VIII status
3. Causality density and location estimates by critical event
4. Ability of host nation to care for civilians

## Aviation Planner/LNO (if available)

1. Coordination of airspace requirements.
2. Fixed and rotary wing lift assets.
3. LZ's, FLS's, FARP's and other air infrastructure.
4. Threat and friendly ADA review.

## 5.4 IPB CONSIDERATIONS

## IPB CONSIDERATION IN THE SUSTAINMENT PLANNING PROCESS

### TERRAIN IMPLICATIONS:

- Can the terrain support sustainment operations?
  - Are host nation (HN) assets available for logistics operations?
  - Any existing structures/built-up areas present?
  - Any usable medical facilities
  - Is there any overhead storage/work areas?

- What are the ground and air avenues of approach (AA) that could interfere with sustainment operations? Offensive operations could produce by-passed or stay behind enemy elements that must be recognized and averted by sustainment assets to be able to maintain continuous support.

- Where are the infiltration lanes that could be used by the enemy?
  - Identify and locate the routes the enemy could use to move insurgents, light infantry and/or unconventional warfare units into the organization's AOR.
  - Is there any area in the organization's AOR that could provide concealed positioned to these enemy units?

- Identify possible AAs, LZs, DZs, and MSR ambush locations in the organization/Sus Bde AO.

**WEATHER IMPLICATIONS:**

- What will be the effect on the entire road network (hard surfaced and unimproved road surfaces) as a result of different types of precipitation (rain, snow, fog/mist, ice) and temperature?
  - Will a rain soaked unimproved dirt road in a tree line support the weight of fuel HEMTTs or 5K – 7.5K tankers? How about an M1070 HET loaded with a M1A2 weighing 138.5 tons?
  - How will an iced over hard surface MSR effect LOGPAC operations?
  - Will an unplowed, snowed over MSR affect replenishment operations (RO) travel time?

- Will the temperature have any effect on:
  - Friendly forces TA-50 (hot and cold weather)
  - Classes of supply
  - Storage of CL I, bottled water, and VIII
  - Consumption of CL III (Bulk & Packaged) or IX (filters, tire chains, batteries, starters)?
  - Production of potable water (frozen pipes, iced over ponds, creeks, etc)?

- How would poor visibility/illumination affect:
  - Enemy infiltration
  - Force Protection
  - Driving/resupply activities (slower convoy speeds, accidents)

**OTHER IMPLICATIONS:**

- Security:
  - Does the area offer adequate cover/concealment?
  - Do we have observation/overwatch positions along possible AAs / LZs?
  - Can we disperse our assets to reduce possible collateral damage?
  - Can we minimize our unit's signature?
  - MSR/ASR security. Are there chokepoints or possible ambush sites?

- General:
  - Does the area afford good commo? Can the maneuver unit talk to the FSC and the BSB LOC (20-30 km away)? Can the task organized FLE OIC communicate with the BSB/CSSB?
  - Is the road network adequate and trafficable? Can the turf support and allow good movement within the AO for the vehicles that will occupy it?
  - Is the AO in proximity to the MSR, not on the MSR but near it? By doing so it reduces unit signature and might take the unit off an AA.
  - Potable water/raw water source location (available, frozen over)
  - Access to MEDEVAC LZ?
  - Existing bridges capable of handling full HEMTTS, 5K tankers and HETS evacuating M1s (140 tons)? What is the height clearance for overhead bridges?

- Any water/rail capability? Although not normally used at Sus Bde level, these assets may be available.
- Are there airfields located nearby for emergency use?

## SUSTAINMENT CONSIDERATIONS IN DEVELOPING THE MCOO

- Does the terrain offer an area suitable for sustainment operations? (Remember, M1070 HETS do not function well in highly sandy off road areas)
- Is it away from possible AAs and mobility corridors?
- Is this area close to a useable road network?
- Does the MSR travel through primary or secondary engagement areas?
- Are there any obstacles that could restrict/divert sustainment/replenishment operations such as bridge restrictions (classification and overhead clearance), choke points, road surface/trafficability concerns?

# 5.5 IPB to ORDERS PROCESS COMPARISON

| STAFF ACTION | IPB TASKS |
|---|---|
| BCT (BSB)/SUS BDE (CSSB) WARNING ORDER | Define the operational (i.e. battlefield) environment |
| | Begin weather and terrain analysis |
| | Develop doctrinal template |
| RECEIVE OPORD | Begin S-2 Mission Analysis |
| | Develop MCOO |
| | Evaluate the threat, situational template |
| | Determine threat capabilities |
| MISSION ANALYSIS BRIEF | Current weather situation |
| | Current enemy situation |
| | Terrain analysis |
| | Situation Template Overlay |
| COMMANDER'S GUIDANCE | Guidance on CCIR (PIR, FFIR) & EEFI |
| COA DEVELOPMENT | Develop event template for each COA |
| | Develop IC collection matrix for each COA |
| SYNCHRONIZATION | Collection Plan for approved COA |
| | Begin intelligence portion of OPORD |
| | Refine IC collection matrix |
| OPORD PRODUCTION | Complete Annex B, Intelligence IC Plan |
| | Disseminate and save all intelligence updates |

## IPB Products

| STAFF PHASE | PRODUCT |
|---|---|
| RECEIVE MISSION | Define the Operational Environment |
| | Doctrinal Template (Order of Battle and Timeline) |
| MISSION ANALYSIS | Key Terrain/MSR/ASRs |
| | Situation Template |
| WARGAMING | Identify enemy actions |
| SYNCHRONIZATION | Sketch in enemy time line phases when applicable |
| OPORD DEVELOPMENT | Complete Annex B for OPORD |

## 5.6 SUSTAINMENT MISSION ANALYSIS INITIAL WORKSHEET

1. Each key staff member should use this initial worksheet as an internal "scratch sheet" to gather data for updating their Staff Estimates and for transfer to the final Mission Analysis Worksheet to be turned in to the S-3 (Para 5.7, Sustainment Mission Analysis Worksheet)

2. Consider all Sustainment Functions (HR, Supply, Maintenance, Field Services, Transportation, CHS, EOD, Religious/Fin Svc) as it relates to each Plans Staff's area of concern.

3. Coordinate your information with the other planners.

4. Retain these worksheets within the staff section and update as new information is developed.

## SUSTAINMENT MISSION ANALYSIS INITIAL WORKSHEET

## 1. HUMAN RESOURCES SUPPORT (formerly "MANNING")

   A.   Any specified, implied or essential tasks:

   B.   Any Constraints

   C.   Facts

      (1)   Status of units

      (2)   Critical MOS's/Shortages

      (3)   Expected replacements:

      (4)   Other

   D.   Assumptions:

      (1)   Casualty rates:

      (2)   EPW, Refugee, HNS requirements

      (3)   Projected losses:

## HUMAN RESOURCE SUPPORT (Cont.)

    **(4)** Other

  E. Conclusions:

    (1) Projected Status on D-Day:

  F. Shortfalls:

  G. Risk Assessment

  H. Any CCIR

  I. Analysis:

  J. Recommendations

## 2. SUPPLY - ARMING

  A. Any specified, implied or essential tasks:

B.  Any Constraints

C.  Facts

    (1)  Class V Status in Days of Mission Support

    (2)  Distribution System

    (3)  Restrictions:

    (4)  Critical Shortfalls

D.  Assumptions:

    (1)  Resupply rates:

    (2)  Host Nation Support

    (3)  Other

E.  Conclusions:

    (1)  Projected Status on D-Day:

F.   Shortfalls:


G.   Risk Assessment


H.   Any CCIR


I.   Analysis:


J.   Recommendations


## 3. SUPPLY - FUELING

A.   Any specified, implied or essential tasks:


B.   Any Constraints


C.   Facts

   (1)   Class III(B) Status in Days of Mission Support

   (2)   Distribution System

(3)   Restrictions:

(4)   Critical Shortages

D.   Assumptions:

   (1)   Resupply rates:

   (2)   Host Nation Support

   (3)   Other

E.   Conclusions:

   (1)   Projected Status on D-Day:

   (2)   Projected Distribution System

F.   Shortfalls:

G.   Risk Assessment

H.   Any CCIR

## SUPPLY - FUELING (Cont)

I.  Analysis:

J.  Recommendations

## 4. MAINTENANCE (formerly "FIXING")

A.  Any specified, implied or essential tasks:

B.  Any Constraints

C.  Facts

  (1)  Maintenance Status:

  (2)  Class IX Status (Critical Items):

  (3)  Critical Shortages:

  (4)  Class VII Status

D.  Assumptions:

  (1)  Host Nation Support:

(2)   Other

E.   Conclusions:

(1)   Projected Status on D-Day:

F.   Shortfalls:

**G.**   Risk Assessment

H.   Any CCIR

I.   Analysis:

J.   Recommendations

## 5. TRANSPORTATION (formerly "MOVING")

A.   Any specified, implied or essential tasks:

B.   Any Constraints

## **TRANSPORTATION (formerly "MOVING") (Cont)**

   C.   Facts

       (1)   Status of Transportation Assets:

       (2)   Critical LOC and MSR/ASR Status:

       (3)   HET Lines/Limits AND CROP/Flatrack Collection Points

       (4)   Critical Shortages:

   D.   Assumptions:

       (1)   Host Nation Support

       (2)   Other

   **E.**   Conclusions:

       (1)   Projected Status on D-Day:

       (2)   Transportation Priorities

F.   Shortfalls:

G.   Risk Assessment

H.   Any CCIR

I.   Analysis:

J.   Recommendations

## 6. <u>FIELD SERVICES, CHS SUSTAINMENT</u>

A.   Any specified, implied or essential tasks:

B.   Any Constraints

C.   Facts

    (1)   Patient-holding capacity, evacuation policy and available evacuation assets

        a.   Level I (BAS):
        b.   Level II (BSMC/SBMC):
        c.   Level III (CSH):

**SUSTAINMENT (Cont)**

    (2)   Shower, Laundry, Clothing, Repair (SLCR) Loc/ Status and Availability:

    (3)   Mortuary Affairs Evacuation Point (MACP) Loc, Status, and Availability

    (4)   EOD Status and Availability:

    (5)   Financial Management Support Status and Availability:

    (6)   Religious, Legal and Band Support Status and Availability:

    (7)   Status of Overall Field Services

    (8)   Critical Shortages

  D.  Assumptions:

    (1)   Casualty rates:

    (2)   Projected Losses:

    (3)   Other

  E.  Conclusions:

F.   Shortfalls:

G.   Risk Assessment

H.   Any CCIR

I.   Analysis:

J.   Recommendations

## 5.7 SUSTAINMENT MISSION ANALYSIS ABBREVIATED TASK WORKSHEET

### MISSION ANALYSIS WORKSHEET

**Section:**                                     **DTG:**
**Officer:**

| 1. Specified Tasks | Reference |
|---|---|
|  |  |
|  |  |
|  |  |
|  |  |
|  |  |
|  |  |
|  |  |
|  |  |

| 2. Implied Tasks | |
| --- | --- |
| | |
| | |
| | |
| | |
| | |
| | |
| | |
| | |
| | |

| 3. Constraints | |
| --- | --- |
| | |
| | |
| | |
| | |
| | |
| | |
| | |
| | |
| | |

| 4. Assumptions | |
| --- | --- |
| | |
| | |
| | |
| | |
| | |
| | |
| | |
| | |

| 5. Facts | Reference |
|---|---|
| | |
| | |
| | |
| | |
| | |
| | |
| | |
| **6. Concerns** | |
| | |
| | |
| | |
| | |
| | |
| | |
| | |
| **7. Requests** | |
| | |
| | |
| | |
| | |
| | |
| | |
| | |
| | |

**Note: Identify mission essential tasks with a \*.**
Note: Ensure classification is printed on document as a header and footer.

## 5.8 CONSIDERATIONS UNDER EACH SUSTAINMENT FUNCTION

The areas of consideration listed below *are not intended as an all-encompassing checklist and may not always be applicable.* Rather, they are intended as a point of departure for Sustainment planners developing a support concept. Although the items are considered, they are not necessarily addressed in the support concept unless they are critical, non-SOP, or unusual.

1.  Items for overall consideration:

    a.  Support boundaries, support areas, and support relationships.

    b.  Priorities of routes/events (timing).

    c.  Support of attached or detached forces, (Cavalry, light infantry, SOF, out-of-sector support, heavy/light mixes, etc – if required)

    d.  Sustainment MSO actions in the assembly area (AA), staging areas, and attack positions (if any) and any MRO.

    e.  Programmed locations and projected displacements of sustainment support units and areas.

    f.  Support provide by/to higher or adjacent units or other unusual support arrangements; e.g. refuel on the move (ROM), FARP Opns, caches, Special Operations Forces unique requirements, etc.

    g.  Sustainment actions that support security and /or deception plans and /or operations.

h.   Foreign nation support and /or host nation support arrangements.

i.   Sustainment organization task organization (Sustainment unit's capability versus supported units' requirements)

j.   Unusual and /or critical impact of weather, terrain, and security on sustainment operations.

k.   Major Replenishment Operations (MRO) that support unit refit & reset.

l.   Special considerations for joint (Air Force, Navy, USMC0 or combined (Allied) sustainment operations.

2.   Items to consider in each phase of the operation:

a.   **Maintenance**: Maintenance priorities (air, ground). Anticipated workload (battle damage and maintenance failure rates/projections). Battle damage assessment and repair (BDAR) procedures. Maintenance repair time lines. Controlled substitution or cannibalization procedures. FMT/CRT employment, locations/displacement of maintenance/repair part supply units. Support from other sources. Distribution methods for classes VII and IX. Evacuation procedures may include recovery procedures. Location and placement of M1070 HETs within AOR. Significant risks involved with recovery.

b.   Transportation: Transportation requirements (logistic versus tactical). Movement and route use priorities (units and/or commodities). Traffic control requirements. Transportation unit/asset displacements. Throughput operations. Trailer Transfer Point arrangements (TTPs) or cargo transfer/terminal operations. Alternate modes of transportation; e.g. rail, foreign/host nation support. Lines of communication (LOC) and MSR security, supply routes, route maintenance requirements (effects of weather, enemy, and engineer support). Mode selection heavy-equipment transport (HET) priorities and backhaul priorities. Movement Control Team (MCT) availability. Support from joint services. Significant risks involved.

c. Supply: Day of Supply Availability and O/H. Classes of supply I, II, III, III(P), IV, V, VI, VII, and IX (less VIII). Supply point or unit distribution methods. Support from other sources. Refugees. Quality of life of the soldier and their family. Current status (in vehicles and bulkcarriers/storage). Bulk refueling procedures. Refuel-on-th-move (ROM activities. FARP operations. Reful assets and system capabilities, fuel allocations. Displacement of fuel/refueling assets. Basic and operational load status. Required Supply Rate (RSR) versus Controlled Supply Rate (CSR) for Class V & VIII. Forecasted requirements and ammunition prestocking arrangements. CSR sub allocation. ATHP, ASA and ASP locations (only general locations, grids on the LCOP overlay). Distribution methods, Combat/Mission-configured load (CCLs/MCLs). Emergency resupply procedures. Expenditure restrictions (e.g. no more than what percent of the CSR may be expended to support the covering force?) Monitoring and reporting requirements. Field storage requirements and missile maintenance.

d. Combat Health Support: Projected casualties and their effect on combat readiness. Establishing or adjusting personnel and medical support priorities. Locations of medical treatment facilities. Evacuation procedures for killed in action (KIA)/wounded in action (WIA).

e.  Field Services: Location of Sus Bde Field Service units and capabilities. Location of mortuary affairs personnel, collection points. Location of aerial delivery units, clothing exchange, laundry, showers, textile repair, and food services.

f.  Explosive Ordnance Disposal: Location of EOD units and capabilities. Identifying procedures for neutralizing domestic or foreign conventional, chemical, and biological munitions and devices that present a threat to military operations and civilian facilities.

g.  Human Resource Support: Personnel services, EPW procedures, Friendly confinement requirements/procedures. Identifying personnel support to service members, their families, DA, civilians, and contractors. Location of personnel accounting activities, casualty management, postal operations, and moral, welfare, and recreation (MWR) facilities and equipment.

h.  Financial Management Operations: Location of financial services and resource management services.

i.  Religious, Legal, and Band Support: Location of religious support operations, legal operations, and band support.

## 5.9 CONSIDERATIONS FOR SUPPORTING OFFENSIVE OPERATIONS.

1.  If offensive momentum is not maintained, the enemy may recover from the shock of the first assault, gain the initiative, and mount a successful counterattack. Therefore, the sustainment priority must be to maintain the momentum of the attack.

2.  A successful attack may develop into an exploitation or pursuit, and the sustainment planner must be flexible enough to support either type of operation. The following techniques and considerations apply to sustainment offensive planning:

    *   Position essential sustainment assets, such as ammunition, petroleum, oils, and lubricants (POL), and maintenance, in advance within the FSC, and ensure that basic loads remain replenished.

    *   Establish maintenance priorities based on the commander's guidance or intent and the factors of mission, enemy, terrain, troops, time, and civilian considerations (METT-TC). Priorities may change as different phases of an operation are completed.

    *   Recover damaged vehicles only to the main supply route for further recovery by TF assets.

    *   Plan for increased consumption of POL

    *   Push planned and pre-configured logistics packages of essential sustainment items.

    *   Plan for increased vehicular maintenance, especially over rough terrain.

    *   Make maximum use of forward maintenance teams (FMTs) with supported TF/CABs.

    *   Request unit distribution at forward locations.

    *   Increased use of meals-ready-to-eat (MRE) and bottled water.

- Use of captured enemy supplies and equipment, particularly support vehicles and POL. Before use, test for contamination.

- Suspend most field service functions except airdrop and mortuary affairs.

- Prepare for increased casualties and additional evacuation and mortuary affairs requirements. Plan replacement operations based on known and projected losses.

- Select supply routes, logistics release points, and subsequent FSC Support Area locations based on map reconnaissance.

- Plan and coordinate enemy prisoner of war (EPW) operations; expect more POWs.

Consider the increasing distances and longer travel times to ammunition supply areas (ASAs) and ammunition transfer holding points (ATHPs)

- Ensure that sustainment MSO preparations for the attack do not compromise tactical plans.

3. These considerations apply to some degree to all offensive operations. The change from one type of operation to another, such as from a hasty attack to a pursuit, does not require a major shift in sustainment plans and procedures. However, the priorities and requirements for support may change. The Brigade Combat Team Executive Officer (XO), assisted primarily by the S-4 and in conjunction with the BSB Cdr, organizes the BCT/task force's sustainment assets to permit uninterrupted support. The main purpose of sustainment in the offense is to maintain the momentum of the attack.

**5. 10 CONSIDERATIONS FOR SUPPORTING THE DEFENSE.**

1.  The immediate purpose of the defense is to cause an enemy attack to fail, or in contrast to offensive operations, to break the momentum of the attack.

2.  As in offensive operations, perhaps the most critical time in the defense is the preparation stage. General considerations in preparing for defensive operations include the following:
    *   Pre-position limited amounts of ammunition, POL, and barrier material in centrally located battle positions in forward areas. Make plans to destroy those stocks if necessary.

    *   Resupply during limited visibility to reduce the chance of enemy interference.

    *   Plan to reorganize to reconstitute/regenerate lost sustainment capability. Identify personnel from the field to train as potential replacements to reestablish lost capability.

    *   Use maintenance support teams in the UMCP to reduce the need to recover equipment to the Brigade Support Area (BSA). Consider pre-positioning of M1070 HETs as far forward as possible.

    *   Consider the additional transportation requirements for the movement of Class IV barrier material, mines, and pre-positioned ammunition, plus the sustainment requirements of additional engineer units assigned for preparation of the defense.

    *   In defensive operations, pre-position ammunition on occupied and prepared positions. However, plans must be made for the control of this ammunition.

## 5.11 PREPARATION FOR MISSION ANALYSIS BRIEFING

## PREPARATION FOR MISSION ANALYSIS BRIEFING

1.  The S-2/ S-2 NCO prepares the MCOO, enemy Situation
    Template overlays (SITTEMP's), (enemy intent & objectives,
    COAs, and terrain analysis) and Event Templates. The S-2
    briefs as if he is the enemy commander (i.e., " I intend to..."
    "I will..." "My objective is to...").

2.  The S-2/S-2 NCO develops (1) the enemy's most likely COA
    based on doctrine and situation, and (2) the enemy's most
    dangerous course of action, if he employed it, against the
    brigade/division. In many cases, the most likely is the most
    dangerous but not always. These enemy COAs will later form
    the basis for friendly COA development; we should develop
    at least three friendly COAs against the "most likely" and the
    "most dangerous."

3.  The S-3 prepares friendly OPS overlays. Spt Ops Off prepares
    the Support Concept overlay. Include on the OPS overlay:
    Brigade, Division AO/AI, (*Corps AO for Sus Bde),* concept 1
    and 2 levels higher, and friendly COA's currently under con-
    sideration by Division Plans Staff. Build the Support Concept
    overlay from the initial Support Concept overlays received
    from the Div G-4 (in the case of Sus Bde and CSSBs) or from
    the Bde S-4 (in the case of BSBs) following WO #1.

4.  **Select for briefing only those bullets of information gath-
    ered during mission analysis that are of primary importance
    to the CDR.** The XO/S-3 keeps the entire list for future
    information and refinement.

5.  Complete relative combat power for friendly and enemy as
    it is at this time.

6.  Conduct analysis of relative support requirements based on requirements of supported units' verses capabilities of supporting units.

7.  When considering shortfalls or "War stoppers", capture solutions, recommendations and additional assets required from other sustainment units that could resolve or eliminate the shortfalls and war stoppers.

8.  Prepare proposed mission statement for CDR's approval.

9.  Have "Sequence of Command and Staff Actions" chart and "arrow sticker" for use during the briefing.

10. Conduct a rehearsal of the mission analysis briefing for the Executive Officer.

11. Appoint two scribes to take notes and annotate overlays throughout the rehearsal and the briefing and to document commander's intent and guidance.

## 5.12 AFTER MISSION ANALYSIS BRIEFING

### AFTER MISSION ANALYSIS BRIEFING

1.  Prepare chart with elements of Commander's Guidance from mission analysis briefing. As a minimum Commander's Guidance should address:

    a.  Specific courses of action to consider or not to consider, both friendly and enemy, and the priority for addressing them. ———

    b.  The CCIR.

    c.  Levels of acceptable risk.

    d.   The Intelligence Collection (IC) guidance.

    e.   Deception guidance (if applicable).

    f.   Fire support and any Effects Based Operations (EBO) guidance.

    g.   Security measures to be implemented.

    h.   Specific priorities for each Sustainment Function (MAFFMS).

    i.   Any revisions or modifications to the time plan.

    j.   The type of order to issue.

    k.   The type of rehearsal to conduct.

2.   Consolidate a request for additional assets desired from the next sustainment organization (Sus Bde/CSSBs).

3.   Prepare and issue Warning Order #2. (should contain at a minimum)

    a.   The restated mission.

    b.   The commander's intent.

    c.   The unit's AO (a sketch, overlay, or some other description).

    d.   The CCIR.

    e.   Risk Guidance.

    f.   Reconnaissance to be initiated by subordinate units.

g. Security measures.

h. Deception guidance (if applicable)

i. Specific priorities for each Sustainment Function.

j. The time plan for each remaining step of the planning and preparation for the operation.

k. Guidance on rehearsals.

4. Revisit Facts and Planning Assumptions and revise essential tasks and restated mission as necessary.

## Blast from the Past
### Commander's Guidance

**"I do not propose to lay down for you a plan of campaign ... but simply to lay down the work it is desirable to have done and leave you free to execute it in your own way."**

**General Ulysses S Grant to Gen William T. Sherman, April 1864**

*CHAPTER 6*

# COURSE OF ACTION DEVELOPMENT

## ✮✮✮

**COURSES OF ACTION (COAs).** COAs are stated as alternative concepts of operation or support – developed after task analysis is complete, objectives are stated, and constraints identified. Recommended COAs should be based on current *Staff and Commander's Estimate* and COA criteria analysis. The adopted COA is the basis for the concept of operation (Para 3a) in the order/plan.

Two (2) systems for Course of Action Development are available for this step.

1.    Commander Directed Single Course of Action
2.    Full Staff Multiple Course of Action Development

1.    **Commander Directed Single Course of Action** is conducted at the discretion of the commander. The commander provides a single Course of Action to the staff. The staff then moves directly to Course of Action Evaluation (Wargaming). This process will be used primarily in time constrained situations and in other situations selected by the commander. The commander will, at a minimum, consider the steps shown below for the Full Staff Multiple Course of Action Development. The commander must remain ready to modify or change the directed Course of Action if Wargaming reveals it to be unsuitable, unfeasible, unacceptable or incomplete.

2. **Full Staff Multiple Course of Action Development** is the formal process used when selected by the commander. The process is detailed below.

## FULL STAFF MULTIPLE COURSE OF ACTION DEVELOPMENT

1. Prepare generic unit symbols (stickies) for friendly units (supported, supporting) at BN level (S-3) and for enemy forces (maneuver, FA, ADA, AHB's) at BN level (S-2/NCO). Show enemy operations forces down to platoon level if at all possible. These are used to array forces for COA development. Symbols MUST show relative combat power for each.

2. The S-2/S-2 NCO reviews Friendly and Enemy Relative Combat Power and complete the Event Template.

3. The SPO reviews "Relative Support Load" for each supporting unit. "Relative Support Load" is an analysis of the support demands (requirements) placed on each support unit (capabilities) as developed in the Spt Opns cell prepared logistics estimates of requirements, capabilities, shortfalls and recommended solutions.

4. XO lists and disseminates CDR's guidance for determining validity of COAs.

5. S-3 develops tactical COA's against "enemy most like COA" and "enemy most dangerous COA" for templated threats to the sustainment organization and the customer (i.e. the supported unit).

6. Spt Ops Off develops support COA's for support of each friendly maneuver COA currently under consideration by the supported unit.

7. Each COA will have a sketch and concept of operation paragraph using the battlefield framework of Decisive (DE), Shaping (SE) and Sustaining. Other planners can assist in COA development as needed. These COAs must be flexible to accommodate "most likely" and "most dangerous" enemy and friendly COAs, they must meet the guidance and intent of the commander, and they must be significantly different from one another. S-3 and SPO coordinate their tactical and support COA's. **The goal is** "how does the sustainment organization synchronize and execute effective and efficient distribution down to the soldier level."

8. Other planners return to their work areas for continued planning and information gathering while COAs are being developed. All planners return at the appropriate time to review COAs. All planners get an initial shot at the COAs to screen for validity, soundness, and general content. All planners have to understand the COAs before presenting them to the XO for review. Each COA must meet criteria of suitability, feasibility, acceptability, distinguishability, and completeness

9. Upon review and approval by XO, sketches and concept of operations paragraphs are prepared for briefing.

10. Other charts and overheads are prepared in accordance with the COA Briefing Format at Chapter 14.

11. Prepare relative combat power for each COA down to regiment/brigade and battalion level. Prepare any overheads, charts, and standard drops for briefing.

## GUIDANCE GIVEN TO EACH PLANNER

1. Determine decisive points and times to focus the main effort.

2. ID purpose to be achieved by the main and supporting efforts.

3.  Determine essential tasks to subordinates (ensure all tasks from higher order are addressed, assigned or delegated to some unit). Assign assets to sub units (Task Organization).

4.  Assign control measures (minimum necessary to achieve synchronization of operation) and phases.

5.  Prepare COA statement and sketches:
    a.  Restated mission.
    b.  Restate/Expansion of commander's intent.
    c.  Designation of decisive point/main effort, supporting efforts and purpose of each.
    d.  Array tactical and support forces within the supported units' form of maneuver.
    e.  Critical factors/elements underlying the plan.
    f.  Phases of operation.
    g.  Idea on timelines for each event and decision point.
    h.  Idea on branches and sequels.

## STEPS IN COURSE OF ACTION DEVELOPMENT

1.  Analyze Relative Combat Power and Relative Support Load. **(S-3 & SPO)**

2.  Generate options. **(ALL)**
    a.  A good COA should be capable of executing all distribution operations while defeating all feasible enemy COAs and supporting all supported units' COAs.
    b.  COA options should focus on distribution techniques that circumvent enemy COAs while supporting friendly maneuver/sustaining COA's, each arranged in order of probable adoption.
    c.  Staff determines the decisive points where the unit will focus the support effort relative to terrain, enemy and time to enable the supported units to achieve their purpose.

3. Array initial forces of Sustainment units. This includes location, composition, task, and purpose for each sustainment element (i.e. BSA, LSA/FOB, CRSP, CSC, FLE, AXP, UMCP, EPW Holding area). **(S-3 & SPO)**

4. Develop concept of support. **(S-3 & SPO)**
   a. The purpose of the operation.
   b. A statement of where the commander will accept tactical and logistical risk.
   c. Identification of critical friendly events and phases of the operation (if phased).
   d. Designation of the main effort, along with its task and purpose.
   e. Designation of supporting efforts, tasks and purposes, linked to support the main effort.
   f. Support to the reserve, to include location, composition, task, and purpose.
   g. Support to deep, close, and rear operations.
   h. R&S operations of Sus Bde/CSSB/BSB units.
   i. An outline of the movements of the Divisional forces and SUSTAINMENT BRIGADE unit movements.
   j. Identification of support options that may develop during the operation.
   k. Location of attack objectives and counterattack objectives.
   l. Responsibilities for area of operations.
   m. Concept of fires (if applicable).
   n. Prescribed formations or dispositions when necessary.
   o. Priorities for each Maneuver Support (MS) and Sustainment element by tactical logistics function. (Internal & external)
   p. Consideration of the effects of enemy weapons of mass destruction (WMD) on the force.

5. Assign headquarters. **(S-3)**

6.  Prepare Course of Action statements and sketches. **(S-3 & SPO)**
    a.  How to accomplish the mission and explain the concept of support.
    b.  As a minimum, it will include:
        (1)  Array of supported and supporting forces and logistics facilities.
        (2)  Planning unit and subordinate unit boundaries that establish the AO.
        (3)  The FEBA or LD/LC, control measures and subsequent phase lines.
        (4)  Reconnaissance and Surveillance (R&S) graphics.
        (5)  Ground and air axes of advance, MSR's.
        (6)  Assembly areas, battle positions, strong points, engagement areas, and objectives.
        (7)  Designation of the main and supporting efforts.
        (8)  Enemy known or templated locations with FA range fans.

## SUSTAINMENT CONSIDERATIONS IN COA DEVELOPMENT

**Sustainment Planners should focus on logistical factors that constrain the tactical operations**

- Key is to identify and eliminate any COA that is not supportable.

- Identify limitations that planners must be concerned with (CL IV availability for barrier plans, CL V CSR vs RSR, vehicle/driver availability)

- Identify the cost or risk in terms of resources for each COA

- Update logistics and personnel estimates as additional information becomes available

**Key questions for the Sustainment planners are:**

- How will the Sustainer achieve distribution operations in an effective and efficient

- Will sustainment support require relocation (BSB) or echelon (Sus Bde/CSSB) during the operation?

- MSR and ASR traffic ability?

- Are the line haul or local haul distance factors exceeded?

**Specific items to focus on for COA development**

- BSA/LSA/TF-CAB Support Area, CSC and CRSP locations, Level II and III medical facilities.

- MSR plan for the conduct of replenishment operations (RO) of the units

- Use of logistics release points (LRPs)

- Medical and maintenance recovery along MSRs

- SECFOR availability for convoy security. Availability and employment of IED defeating electronic warfare (EW) systems.

- Will the BSB need to move to support the COA?

- Will the Sustainment Brigade need to echelon/establish a CSC, TTPs, Mini-mart, or CRSPs?

- Are any Forward Logistics Elements (FLEs) required?

# QUALITIES OF COA'S

1. **Suitability:** It must accomplish the mission and comply with the commander's guidance.

2. **Feasibility:** The unit must have the capability to accomplish the mission in terms of available time, space and resources.

3. **Acceptability:** The tactical or operational advantage gained by executing the COA must justify the cost in resources, especially casualties.

4. **Distinguishability:** Each COA must differ significantly from any others. Significant differences may result from use of reserves, different task organizations, day or night operations, or a different scheme of maneuver.

5. **Completeness:** It must be a complete mission statement to include who, what, when, where, and why.

## PREPARATION FOR COA BRIEFING

1. Rehearse briefing. One person briefs while another planner points. (Chapter 14)

2. Be prepared to display all friendly COAs side-by-side for final review by CDR.

3. Address concept of logistics/sustainment for all COAs.

4. Show end state disposition of friendly forces in COA sketches.

5. Identify a time line (red timelines for enemy movement against our defense) (blue timelines for friendly movement against enemy defense) for each COA.

6. Ensure the following are visually displayed for briefing:
   - Map showing AOR, friendly and enemy units on 1:50,000 (*1:250,000 at Sus Bde*)
   - Mission statement and Intent 1 and 2 levels up.
   - Narrative for each enemy COA.
   - Division restated mission.
   - Task Organization (highlight any additional assets added from higher since last brief).

7. Display relative combat power for friendly and enemy (at battalion or brigade/regiment level) for viewing with each COA.

## PRODUCTS FROM COA BRIEFING

1. Additional commander's guidance on selected COAs for war gaming.

2. Time and Location for Decision Briefing.

3. COA statements and sketches

## 6.1 COURSE OF ACTION DEVELOPMENT CHECKLIST

### STEP 1 REVIEW COMMANDERS MISSION ANALYSIS GUIDANCE

| TASK DESCRIPTION | PERSONNEL |
|---|---|
| Extract and publish Commanders Guidance | ALL/Clerk |
| Update Restated Mission | XO, S-3 |
| Update/Brief Subordinate Unit Status | STAFF |
| Update/Brief RFIs received | OPS NCO |

## STEP 2 DEVELOP COURSES OF ACTION

| TASK DESCRIPTION | PERSONNEL |
|---|---|
| Analyze force ratios | S-3 |
| Array initial forces | S-3 |
| Draft Commanders Intent | XO, S-3 |
| Develop Scheme of Maneuver per COA | ALL |
| Determine C2 means and maneuver control measures | S-3 |
| Prepare COA statements and Operational Sketches | S-3, ANY APPLICABLE STAFF |

## STEP 3 ANALYZE AND COMPARE COURSES OF ACTION

| TASK DESCRIPTION | PERSONNEL |
|---|---|
| Extract and publish Commanders Guidance | S-3 Clerk |
| Develop proposed CCIR | ALL |
| Conduct initial wargame each COA. The focus of the Battle Staff is more on the entire sector than on each battle. The purpose of the initial wargame is to allow each Battle Staff Section to gather enough insight on a COA to make a recommendation to the commander | ALL |
| Determine decision criteria and assign weighting values to criteria | ALL |
| Make recommendation | ALL |

## STEP 4 PREPARE AND CONDUCT COA DECISION BRIEF

| TASK DESCRIPTION | PERSONNEL |
|---|---|
| Provide COA decision brief input to the XO or S-3 NCOIC | ALL |
| Review COA decision criteria and COA comparisons | ALL (as necessary) |
| Site setup for briefing | S-2/3 NCOs |
| Prepare slides and handouts | S-2/3 NCOs |
| Rehearse briefing to XO | ALL Briefers |
| Conduct briefing | ALL |
| Receive Guidance | ALL |

## 6.2 BSA and FORWARD LOGISTICS ELEMENT (FLE) SELECTION CRITERIA (BSB Only)

1. **Approval Authority.** In concert with the BSB Bn Cdr, the BSB S-3 will designate the general location of the primary and alternate BSAs and/or FLEs. The S-3 determines the exact location based on input and guidance from the Battalion Commander, Battalion XO, Battalion SPO and the Brigade S-4.

2. **Size.** Minimum size of the Brigade Support Area depends on factors of METT-T (Mission, Enemy. Terrain, Time Available, Troops Available, and civilian considerations) and it normally requires 2-3 square kilometers. Minimum size of the FLE is based on the support role it is required to perform.

3. **Criteria.** Primary considerations in the selection of the BSA (or FLE location) are: survivability and defendability (out of artillery range and good overhead concealment), mobility, accessibility and responsiveness. In selecting a BSA/FLE site, the following criteria will be considered:

00 Log Spt Responsiveness to Tactical Requirements
  o CL I-IX. Svcs
  o Must consider time / distance factors for all supported units
  00 Sufficiency of AO
  o Access to Ground LOCs
  o Ease of Gnd Mvt/Traffic Plan
  o DZs
  o LZs
  o HLZs
  o Air/Sea Ports
  o Water source for ROWPU teams, access to a water source
  o Size/Dispersion
  o Hardstand
  o Supply routes / dirty routes
00 Command. Control, Communications
00 Risk
  o Security
    - OCOKA (Observation. Cover & Concealment. Obstacles,
    - Key/Decisive Terrain, and Avenues of Approach)
    - Fields of Fire
  o Distance from Enemy Indirect Fire
  o Safety
00 Supports Sus Bde planned MRO/MSOs

Items to consider:
   Expandability of area (e.g. what if we get more assets prior to the battle?)

4.   **Forward Logistics Element/Base Criteria**. If a FLE is in consideration as a COA, as a minimum, the following five (5) criteria must be addressed.

* **Mission**. What is the mission of the FLE (Who, What, Where, When, Why – Task & Purpose)
* **Duration**. FLEs are not indefinite structures that can be sent out for long period of time.
* **Command and Control.** Who is in charge (by name) and how does the unit communicate with the FLE (by communications device)?
* **Security**. How does the FLE provide its own security or how is it tied in to other unit's security plan?
* **Composition**. What specific elements and equipment make up the FLE? Required equipment and elements become a tasking to subordinate units in the final OPORD preparation.

## 6.3 BSA/FLE DISPLACEMENT CRITERIA

* BSA & FLE Displacement criteria occur when:

  ✓ Ordered to do so by higher HQ

  ✓ Required to maintain signal support

  ✓ Boundary changes forward or rearward

  ✓ Within tube Artillery or insurgent mortar/rocket range

  ✓ MSR interdicted or closed over 24 hours

  ✓ Enemy eyes on confined

  ✓ LOCs become extended by time and/or distance, making ft to difficult to maintain continuous support to maneuver units

## 6.4 BSA/FLE Positioning Criteria

This chart may be useful for reconnaissance as well as decision making. Weights may be assigned to each dependant upon **Mission, Enemy, Terrain, Time, Troops, and Civilian Consideration (METT-TC) Available.**

| CRITERIA | POSSIBLE SITES | | | | | |
|---|---|---|---|---|---|---|
| | WT | 1 | 2 | 3 | 4 | 5 |

*LOG SPT RESPONSIVENESS TO TACTICAL SITUATION*
* Supply
* Maintenance
* Medical
* Services
* Transportation
* Ground LOC Distance & Condition

*SUFFICIENCY OF BRIGADE SUPPORT AREA*
* Trafficability
* Water Source
* Road Network
* Helicopter LZs
* Air/Sea Ports
* Hardstand
* Drainage

*COMMAND, CONTROL, COMMUNICATIONS RISK*
* Security – OCOKA (Observation and fields of fire, Cover and concealment, Obstacles, Key/Decisive terrain, and Enemy Avenues of Approach)
* NBC Effetcs

* Distance from Enemy Indirect Fire
* Support Deception
* Safety

*LOCATION SUPPORTS REORGANIZATION*

CONCLUSION: SITE ___ IS THE BEST COA

## 6.5 THE SUSTAINMENT OVERLAY (AKA "THE LOGISTICS COMMON OPERATING PICTURE or "LCOP")

1.  The sustainment overlay (or LCOP in digital C2 TOCs) is a graphic representation of the tactical allay of support areas and units. Ideally, it accompanies copies of the OPLAN and/ or OPORD distributed to subordinate HQ and is used as a graphic backdrop to the support concept briefing. The list below is a representative example of elements that could be expected to locate in the BSA and key logistical resources areas that will occur with the units area of operation. •This overlay must be synchronized with the operations overlays.

    * Command Posts: Sus Bde, CSSB, BSB and local Division TOC
    * Alternate/Proposed BSA, TF/CAB SA, and FLE Locations
    * MSRs, from the TD Sus Bde to the BSA including FDRPs and TCPs
    * SRs and Dirty Routes within the sector
    * LRPs and LZs
    * Boundaries for Sustainment Unit responsibilities.
    * BSB Distribution Company CP
    * Class I point & Water point
    * Class II, III, IV, and VII (if applicable) point
    * ASA (Sus Bde) and/or ATHPs active/planned within AOR
    * Salvage collection point

- Mortuary Affairs Collection Point (MACP)
- BSB Forward Maintenance Company CP
- Class IX point
- Support Maintenance Company shops
- UMCPs and MCPs
- BSB Medical Company/Support Brigade Medical Company CP/Class VIII Point
- Battalion Aid Stations
- Smoke Platoon
- Decontamination Point
- Reconnaissance Squad
- Military Police Platoon
- EPW Collection Point
- Military Intelligence Team
- ADA Battery (-)
- Network Support/Signal Units within AOR
- Aviation Elements

## A Typical BSA Configuration

## 6.6 SUSTAINMENT UNIT LOCATION GUIDELINES

1.  Position CP's near the center of the FOB/LSA/BSA Perimeter for C2 and security reasons.

2.  Balance the advantages of dispersion (reduced destruction from a single enemy rocket/mortar strike) with the disadvantages ($C^2$ constraints and extended perimeter).

3.  Make supply points accessible to both customers and re-supply vehicles and helicopters.

4.  Keep Class III points away from other supplies to prevent contamination. They should also be located at least 100 ft from water supplies.

5.  Locate the ATHP at least 180 meters from other supplies and 620 meters from the nearest inhabited tent.

6.  Position MACP and salvage points near the MSR possibly near the ATHP to maximize back- haul mission of vehicles used for ammunition re-supply.

7.  Locate the Class I point near the water point whenever water sources allow.

8.  Locate the clearing station away for likely target areas (ATHP, Class III points, bridges, road junction) but near evacuation routes and open area for landing air ambulances.

9.  Locate maintenance sites to be accessible to customers, including recovery/evacuation vehicles.

10. Ensure maintenance shops, along with parking and equipment holding sites are on firm ground.

11. Position Network Support/Signal assets and any attached MP platoon HQ near the BDE/BSB CP to enhance support and security.

12. Position the ATHP near the rear of the BSA and near but off the MSR so that the large number of PLS systems and trailers bringing ammo into the area do not clog up the MSR with in the BSA. The ATHP requires sufficient area to perform transload operations without interfering with BSA traffic.

13. Position units with the heaviest fire-power, such as the FSC maintenance platoon, along the most threatening avenue of approach.

## 6.7 BSB MOVEMENT TECHNIQUES

Primary goal is to provide continuous support to the BDE while displacing the BSB

## 1. MOVEMENT OF THE BSB WITHIN THE BDE FORMATION
- Enemy contact not expected
- Long road march to TAA
- Requires BDE to resupply prior to movement to allow the BSB to pack up
- MSTs should move with TFs, BSA moves as a unit
- Relies heavily on theater/corps support
- "Tailgate" support sho        uld be available

— Maintenance

— Medical

* MST and maj assy w/ TF
* Transport "delayed casualties.

* 30 min repair limits
* MEDEVAC

* Recovery plan
* Some Ambulances w/ BSA

* O/O MCPs identified
* Air Evac coordinated

* Drag NMC Veh w/ short repair times

- Bulk Refuel
\* SRO by Sus Bde (TD/CSSB
\* Alternate refuel plan

- Mortuary Affairs
\* Collection Plan
\* Transportation Plan

## 2. ATTACHMENT OF CRITICAL SUSTAINMENT ASSETS TO BCT
### "TUCK UP PACKAGES"
**Advantages**

- Most responsive method
- Combat essential CL III, V, medical and water sent w/ each TF
- Supply point distribution for all other customers
- Primarily used during Offensive Operations
  - Operational distances are great
  - Secure LOCs are uncertain
  - Log turnaround time too long to support the TFs

**Disadvantages**

- High risk to scarce resources (eg 5K Tankers ambulances etc)
- Results in longer resupply times for BSB assets or requires CSSB to push far fwd,
- Limits support for other customers in the BSA
- Limited capability to transport Class V forward

## 3. SUPPORT FROM THE BSB: DISPLACE AS AN ENTITY

- Best used when BCT is operating with clearly defined phases with identifiable windows b/w operations (e.g. river crossings)
- Supply point distribution from the BSB
- BSB jumps partly or in whole during time provided by window

- Sustainment black out for BCT for 12-24 hours as BSB re-establishes
- May be used ICW tuck up packages to minimize support disruption
- BSA must be resupplied by the Sus Bde (MSO) prior to jump in order to re-establish sustainment ops at new site
- Close out times, start up times and new locations must be coordinated w/the Sustainment Brigade, the BCT and (time permitting) the Div G-4.
- Consider jumping the BSB ahead of the BCT if new BSA is secure. Jump when least detrimental to BCT.

## 4. BSB DISPLACEMENT BY ECHELONS

- Used when continuous support is required
- Supply point distribution at both ends
- Critical CSS assets are split, displace by bounds
- Sections that can be easily split
  - BSB TOC
  - Water (FAWPSS or SMFT)
  - Class III tankers
  - Major assembles
  - MSTs (displace with TFs MCPs)
  - Medical (ambulances, treatment squads)
- Sections that cannot be easily split
- Water production
  - Class I
  - Class II/IV
  - Mortuary Affairs
- ATHP has limited capability to split operations
- Critical Class V may be pushed fwd using organic tractors
- SPO deploys w/ forward element
- BSB TOC remains in rear until BCT Sustainment Cell (S-1/4) CP assumes control

- Asst SPO remains with TOC to coordinate sustainment at old site
- Support Ops provides BCT, Div G-4, and Sus Bde SPO with shut down and start up times and grids for new locations once established

# COA ANALYSIS (WAR-GAMING)

★★★

## WAR-GAMING

After the COA briefing, select staff gathers in the Plans area to begin war-gaming the COAs that survived the COA briefing. War-gaming is a disciplined process with rules and steps that attempt to visualize the flow of the operation – in this case the conduct of distribution operations. Planners take necessary time to return to their staff sections to develop further information, gather additional tools, etc. and return at the appointed time.

## PURPOSE OF WAR-GAMING

1. Determine how to maximize '*sustainment*' combat power.
2. Provides identical vision of the battle.
3. Anticipate battlefield events.
4. Determine conditions and resources for success.
5. Decide how to apply support capabilities.
6. Focus IPB on enemy strengths/weaknesses, center of gravity, desired end state and decisive points in both the shaping and decisive efforts, with focus on the main and supporting efforts.
7. ID coordination necessary to synchronize results.
8. Determine most flexible COA.

## WAR-GAMING PROCESS

1. Considers friendly disposition, strengths and weaknesses.
2. Considers enemy assets and probable COAs.
3. Based on characteristics of AO.
4. Focuses the staff on each phase of operation in a logical sequence.
5. Iterative process of action, reaction and counteraction.

## WAR-GAME RESPONSIBILITIES

1. **XO**: Responsible for coordinating actions of the staff during the war game.
2. **S-1**: Analyze potential battle losses and personnel support.
3. **S-2/Intel NCO**: Role play enemy commander; develops enemy decision points, reaction to friendly actions, enemy losses. Participates in the Rear Battle Targeting meeting and identifies High Value Targets for Rear Battle. Be sure to also reflect any MSR/ASR inhibitors that could potentially interfere with distribution operations.
4. **S-3**: ID information requirements, refines event template to include NAIs, refines sustainment unit Sustainment Sync matrix with DPs, TAIs, HVTs; refines situation template, ID area of interest. Selects the war gaming method. Maintain Sustainment synch matrix/ sketch notes.
5. **S-4**: Analyze internal sustainment unit internal logistics and effects on ability to support sustainment operations to the customer.
6. **SPO**: Critical requirements for each sustainment function, assesses status of all sustainment functions; ID potential shortfalls and recommends actions to eliminate; assesses movement times and assets to support each COA.
7. **All Staff Members**: Determine force requirements for external support, risks, and each COAs strengths and weaknesses.

## WAR-GAMING STEPS

Gather the necessary tools: current coordinating staff estimates, event templates, recording method, completed COAs to include maneuver and R&S graphics, means to post enemy and friendly unit symbols, map of AO (blank synch matrices, butcher paper, blank overlays to record DST during war gaming, etc.).

1. List all friendly forces.
2. List assumptions (Review previous assumptions for continued validity and necessity).
3. List known critical events and decision points.
4. Determine evaluation criteria.
5. Select the war game method (Revisit the war gaming procedure as necessary).
6. Select a method to record and display results (Identify a scribe to post all notes from war gaming onto the synch matrix and a planner to record the DST).
7. War game the battle and assess results (Establish timelines for war gaming and post on a blank overlay the enemy or friendly timelines for movement. Begin a list of additional assets to be requested from Corps as a result of war gaming.

## EVALUATION CRITERIA

1. This portion of the sustainment planning process will allow you to determine which customer COA can best be supported from a sustainment perspective. In order to do this, screening and evaluation criteria must be defined. Screening criteria screens out unsatisfactory and unfeasible COAs. Evaluation criteria, is evaluated further for suitability, feasibility, and acceptability.

2.  The following list contains examples of evaluation criteria:

    a.  Command and control: provides unity of command
    b.  Commander's intent; best supports to objectives of the commander
    c.  Location: provides suitable location to support sustainment/CHS operations.
    d.  Routes: provides the most responsive and safest means for moving supplies and personnel.
    e.  Risk: requires minimal risk to unit/personnel
    f.  Security: provides best security posture for sustainment/CHS assets
    g.  Re-supply operations: promotes ease of re-supply in an expedient manner
    h.  Medical evacuation: best use of medical and non-standard evacuation assets that will maintain a continuous flow of rapid casualty evacuation.

## WAR-GAMING SEQUENCE (See 7.1)
## DURING WAR-GAMING

1.  Develop additional planning assumptions, as necessary.
2.  Capture PIR/IRs during each war gaming turn from PIR/IRs developed during Mission Analysis.
3.  List additional assets to be requested from other Sustainment Brigades or ESC.
4.  **TIP**: Keep the war-gaming moving and on track. Scribe doesn't have to write everything down. Each planner should be keeping notes, by WFF, of the significant elements of the war gaming that apply to him.
5.  The S-2/Intel NCO plays the part of the enemy commander and fights the battle from two perspectives: the enemy's "most likely course of action" and the enemy's "most dangerous course of action." If there are two distinct enemy COAs, then each friendly COA must be considered against them.

Again, do not forget to factor in possible (but realistic) factors into MSR/ASR status that could potentially effect distribution operations.

6. At the end of each "war-gaming iteration," assess friendly and enemy loss percentages and present combat power and support capabilities.

## ITEMS THE COMMANDER AND STAFF SHOULD IDENTIFY, REFINE, DEVELOP OR FINALIZE AS A RESULT OF WAR-GAMING COAs

1. Refining or modifying the COA, to include identifying branches and sequels that become on-order or be prepared missions.
2. Refining locations and timing of the decisive points.
3. Identifying key or decisive terrain and determining how to use it.
4. Refining the enemy event template.
5. Refining task organizations, to include forces retained in GS of the command.
6. Identifying tasks the unit must retain & tasks to be assigned to subordinate commanders.
7. Allocating maneuver, maneuver support, and sustainment assets to subordinate commanders to accomplish their missions.
8. Developing a Sustainment Synchronization Matrix and Decision Support Template.
9. Estimating the duration of each critical event as well as of the entire operation.
10. Projecting the percentage of total enemy forces defeated in each critical event, and overall.
11. Identifying likely times and areas for enemy use of WMD and friendly CBRNE defense requirements.
12. Identifying the location and commitment of the reserves.
13. Identifying the most dangerous enemy COA.

14. Identifying the location of the commander and unit command posts.
15. Identifying additional critical events.
16. Identifying additional requirements for maneuver support and sustainment support.
17. Determining requirements for deception and surprise.
18. Refining C2 requirements, to include control measures and updated graphics.
19. Finalizing CCIR and IR with the latest time information is of value (LTIOV) or latest event information is of value (LRIOV).
20. Finalizing the R&S plan and graphics for the basis for the collection plan.
21. Refining CCIR and incorporating them into the R&S plan and graphics.
22. Developing Fires, Protection, information/influence activities (IIA), and sustainment plan and graphics.
23. Identifying or confirming the locations of decision points, NAIs, and TAIs, and the information needed to support the decision points.
24. Determining the timing of force concentrations.
25. Developing the intelligence collection and dissemination plan.
26. Determining movement times and tables.
27. Identifying, analyzing, and evaluating strengths and weaknesses of the COA.
28. Integrating the targeting process, to include identifying or confirming high pay-off targets and determining attack guidance.
29. Synchronizing Class III (fog oil) ISO smoke operations.
30. Identifying additional hazards, assessing their risk, developing control measures to reduce risk from all identified hazards, and determining residual risk.

# WAR GAMING OUTPUT

1. War game results. Which COA best supports both efficient and effective distribution operations.
2. Task Organization. (It's OK to cross level pure companies such as Truck Companies into multifunction transportation units, such as cross attaching a HET Platoon from a HET Company with a PLS Platoon from a Medium Truck company possessing PLS systems.
3. Mission to subordinate units. Remember – if you opt to create a Forward Logistics Element, one unit needs to pick up the C2 portion.
4. CCIR. These should change from those initially developed in Mission Analysis.

# PRODUCTS FROM WAR GAMING

1. Refined Courses of Action
2. Synch Matrix for each war game.
3. Decision Support Template/DSM for each war game.
4. Potential branches and sequels – contingency planning if required
5. List of areas of concern to be engaged during shaping and decisive operations.
6. Sustainment combat power at the end of the war game for friendly and enemy and support capabilities for friendly forces.
7. Updated running estimates and assumptions.

## 7.1 The Wargaming Sequence.

### Wargaming Sequence

1. Visualize the operation.
2. Considerations in developing COA's based upon METT-T
   a. Movement planning (air, ground).
   b. Task organization
   c. FOB/LSA/CRSP/TTP/CSC/Base cluster locations
   d. Availability of addition support (MP, SECFOR, EN, ADA, higher headquarters, etc.)
   e. Security /Force Protection measures
      (1) Entry to AO
      (2) Convoy operations
      (3) Critical equipment sites [Example: ROWPU, FSSP, FARE, FAWPSS].
3. List advantages and disadvantages (remain unbiased).
4. Assess feasibility of COA.
5. Avoid comparing COA's until comparison phase.
6. Avoid premature conclusions.

# THOUGHTS ON WAR-GAMING

"When he looked at a map, Zhukov did not just reproduce the picture of the past engagement; he could foresee the nature of the future encounter and in a matter of minutes play out as it were, the various scenarios first for himself and then for the enemy. He could put himself in the enemy's place for a while so that when he became himself again he could evaluate the intentions of the enemy."

FROM; A. CHAKOVSKLY, THE BLOCKADE IN FUNDAMENTALS OF TACTICAL COMMAND AND CONTROL, BY D.A. IVANOV ET AL. (MOSCOW, 1977), P.203

15

*CHAPTER 8*

# COURSE OF ACTION COMPARISON

✮✮✮

1.  After war gaming, the staff prepares to do comparison of the courses of action. The course of action comparison starts with each staff officer analyzing and evaluating the advantages and disadvantages of each COA from their perspective. The planners return to their work areas, as time permits, to begin their individual COA comparison. Each planner must take the comparison criteria and individually apply them to each COA, paying particular attention to developing rationale to support his decision about which COA is best supported by his/her War Fighting Functional Area. When the planners reconvene, each staff member presents his/her findings for the others' consideration. Using the evaluation criteria developed earlier, the staff then outlines each COA, highlighting its advantages and disadvantages with respect to each other. Planners have the opportunity to make points pro and con about each COA.

2.  The staff compares feasible courses of action to identify the one that has the highest probability of success against the most likely enemy course of action and the most dangerous course of action. The selected COA should also:

    a.  Pose the minimum risk to the soldiers, equipment, and mission accomplishment.
    b.  Best position the force for future operations.

    c.   Provide the best flexibility to meet "unknowns" during execution.

    d.   Provide maximum latitude for initiative by subordinates.

3.   The actual comparison of COAs is critical. The staff may use any technique that facilitates reaching the best recommendation and the commander making the best decision. The most common technique is the Decision Matrix (ATTP 5-0.1, Figure 4-16). Each staff officer may use his/her own matrix, using same evaluative criteria, for comparison in his/her own field of interest. Decision matrixes cannot alone provide decision solutions. The matrix should use the evaluation criteria developed earlier. The XO normally determines the weight of each criterion based on its relative importance. The staff officer responsible for a functional area scores each COA using those criteria. Multiply the score by the weight yields the criterion's value. Comparing a COA by category is more accurate than attempting to aggregate a total score for each COA.

**COA Comparison (the Leavenworth "School Solution"):** Let's assume there are three COAs to the compared. The criteria is established and agreed to. For the each criteria, the COA that is best supported gets a "3". The next in order of supportability gets a "2" and the last COA gets a "1". If one sees little or no difference in the last two COAs (for supportability), then each COA gets a "1.5" (the average of the sum of 2+1). Using the same thought process, if all COAs are deemed to be equally supportable against a particular criteria, then they would all get a "2" (average of the sum of 3+2+1). If there were 4 COAs to be compared, then the most supportable would get a "4" and so on. None of the criteria is weighted, initially. If at the end of the comparison and the totaling of the numbers given to each COA against the criteria there is not a clear cut "winner", then the planners should go back to the commander's guidance, pick the one or two most important points and assign a weight to those criteria, do the multiplication and addition again, and see if one COA comes out ahead. This is the comparison method that is taught in ILE (formerly CGSC), and SAMS.

4.   Output from the COA Comparison is the Decision Matrix.

## 8.1 COMPARISON CRITERIA – A METHOD

1.   COA's for Sustainment units are limited in the number and extent of available options due to the assigned missions, available task organization, and METT-T of the situation. As a result, Sustainment C2 units should spend their available time comparing missions to available assets to insure that resources are available to ensure success. Distance, terrain, weather, personnel strength, mission requirements, potential enemy action, and equipment loss all must be taken into consideration. Ultimately, the best COA is the one that conducts effective and efficient "end-to-end" distribution management with little/no loss of life and equipment. Typical COAs are:

a.   For Sus Brigades/CSSBs: Echelonment of a FLE/FLB
Establish a Centralized Receiving and Shipping Pt (CRSP)
Establish a Trailer Transfer Point (TTP)
Establish a Convoy Support Center (CSC) or "Mini-Mart"

b.   For BSBs: Echelonment of FLE/FLB
Split the BSB into two equal elements, capable of independent operations.

2.  All task organization unit assets and capabilities must be recorded and tracked by both the S-4 (internal unit readiness) and Support Operations (external support operations) staff sections due to the multiple capabilities of many pieces of equipment, primarily transportation assets which are the key to any operation.

3.  All COA's must place the battalion and its task organization in a position to support follow-on missions.

## CONCEPT OF SUPPORT

## 8.2 SCHEME OF SUPPORT FOR COURSE OF ACTION DEVELOPMENT

### General Instructions

In the course of COA development, the staff takes the *input* and completes the development process to create the *output* which becomes the Scheme of Support.

**Input**
Restated Mission
Commander's Guidance
Intelligence Estimate

## Process
Analyze support requirements and unit capabilities
Match capabilities with mission tasks
Determine mission requirements
Complete Personnel, Intelligence, Sus, and Support
  Operations Estimates
Determine C2 requirements

## Output
Course of action statements
Intelligence update
Recommended course of action for analysis

## 8.3 SCHEME OF SUPPORT COA DEVELOPMENT WORKSHEET

1.  Identify tasks that require both equipment and material. Make assumptions for consumables (Class III and IX) as necessary.
2.  Identify if shared resources are used for a task (i.e. one tractor for two or more trailers).

| Unit | Tasks | Equipment | Shortfalls/Issues |
|------|-------|-----------|-------------------|
|      |       |           |                   |
|      |       |           |                   |
|      |       |           |                   |
|      |       |           |                   |
|      |       |           |                   |
|      |       |           |                   |
|      |       |           |                   |
|      |       |           |                   |
|      |       |           |                   |
|      |       |           |                   |
|      |       |           |                   |

## 8.4 SCHEME OF SUPPORT COURSE OF ACTION SKETCH

### Annex C to 123 BSB OPORD

| | Phase I: Prep/ Counter-recon | Phase IIA & B: Motorized IN, Mech Armor Fight | Phase III: Consolidation and Reorganization |
|---|---|---|---|
| CONCEPT OF SUPPORT: 123 BSB conducts GAC and LOGAIR missions to provide uninterrupted CSS to the 30 HBCT as they defend in sector. Priority of supplies is Class IV, V, III(B), and water. BPT push out LOGPACs and FLEs to rearm and refit the 30HBCT as they transition into offensive operations. | T: A Co move 1-120 CAB and 1-150 CAV into sector P: Allow units to establish defense T: A Co BPT move 1-252 CAB fwd into sector P: Allow unit to prepare for defense in the event no air is available T: A Co move CL IV & V into sector P: IOT est. Brigade defense | T: A Co BPT push emergency resupply of CL I, III, IV, V, VIII, IX, and water fwd by air or ground P: Allow units to continue the fight T: A Co BPT refuel BDE reserves P: Allow the reserve to remain flexible | T: A Co BPT push emergency resupply of CL I, III, IV, V, VIII, IX and water fwd by air or ground P: Allow units to continue the fight T: A Co O/O push necessary classes of supply forward P: Allow the 30 HBCT to transition into the offense |

Priority of Support:
Priority of support is 1-120, 1-150 CAV/ 1-252 and 1-113 FA

Pr. of Troop movement from TAA to def position:
Air moves 1-150 CAV
210600-UTC: A/1-120, C/1-120
No air avail:
210600-UTC: 1-252, B/1-120, D/1-120

See Appendix 1 to Annex I (External) 123rd OPORD

**Priority of Maintenance:**
o Priority of ground maintenance is M1, M3, Q36, M198, M119, Avenger, Sünger, ROWPU, MHE
o Priority of air maintenance is AH64, OH58D, UH60, CH47

**Routes:**
o All MSRs need to remain open until 23 1800 JUL
o MSRs need to be closed NLT 23 1800 JUL
o At the conclusion of the defense, o/o open MSRs in their AOs to allow for resupply to move forward

**CL IV Movement Assets pushed fwd:**
1-120: 3 x 4K FL, entire operation
1-252: 1 x 10K FL 211800-212400
1-150: 1 x 10K FL 211800-212400

RSR—CSR except the following:

A. 155MM

| HE | APICM | DPICM | HC | RAP | WP | ILL | RAAMS | ADAM | CLGP |
|---|---|---|---|---|---|---|---|---|---|
| 25 | 3 | 50 | 6 | 2 | 6 | 3 | 2 | 1 | 2 |

B. 105MM

| HE | APICM | APERS | HC | RAP | WP | ILL | HEP-T |
|---|---|---|---|---|---|---|---|
| 40 | 40 | 1 | 3 | 6 | 6 | 6 | 2 | 1 |

C. 81MM

| HP | WP | ILL |
|---|---|---|
| 114 | 12 | 6 |

D. 60MM

| HE | WP | ILL |
|---|---|---|
| 60 | 15 | 15 |

E. AT4
20 per company per day

F. Mines

| M21 | VOLCANOES | MOPM |
|---|---|---|
| 3000 | 2 | 10 |

**Class I:**
o Primary source for water resupply is ROWPU
o Iodine tablets are authorized for use first 15 days
o All surface water is non-potable

**Class III(B):**
o Pushed out daily w/ LOGPAC
o 1 HEMTT fueler stays with Cav troop, 2 pushed out w/ LOGPAC
o 23 1500 Jul LOGPAC, 3 fuelers pushed out to Cav, 1 add stays fwd (2 total)

**Class IV:**
o A Co BPT push 1st CL IV push NLT 21 1800 JUL
o Primary means for CL IV movement is air, then ground

**Class VII:**
o Pushed FWD with LOGPACs or as required

**Class IX:**
o Pushed out daily with unit LOGPACs

**LOGPAC:**
o Pushed daily at 0600 and 1700
o Last LOGPAC at 23 1500

**Class VIII**
o Pushed out daily with unit LOGPACs or utilizing ambulance back haul

## 8.5 COURSE OF ACTION COMPARISON MATRIX

| Courses of Action - | Advantages |
|---|---|
| | |
| | |
| | |
| | |
| | |
| | |
| | |
| | |
| | |
| | |
| | |
| | |
| | Disadvantages |
| | |
| | |
| | |
| | |
| | |
| | |
| | |
| | |
| | |
| | |
| | |

**(Copy as many times as needed for each COA)**

## PREPARATION FOR DECISION BRIEFING

1.  S-2/S-2 Intel NCO is prepared to discuss the enemy situation and enemy COAs to refresh those being briefed.
2.  S-3 briefs all friendly COAs. Another planner points, as the concept of operation paragraph is read. He then indicates the comparison criteria chart to the CDR and briefly elaborates on the selected criteria.
3.  Each tasked staff COA planner then is prepared to discuss in detail, by his particular Warfighting function (WFF), the comparison process he/she used to arrive at the decision that one COA was most feasible. Planners must discuss the advantages and disadvantages he considered when comparing the COAs from his/her perspective. **At no time** will a briefer state that there is "no difference between the COAs from my perspective." This is the kiss of death for a planner for it indicates you have little or no imagination, have not completed an in-depth analysis of the COAs, or you simply don't have the deductive thinking process necessary to make recommendations to decision-makers.
4.  After each briefer elaborates on his rationale to support one COA over the others, the S-3 reveals the totals on the comparison chart and takes his seat.

## COMMANDER'S DECISION BRIEFING

1.  After completing its analysis and comparison, the staff identifies its preferred COA and makes a recommendation. If a decision cannot be reached, the XO decides which COA to recommend at the commander's decision brief. The decision briefing format includes: (Chapter 16)

    a.  The intent of the higher HQ (higher and next higher commanders).
    b.  The restated mission.

c. The status of own forces.

d. An updated IPB.

e. Own COAs, including:

    (1) Assumptions used in planning.

    (2) Results of staff estimates.

    (3) Advantages and disadvantages (including risk) of each COA (with decision matrix or table showing COA comparison).

f. The recommended COA.

## PRODUCTS FROM THE DECISION BRIEFING/ COA APPROVAL

1. Approved COA. The commander's decision on which COA to complete development on and prepare an order for.
2. Refine Commander's Intent Statement (if required).
3. Level of risk the Commander is willing to accept.
4. New/approved CCIR to support execution.
5. Specified type of order.
6. Specified type of rehearsal.
7. Refine the Concept of Support (CoS) and Sustainment Sync Matrix.
8. Location and time for Orders Brief.

## DECISION MATRIX
### (COA Analysis)

| CRITERIA | WT | COURSES OF ACTION | | |
|---|---|---|---|---|
| | | 1 | 2 | 3 |
| C2 | | | | |
| CDR'S INTENT | | | | |
| LOCATION | | | | |
| RISK | | | | |
| RE-SUPPLY | | | | |
| ROUTES | | | | |
| RISK | | | | |
| MEDEVAC | | | | |
| TOTAL | | | | |
| WEIGHTED TOTAL | | | | |

LOWER IS BETTER

## 8.6 COA COMPARISON - OFFENSE

| CRITERIA: | DESCRIPTION: |
| --- | --- |
| SIMPLICITY | Facilitates Command and Control, Less complicated graphics, Less likelihood for fratricide |
| FIRE SUPPORT | Facilitates Rear Battle fires, Simple FS measures, Org for combat, Survivability, Control of assets |
| MOB/PROTECTION | Maximizes engineer effort in fewer zones/avenues of approach, facilitates Class IV resupply |
| MASS | Concentrates combat power and support effort for the greatest effect. |
| INTEL | \See the enemy, Disrupt the enemy, Protect the force, Do not let the enemy disrupt the replenishment operation |
| RISK | Which COA allows the greatest chance for enemy to disrupt our support effort or for customers to not be supported |
| ADA | Provides best option for use of assets by maximizing protection for friendly forces |
| FACILITATES END STATE | Option that supports faster defeat of enemy and maximizes the chances for commander's intent for end state of the force |

DECEPTION                Best influences the enemy to our advantage, easiest to employ quickly

SUSTAINMENT              Maximized distribution over greater distances. Strive to develop more local haul operations through distro hubs versus line haul operations

## 8.7 COA COMPARISON - DEFENSE

**CRITERIA:**                **DESCRIPTION:**

SIMPLICITY               Facilitates Command and Control, Less complicated graphics, less likelihood for fratricide

FIRE SUPPORT             Facilitates Rear battle fires, Simple FS measures, Org for combat, Survivability, Control of assets

MOB/C-MOB                Requires least amount of engineer work

MASS                     Concentrates combat power and support effort

INTEL                    See the enemy, Disrupt the enemy, Protect the force

RISK                     Which COA gives the greatest chance for success to the enemy

ADA                      Provides best option for use of assets by maximizing protection for friendly

FACILITATES END
STATE

Option that supports faster defeat of enemy and maximizes the chance for commander's intent for end state of the force

DECEPTION

Best influences the enemy to our advantage, Easiest to employ quickly

SUSTAINMENT

Maximized distribution concentrating on Class IV/V. Strive to develop more local haul operations through distro hubs versus line haul operations

*CHAPTER 9*

# ORDERS PRODUCTION

## <u>OVERVIEW</u>

1.  Plans and orders are the means by which the commander expresses to his subordinates his/her battlefield visualization, intent, and a decision, focusing on the results the commander expects to achieve – their vision of the end state of operations. This gives subordinates the maximum operational and tactical freedom to accomplish the mission which providing only the minimum restrictions and details necessary for synchronization and coordination. Plans and orders should provide the "*what*" rather than the "*how*" to encourage initiative. Plans and orders are the method the commander uses to synchronize military actions. They also help the staff synchronize the commander's decisions and concepts. The amount of detail the commander provides in a plan or order depends on the experience and competence of subordinate commanders, the cohesion and tactical experiences of subordinate units, and the complexity of the operation.

2.  **Operation Plan** – (OPLAN) (Format Para 9.6) is a plan a command uses to conduct military operations.

    a.  States critical assumptions that form the basis of the plan. Assumptions must be revalidated prior to execution of the plan.
    b.  Becomes an OPORD when the conditions of execution occur and an execution time is determined.

3.  **Service Support Plan** – (SSPLAN) (Format Para 9.7)) provides information and instructions covering an operation's service support. Estimates of the command's operational requirements are the basis for the plan. The SSPLAN becomes the service support order when the conditions of execution occur. (Ref Para 9.7)

4.  **Operations Order** – (OPORD) are directives a command issues to subordinate commanders to coordinate the execution of an operation. (Ref Para 9.6)

5.  **Service Support Order** - (SSORD) provides the plan for service support of operations, including administrative movements. If provides information to supported elements and serves as a basis for the orders of supporting commanders to their units. SSORDs may be issued either with an OPORD, or separately when the commander expects the CSS situation to apply to more than one operation plan or order. At division or corps levels of command, the SSORD may replace an OPORD's service support annex, if that happens the staff refers to the existence of the SSORD in paragraph 4 of the OPORD. The G4 (S4) has primary coordinating responsibility for preparing, publishing, and distribution of the SSORD. Other staff officers will provide their parts of the orders concerning their area of responsibility. (Ref Para 9.7)

6.  **Movement Order** (Format Para 9.8) – The movement order is a stand-alone order that facilitates an uncommitted unit's movements. The movements are typically administrative, and troops and vehicles are arranged to expedite their movement and to conserve time and energy when no enemy interference (except by air) is anticipated. The G4 (S4) has primary responsibility coordinating staff responsibility for planning and coordinating movements with input from all other staff sections, primarily the S-3. The G4 (S4) is also responsible for preparing, publishing, and distribution of the movement order

7. **Warning Order** – (WARNO) is a preliminary notice of an order or action that is to follow. Warning orders help subordinate units and their staffs prepare for new missions. Warning orders maximize the subordinate's planning time, provide essential details for the impending operation, and detail major time-line events that accompany mission execution. The amount of detail a warning order includes depends on the information and time available when the order is issued and the information subordinate commanders need for proper planning and preparation. The warning order clearly informs the recipient of what tasks he must do now as well as informs him of possible future tasks. However, a WANO does not authorize execution other than planning unless specifically stated.

8. **Fragmentary Order** – (FRAGO) (Format Para 9.9) provides timely changes of existing orders to subordinate and supporting commanders while providing notification to higher and adjacent commands. Commanders may authorize members of their staff to change existing orders by issuing Fargo's in their name. A FRAGO is either oral or written and addresses only those parts of the original OPORD that have changed. The FRAGO differs from an OPORD only in the detail of detail provided. It refers to previous orders and provides brief and specific instructions. The higher headquarters issues a new OPORD when there is a complete change of the tactical situation or when many changes make the current order ineffective.

## GENERAL INFORMATION – A COURSE OF ACTION IS SELECTED!

1. Based on the commander's decision and final guidance, the S-3 (with assistance of the SPO) refines the COA and completes the plan and prepares to issue the order. The plan or order is prepared to implement the selected COA by turning it into a clear, concise concept of support and concept of operation for the decisive, shaping and sustaining battles.

The COA statement will become the concept of support and operations statement. The COA sketch is the basis for the sustainment and operations overlays/LCOP. Orders and plans provide all necessary information subordinates require for execution, but without unnecessary constraints that would inhibit subordinate initiatives.

2.  The concept of support is the key to the sustainment unit order. It is the commander's clear, concise statement of where, when and how he intends to concentrate the support effort to accomplish the mission IAW the higher commander's intent and to accomplish support to his customer. It includes actions within the tactical logistics functions and battlefield organization, weighting of the main effort, priorities of support, and specific command and support relationships. The relationships are then included in the Task Organization and Organization for support.

3.  During orders production, the staff implements accident risk controls by coordinating and integrating them into the appropriate paragraphs and graphics of the OPORD. It is essential to communicate how controls will be put into effect, who will implement them, and how they fit into the overall operation.

4.  Finally, the commander reviews and approves orders before the staff reproduces and briefs them.

# PREPARATION FOR ORDERS BRIEFING

Most of the products created for the previous briefings now form the basic order.

- Intelligence Estimate becomes para 1a and 1d (OPLAN only) of the basic order. This information also forms the basis of ANNEX B.
- The Higher Headquarters order provides information for para 1b and 1c of the basic order.
- S-2 Mission Analysis becomes part of para 1b, 1d (OPLAN only), and para 2 of the basic order.
- Personnel Estimate provides information for para 1d (OPLAN only) and personnel sub-paragraphs in para 4 of the basic order.
- Logistic Estimates provide information for para 1d (OPLAN only) and para 4 of the basic order.
- The Commander's Guidance and Intent provides information for Task Organization and para 3 of the basic order.
- COA statement and sketch forms the basis for para 3a of the basic order.
- War gaming products (synchronization matrix) provides information for Task Organization, para 3a, 3b, 3c, 3d, para 4, and para 5.

## 9.1 Staff Responsibility for Orders and Annexes

The following staff sections are responsible for writing (or assist with) specific portions of the OPORD and annexes. At the battalion level, only a portion of the annexes listed in ATTP 5-0.1 are needed for most operations.

| Para | TITLE | PRIMARY | ASSIST | ASSIST |
|------|-------|---------|--------|--------|
| 1 | Situation | S-2 | | |
| 2 | Mission | XO | S-3 | |
| 3 | Execution | | | |
| | Scheme of Support | SPO | BC | XO |
| | Scheme of Defense | S-2 & S-3 | BC | XO |
| 4 | Sustainment | | | |
| | Support Concept | S-4 | | |
| | Material and services | S-4 | | |
| | Medical Eva and Hospitalization | S-1 | | |
| | Personnel | S-1 | | |
| | Civil Military Operations (Para 3g) | S-1 | | |
| 5 | Command and Signal | S-2/3 | XO | |

| ANNEX | TITLE | PRIMARY | **ASSIST** | ASSIST |
|---|---|---|---|---|
| A | Task Organization | S-3 | XO | SPO |
| B | Intelligence | S-2 | | |
| C | Operation Overlay | | | |
| | Appendix 1 – Scheme of Support | SPO | BC | XO |
| | Appendix 2 – Scheme of Defense | S-3 | BC | XO |
| E | Protection | S-3 | | |
| F | Sustainment | | | |
| | Appendix 1 – Supply | S-4 | SPO | |
| | Appendix 2 - Transportation | S-4 | SPO | |
| | Appendix 3,4, 5 | S-1 | | |
| H | Signal | S-6 | S-3 | |
| K | Civil Affairs Operations | S-1 | | |
| L | Recon & Surveillance | S-3 | S-2 | |
| R | Reports | XO | S - 3 &S-1 | SPO |

At the Sustainment Brigade, the flowing is a breakdown of applicable annexes.

ANNEX A   TASKO                                           S-3
ANNEX B   Intelligence                                   S-2
ANNEX C   Operations, Synch Matrix, Graphics   S-3, SPO
ANNEX D   Fires                                          S-3
ANNEX E   Protection                                     S-3
ANNEX F   Sustainment                                    S-4/S-1
ANNEX G   Engineering                                    S-3
ANNEX H   Signal                                         S-6
ANNEX I   Not Used                                       **N/A**
ANNEX J   Inform and Influence Activities (IIA) S-3
ANNEX K   Civil Affairs Operations                       S-1
ANNEX L   Reconnaissance & Surveillance   S-3 (assist by S-2)
ANNEX M   Assessment                                     S-3

| ANNEX N | Space Operations | **N/A** |
|---|---|---|
| ANNEX O | Spare | **N/A** |
| ANNEX P | Host Nation Support | S-1, SPO |
| ANNEX Q | Spare | **N/A** |
| ANNEX R | Reports | S-3 |
| ANNEX S | Special Technical Operations | S-3 |
| ANNEX T | Spare | **N/A** |
| ANNEX U | Inspector General | S-1 |
| ANNEX V | Interagency Coordination | S-3 |
| ANNEX W, X, Y | Spare | **N/A** |
| ANNEX Z | Distribution | S-3 |

2.  Notes regarding the preparation of OPLANs/OPORDs are at Chapter 25.

## DURING THE ORDERS BRIEFING

The Orders Briefing Format is at Chapter 17. As we near the end of our 1/3 time hack we must be flexible and prepared to make any necessary corrections, additions, deletions to the order as a result of the briefing.

## PRODUCTS FROM THE ORDERS BRIEFING

1.  Written OPLAN/OPORD.
2.  All Annexes to the OPLAN/OPORD.
3.  All overlays in the necessary numbers in 1:100,000 scale.

## DAILY PLANS UPDATE TO THE CDR

**S-3** provides a daily update to the CDR and/or XO in the Plans area on a daily basis usually at 0900 hours. The format for this informal briefing is at Chapter 18.

## BRANCHES AND SEQUELS

**S-3** is responsible for continuous planning for the current operation and future operations.

**Branches** are contingency operations or course of action (an option built into the basic plan or course of action) for changing the mission, disposition, orientation, or direction of movement of the force to aid success of the operation based on anticipated events, opportunities, or disruptions caused by enemy actions and reactions as determined during the war gaming process. These plans must have as much detail as possible to them and should have gone through the MDMP (Time constrained), War gaming, and approval process.

**Sequels** are contingency operations that may be executed after or following the current operation. Plans for these are based on the possible outcomes (victory, stalemate, or defeat) associated with the current operation. These plans must also go through the MDMP (Time constrained), War gaming, and the approval process.

As time permits, all contingency plans must be prepared as FRAGOs with as much detail as possible and must be in the hands of those responsible for executing them. Planning is an ongoing process. The enemy will almost never act or react exactly as we might think he will, but our plans must take into consideration all the probable courses of action he might take and allow for the flexibility necessary to change our operations to meet his challenge.

## 9.2 DEVELOPMENTAL GUIDELINES FOR PARAGRAPH 4 (SUSTAINMENT)

1.  General rules for paragraph 4a.

    a.  Use language that is clear, concise, and comprehensive. Avoid technical terminology.

b.   Focus on what the non-sustainment commander needs to know about how the operation is sustained. This makes paragraph 4a the logistic equivalent to the concept of the operation.

c.   Consider the sustainment functions in the context of actions by phase of an operation or, before, during, and after the operation. The operative term is 'consider'. The intent is not to address each function unless it is critical or unusual. The support concept is organized into a framework based on operational phasing, or presented as before, during, and after Operations format.

d.   The support concept establishes priorities of support by phase or before, during, and after the operation. The commander at each level establishes these priorities in his intent statement (e.g., main effort) and in the concept of the operation (paragraph 3). This could include prioritizing such things as personnel replacements; maintenance and evacuation, by unit and by system (aviation and surface systems would be given separate priorities); fuel and/or ammunition; road network use by unit and/or commodity; and any resource subject to competing demands or constraints.

e.   Synchronize the support concept with the concept of the operation. Remember – your *'Concept of Operation'* should nicely dovetail into your higher headquarters *'Concept of Support'*.

f.   Formations comprised of units that are not part of the same organization or don't have habitual relationships may not share a common TSOP and may require a more lengthy support concept. Conversely, the more comprehensive the TSOP, the briefer the support concept.

g.  The more complex the operation (a multi-phased operation or operations larger formations conduct), the more critical the sustainment synchronization.

h.  Routine, doctrinal, or constant information is not included in the support concept. It is incorporated into the unit TSOP.

i.  Detailed and numerical data relevant to the operation, and of primary interest to unit logistic personnel, may be in another subparagraph of 4 or in the service support annex.

j.  It is important to understand the next higher commander's support priorities and where your particular unit fits into those priorities.

2.  Sustainment planners need to review the support concept and ensure it meets the commander's needs. There are several basic questions the Sustainment planner should ask:

a.  Is the support concept easily understood, and is it comprehensive and concise?

b.  Does it provide visualization (word picture) of the overall support concept?

c.  Is the support concept synchronized with and does it support the concept of the operation (paragraph 3)?

d.  Does it consider, and address as required, the sustainment functions by phase of an operation or in the context of before, during, and after?

e.  Does it establish priorities of support by phase and do these priorities correlate with the priorities established in the commander's intent, paragraph 3, and other directives from higher?

f.  Is it written for the non-sustainment commanders and their primary staffs and focused for supported units?

g.  Does it address all critical, non-SOP, or unusual aspects of support?

## SUSTAINMENT (Paragraph 4a) FORMAT

1.  **Support Concept**. Paragraph 4a will provide all overall view of the support concept. Its intent is to provide the non-Sustainment commanders and their primary staffs an image of how the operation will be logistically supported. If the information pertains to the entire operation, or if it pertains to more than one unit, include it in the introductory portion of paragraph 4a. Change it in tile ensuing subparagraphs when needed. This could include:

- A brief synopsis of the support command mission.
- Support command headquarters and/or support area locations, including locations of next higher logistics bases if not clearly conveyed in the sustainment overlay/ LCOP.
- The next higher level's support priorities and where the unit fits into those priorities.
- Priorities that remain unchanged throughout the operation.
- Units in the next higher Sustainment organization supporting the unit.
- Significant and/or unusual sustainment issues that might impact the overall operation.
- The use of host nation support.
- Any significant sustainment risks.

a. **PHASE I** (starts with "event" and ends with "event").
   - Sustainment focus (Decisive Operation (DO), ME, and SE)
   - Priorities:
     — By unit.
     — For personnel replacements.
     — Maintenance and/or recovery and evacuation priorities (by unit and equip type)
     — Movement.
     — By class of supply.
   - Critical events or other pertinent information needed to communicate how logistics support will be conducted for the operation. Use the sustainment functions for information to include in the support concept.

b. **PHASE II** (starts with "event" and ends with "event"). If there are any differences or changes, state them in this paragraph.
   - Sustainment focus (DO, ME, and SE)
   - Priorities:
     — By unit.
     — For personnel replacements.
     — Maintenance and/or recovery and evacuation priorities (by unit and equip type).
     — Movement, — By class of supply.
   - Critical events or other pertinent information needed to communicate how logistics sup-port will be conducted for the operation. Use the sustainment functions for information to include in the support concept.
   - Critical decision points.

c. **PHASES III, IV and V** (starts with "event" and ends with event'). If there are any differences or changes from previous phases, state them here, -

- Sustainment focus (DE, ME and SE). Remember, your sustainment focus needs to support your higher headquarters/supported units 'Decisive Effort'.
- Priorities:
  — By unit.
  — For personnel replacements.
  — Maintenance and/or recovery and evacuation priorities (by unit and equip type).
  — Movement.
  — By class of supply.
- Critical events or other pertinent information needed to communicate how logistics support will be conducted for the operation. Use the sustainment functions for information to include in the support concept.
- Major Resupply Operation (MRO) (referenced in the last phase).
- Preparing for future operations (last phase).

d. Paragraphs 4b through 4e are normally more detailed and are included in the service support annex. They are not part of the support concept.

e. Concept of support written before, during, and after format. Follow the same guidance as by phase.

# 9.3 SUPPORT CONCEPT MATRIX (DIVISION)

## 9.3 SUPPORT CONCEPT MATRIX (DIVISION)

| SUSTAINMENT FUNCTIONS | PHASE I (Move from TAA to ATK POS - DTG) | PHASE IIa (ATK to Defeat Lead Divisions) | PHASE IIb (Counterattack) | PHASE III (Hasty Defense) |
|---|---|---|---|---|
| PRIORITY OF SUPPORT | 52: CAB, 37 FIB, 2 BDE, 3 BDE, 1 BDE | 2 BDE, 3 BDE, 52 CAB, 37 FIB, 1 BDE | 3 BDE, 2 BDE, 52 CAB, 1 BDE, 37 FIB | 1 BDE, 2 BDE, CAB, 3 BDE, 37 FIB |
| **HR** HUMAN RESOURCES SUPPORT | PRI REPL: CAB, 37 FIB, 2 BDE, 3 BDE, 1 BDE | PRI REPL: 2 BDE, 3 BDE, CAB, 37 FIB, 1 BDE. SHIFT TO 1 BDE IF COMMITTED. REPL OPS SUSPENDED UNTIL PL DESK | PRI REPL: 3 BDE, 2 BDE, CAB, 1st BDE, 37 FIB | PRI REPL: 1 BDE, 2 BDE, CAB, 3 BDE, 37 FIB. REPL OPS RESUME. |
| SUPPLY (CL I, II, III(p), III(B), IV, V, VI, and VII) | PRI CL III: CAB, 3 BDE, 2 BDE, 1 BDE. PRI CL V: HELLFIRE, 25MM, TANK ATGM, 155 DPICM | PRI (LESS CL V): 2 BDE, 3 BDE, 52 CAB, 37 FIB, 1 BDE. PRI CL V: 120MM HEAT, TOW, 155 DPICM | PRI (LESS CL V): 3 BDE, 2 BDE, CAB, 1 BDE, 37 FIB. REPLENISH CL III UBLs. PRI CL V:155 DPICM, HELLFIRE, TOW, TANK. REPLENISH UBLS | PRI ALL CLASSES: 1 BDE, 2 BDE, CAB, 3 BDE, 37 FIB. |
| MAINTENANCE | PRI MAINT: M109, M1, M2/3, 5K Tankers, PLS, and M88. PRI MAINT CAB: AH-64, OH-58D, and UH-60 | PRI MAINT: M1, M2/3, M109, MHE. PRI CAB MAINT: UNCHANGED | PRI – NO CHANGE | PRI MAINT: M1, M109, M2/3, M88. PRI CAB MAINT: UNCHANGED |
| TRANSPORTATION | PRI FWD: DS 37 FIB, MNV UNITS, III, V. PRI REAR: MED, EQUIP EVAC, REFUGEES. | PRI FWD: MNV UNITS, DS 37 FIB, III, V. PRI REARWARD: MED, MAINT EVAC, EPWs, REFUGEES | PRI FWD AND REARWARD UNCHANGED. | PRI FWD: IX, VI, III, V. PRI REARWARD: UNCHANGED |
| FIELD SERVICES | FS PROVIDED BY 13th CSSB IN LSA LAMP. | FS OPERATIONS SUSPENDED UNTIL PL DESK. KIA EVAC TO MA | FS – NO CHANGE | FS OPS RESUME IN SUS BDE LSA. |
| CHS | 842d FST & FSMT DS TO 303D FSB, 843D FST & 1 FSMT DS TO 202D FSB, 1FSMT W/ 404TH FSB, MSMT AREA COVERAGE DREAR ASMT W/ DASB | 2XCH-47 AVAIL FOR MASS CAL. CSH LOCATED IN LSA BELL | 2XCH-47 AVAIL FOR MASS CAL. CSH LOCATED IN LSA BELL. SBMC LOC IN LSA LAMP | |
| EOD | EOD SPT AVAIL IN LSA LAMP | NO CHANGE | NO CHANGE | NO CHANGE |
| FINANCIAL MGT SPT | CORPS PROVIDES FINANCE SPT IN UNIT SPT AREAS | FIN OPS SUSPENDED UNTIL PL DESK | NO CHANGE | FIN OPS RESUMED |
| RELIGIOUS / LEGAL / AND BAND SPT | BAND SUPPORT AVAIL UPON REQUEST TO G3 | DIV BAND PROVIDES FORCE PROTECTION TO DMAIN CP | NO CHANGE | NO CHANGE |

## 9.4 BRIEFING THE SUPPORT CONCEPT

1. The Sustainer's's role in the overall OPLAN/OPORD briefing is to brief the support concept, but he/she must first understand the general concept of the operation and the commander's intent. This briefing facilitates communicating the support concept to the commander and the subordinate commanders. The support concept briefing should address the critical, non-SOP, or unusual aspects of logistic support by phase of an operation by critical sustainment functions. Doctrinal, usual, or SOP matters should not be addressed unless there is a deviation in support relationships or normal methods. The Sustainment planner briefs the support concept, working through the operation by phase. This briefing should go into greater detail than is laid out in the written support concept.

2. **Some rules of thumb for the support concept briefing are:**

   a. Tell commanders what they can expect from sustainment and how many days or hours they can operate based on materiel readiness, quantities of supplies on hand, etc. Use common terms such as DOS or other terms that are meaningful to the commander. Avoid using technical terminology or SOP information.

   b. Address the "culminating point" from a logistic perspective.

   c. Avoid briefing the results of extensive number-crunching that is associated with the logistics estimate process.

   d. The briefer should not read a written product. Rather, use the Sustainment overlay/LCOP and appropriate visual aids, such as a support concept overview matrix (see appendix H), he should show the commander how the support concept is synchronized with and supports the concept of the operation.

e.  The briefing should include locations of critical sustainment (i.e. logistic) assets, headquarters, and events.

f.  Address priorities, shifts in priorities, problem areas and solutions, and critical events.

g.  Bottom line: The logistician must tell the commander what he needs to know.

**IMPORTANT: DO NOT 'FIRE HOSE' THE COMMANDER WITH LOGISTICAL 'DATA'. PROVIDE HIM WITH KNOWLEDGE!!!**

Knowledge is Data (from Staff Estimates) + Analysis (from appropriate Staff person) = Informed (and Knowledgeable) Commander.

3.  Support concept briefing format,

a.  **Introduction** (overview of the support concept and orientation to the map, if required). Orientation to the map is not required if another briefer has done so previously. Do not assume the commander totally knows the terrain. Focus on locating critical sustainment nodes, MSRs, etc.

b.  **Brief the support concept** starting with critical actions that must be accomplished in the first phase of the operation and concluding with critical actions to be accomplished in the last phase. This will prepare for future operations using the sustainment functions as a guide.

c.  **Identify which units have priorities** for each critical sustainment functions (this should correlate with the commander's priorities; e.g., main effort).

d. **Identify the next higher echelon unit** providing support and/or backup support.

e. **Identify any critical shortages/problem areas** for each sustainment function and solution. For example, this can be supported, but ..., or it can be done, but not without risk in ....

f. **Identify any other sustainment problem areas**, arrangements, special requirements, or any other critical aspects addressed elsewhere in the briefing.

## PREPARATION FOR ORDERS BRIEFING

Most of the products created for the previous briefings now form the basic order.

- Intelligence Estimate becomes para 1a and 1d (OPLAN only) of the basic order. This information also forms the basis of ANNEX B.

- The Higher Headquarters order provides information for para 1b and 1c of the basic order.

- S-2 & S-3 Mission Analysis becomes part of para 1b, 1d (OPLAN only), and para 2 of the basic order.

- Personnel Estimate provides information for para 1d (OPLAN only) and personnel sub- paragraphs in para 4 of the basic order.

- Sustainment (Logistics) Estimate provides information for para 1d (OPLAN only) and para 4 of the basic order.

- The Commanders Guidance and Intent provides information for Task Organization and para 3 of the basic order.

- COA statement and sketch forms the basis for para 3a of the basic order.

- War gaming products (synchronization matrix) provides information for Task Organization, para 3a, 3b. 3c. 3d, para 4, and para 5.

## 9.5 The Sustainment Support & Execution Matrices

### Sustainment Support Matrix

**ORDER #**_____,     **DTG:**_____

| | | | | | |
|---|---|---|---|---|---|
| | DATE | | | | |
| | EVENT/PL ITEM | | | | |
| | ENEMY ACTIONS | | | | |
| | FRIENDLY ACTIONS | | | | |
| | SUSTAINMENT DECISION POINTS | | | | |
| **Priority of Support** | FIX | | | | |
| | ARM | | | | |
| | FUEL | | | | |
| | SUSTAIN | | | | |
| | MOVE | | | | |
| | PROTECT | | | | |
| | MAN | | | | |
| | MSR | | | | |
| | ASR | | | | |
| **Requirements** | Class I | | | | |
| | Class II | | | | |
| | Class III | | | | |
| | Class IV | | | | |
| | Class V | | | | |
| | Class VI | | | | |
| | Class VII | | | | |
| | Class VIII | | | | |
| | Class IX | | | | |
| | WATER | | | | |
| | MED LOCs | | | | |
| | MA CP PT | | | | |
| | DC COL PT | | | | |
| | EPW COL PT | | | | |

# Execution Matrix

| Date | | | | |
|---|---|---|---|---|
| Day | | | | |
| Event | | | | |
| Class I | | | | |
| Class I (Water) | | | | |
| Class II | | | | |
| Class III | | | | |
| Class IV | | | | |
| Class V | | | | |
| Class VI | | | | |
| Class VII | | | | |
| Class VIII | | | | |
| Class IX | | | | |
| Transportation | | | | |
| Showers | | | | |
| Laundry | | | | |
| Repair | | | | |
| Maintenance/ Recovery | | | | |
| | | | | |

*Adjust table to meet requirements of assigned missions.*

## 9.6 OPORD/OPLAN FORMAT

_____
(Classification)
(Change from oral orders, if any)

Copy ____ of ____ copies
123$^{rd}$ CSSB
(Place of issue)
(Date-time-group of signature)
(Message reference number)

**OPERATION PLAN (ORDER) _____ (Code name/ number)**

**(U) References:**

**(U) Time Zone Used Throughout the Plan (Order):**

**(U) Task Organization:**

1. **(U)SITUATION**
    a.  (U) Area of Interest. (S-2)
    b.  (U) Area of Operations (S-2)
        (1) (U) Terrain
        (2) (U) Weather
    c.  (U) Enemy Forces (S-2)
    d.  (U) Friendly Forces (S-3)
        (1) (U) Higher HQ's Mission and Intent
            (a) (U) Higher HQ's Two Levels Up.
                1. (U) Mission
                2. (U) Intent
            (b) (U) Higher HQ's One Level Up
                1. (U) Mission
                2. (U) Intent
        (2) (U) Missions of Adjacent Units

e. (U) Interagency, Intergovernmental, and Nongovernmental Organizations.
f. (U) Civil Considerations
g. (U) Attachments and Detachments
h. (U) Assumptions

**2. MISSION (S-3, XO - from analysis)**

**3. EXECUTION**
a. (U) Commander's Intent: (Cdr)
b. (U) Concept of Operations (S-3)
c. (U) Scheme of Support (Maneuver) (SPO)
  (1) (U) Scheme of Movement/Counter mobility
  (2) (U) Scheme of Battlefield Obscuration (if applicable)
  (3) (U) Scheme of Recon and Surveillance (refer to Annex L) (S-3/S-2)
d. (U) Scheme of Intelligence (refer to Annex B) (S-3)
e. (U) Scheme of Fires (refer to Annex D 'Fires' if applicable) (S-3)
f. (U) Scheme of Protection (refer to Annex E) (S-3)
g. (U) Stability Operations (refer to Annex C 'Operations' and Annex K 'Civil Affairs') (S-3/ S-1)
g. (U) Assessment (refer to Annex M 'Assessment' if applicable) (S-3)
i. (U) Tasks to Subordinate Units (S-3)
  (1) (U) Sub-unit Tasks
  (2) (U) Sub-unit Tasks
j. (U) Coordinating Instructions
  (1) (U) Time or condition when a plan or order becomes effective (XO/S-3)
  (2) (U) Commanders Critical Information Requirements (CCIR) (XO/S-3)
  (3) (U) Essential Elements of Friendly Information (EEFI) (S-3)
  (4) (U) Fire Support Coordination Measures (S-3)

(5) (U) Airspace Coordination Measures (S-3)

(6) (U) Rules of Engagement (S-3)

(7) (U) Risk Reduction Control Measures (S-3/S-1)

(8) (U) Personnel Recovery Coordination Measures (S-3/S-1)

(9) (U) Environmental Considerations (S-3/S-4)

(10) (U) Themes and Messages (S-3)

(11) (U) Other Coordinating Instructions (As required)

## 4. SUSTAINMENT (S-1 / S-4)

a. (U) Logistics. (refer to Annex F 'Sustainment') (internal) (S-4)

b. (U) Personnel (refer to Annex F 'Sustainment') (S-1)

c. (U) Army Health System Support (refer to Annex F 'Sustainment') (S-1)

## 5. COMMAND AND SIGNAL (XO / S-3/S-6)

a. (U) Command (XO)

(1) (U) Location of Commander

(2) (U) Succession of Command (see TACSOP if stated here)

(3) (U) Liaison Requirements

b. (U) Control (XO/S-3)

(1) (U) Command Post

(2) (U) Reports (refer to Annex R 'Reports')

c. (U) Signal (S-6)

**ACKNOWLEDGE:**

MENTER
LTC

**OFFICIAL:**
COLE
S-3

ANNEXES:

Annex A     Task Organization (S-3)

Annex B     Intelligence (S-2)

           Appendix 1 Intelligence Estimate

             Tab A Terrain Analysis (Routes, base/ base cluster)

             Tab B Weather

             Tab C Civil Considerations

             Tab D Intelligence Preparation of the Battlefield (IPB)

Annex C     Operation (S-3)

           Appendix 1 Design Concept

           Appendix 2 Operations Overlay/ Graphics

           Appendix 3 Decision Support Template/Matrix

Annex D     Fires

           Appendix 7 Cyber/Electromagnetic Activities (S-2)

             Tab A Electronic Warfare (DUKE/WARLOCK IED Defeat Systems)

Annex E     Protection

Annex F     Sustainment

           Appendix 1 Logistics (S-4)

            Tab A Sustainment Overlay

            Tab B Maintenance

            Tab C Transportation

              Exhibit 1 Traffic Circulation and Control

              Exhibit 2 Traffic Circulation Overlay

              Exhibit 3 Road Movement Table

              Exhibit 4 Highway Regulation

            Tab D Supply

            Tab E Field Services

            Tab F Distribution

            Tab G Contract Support Integration

            Tab H Mortuary Affairs

            Tab I Internment and Resettlement Support

DISTRIBUTION     _____

## 9.7 SUSTAINMENT ANNEX FORMAT

(Classification)
(Change from oral orders, if any)

Copy ____ of ____ copies
123rd BSB
(Place of issue)
(Date-time-group of signature)
(Message reference number)

### ANNEX F (SUSTAINMENT) TO OPORD/OPLAN
_____ **(Code name)**
(number)

**(U) References:**

**(U) Time Zone Used Throughout the Plan (Order):**

1. **(U)SITUATION**
    a. (U) Area of Interest. (S-2)
    b. (U) Area of Operations (S-2)
        (1) (U) Terrain
        (2) (U) Weather
    c. (U) Enemy Forces (S-2)
    d. (U) Friendly Forces (S-3)
    e. (U) Interagency, Intergovernmental, and Nongovernmental Organizations.
    f. (U) Civil Considerations
    g. (U) Attachments and Detachments
    h. (U) Assumptions

2. **MISSION (S-3, XO - from analysis)**

3. **EXECUTION**
    a. (U) Scheme of Sustainment Support (S-3/SPO)

    b.  (U) Tasks to Subordinate Units (S-3)
       (1) (U) Sub-unit Tasks
       (2) (U) Sub-unit Tasks
    c.  (U) Coordinating Instructions

**4.  SUSTAINMENT (S-1 / S-4)**
    a.  (U) Material and Services (SPO)
       (1) (U) Maintenance
          (a) (U) Ground
          (b) (U) Watercraft
          (c) (U) Aircraft
          (d) Field Maintenance
          (e) Sustainment Maintenance
       (2) (U) Transportation
          (a) (U) Ground
          (b) Sea/River/Water
          (c) (U) Air
          (d) (U) Container Management
       (3) (U) Supply
          (a) (U) Class I Rations
          (b) (U) Class II OCIE/Maps
          (c) (U) Class III Bulk (B) and Packaged (P) POL
          (d) (U) Class IV Construction and Fortification Materials
          (e) (U) Class V Munitions
          (f) (U) Class VI Personal Demand Items
          (g) (U) Class VII Major End Items
          (h) (U) Class VIII Medical Supply
          (i) (U) Class IX Repair Parts
          (j) (U) Class X Material for Nonmilitary/Civil Affairs Operations
          (k) Miscellaneous
       (4) (U) Field Services
          (a) (U) Construction
          (b) (U) Light Textile Repair and Showers

  (c) (U) Food Preparation
  (d) (U) Water Purification
  (e) (U) Aerial Delivery
  (f) (U) Installation Services
 (5) (U) Distribution
  (a) (U) Distribution Node(s) Locations
  (b) (U) Tracking Procedures
  (c) (U) Distribution Nodes
  (d) (U) Movement Request Format
  (e) (U) Container Operations
  (f) Movement Control Responsibility
 (6) (U) Contract Support Integration
 (7) (U) Mortuary Affairs
 (8) (U) Internment and Resettlement Support
 (9) (U) Labor
b. (U) Personnel (refer to Annex F 'Sustainment') (S-1)
 (1) (U) Human Resource Support
 (2) (U) Financial Management
 (3) (U) Legal Support
 (4) (U) Religious Support
 (5) (U) Band Operations
c. (U) Army Health System Support (refer to Annex F 'Sustainment') (S-1)
 (1) (U) Medical Evacuation
 (2) (U) Hospitalization
d. (U) Foreign National and Host Nation Support
e. (U) Resource Availability
f. (U) Miscellaneous

## 5. COMMAND AND SIGNAL (XO / S-3/S-6)
a. (U) Command (XO)
 (1) (U) Location of Commander
 (2) (U) Succession of Command (see TACSOP if stated here)
 (3) (U) Liaison Requirements

    b.   (U) Control (XO/S-3)
        (1)  (U) Command Post
        (2)  (U) Reports (refer to Annex R 'Reports')
    c.   (U) Signal (S-6)

**ACKNOWLEDGE:**

                                        MENTER
                                        LTC

**OFFICIAL:**
COLE
S-3

Appendix 1 Logistics (S-4)
   Tab A Sustainment Overlay
   Tab B Maintenance
   Tab C Transportation
      Exhibit 1 Traffic Circulation and Control
      Exhibit 2 Traffic Circulation Overlay
      Exhibit 3 Road Movement Table
      Exhibit 4 Highway Regulation
   Tab D Supply
   Tab E Field Services
   Tab F Distribution
   Tab G Contract Support Integration
   Tab H Mortuary Affairs
   Tab I Internment and Resettlement Support
Appendix 2 Personnel Services Support
   Tab A Human Resource Support
   Tab B Financial Management
   Tab C Legal Support
   Tab D Religious Support
   Tab E Band Operations (N/A)
Appendix 3 Army Health System Support (S-1/Unit Surgeon/ Med Plt Ldr)

## 9.8 MOVEMENT ORDER FORMAT

_____
(Classification)
(Change from oral orders, if any) (Optional)

Copy ____ of ____ copies
123rd BSB
(Place of issue)
(Date-time-group of signature)
(Message reference number)

MOVEMENT ORDER _____

**OPERATION PLAN (ORDER)** _____ **(Code name/ number)**

**(U) References:**

**(U) Time Zone Used Throughout the Plan (Order):**

**(U) Task Organization:**

1. **(U)SITUATION**
   a. (U) Area of Interest. (S-2)
   b. (U) Area of Operations (S-2)
      (1) (U) Terrain
      (2) (U) Weather
   c. (U) Enemy Forces (S-2)
   d. (U) Friendly Forces (S-3)
      (1) (U) Higher HQ's Mission and Intent
         (a) (U) Higher HQ's Two Levels Up.
            1. (U) Mission
            2. (U) Intent
         (b) (U) Higher HQ's One Level Up
            1. (U) Mission
            2. (U) Intent

(2) (U) Missions of Adjacent Units
e. (U) Interagency, Intergovernmental, and Nongovernmental Organizations.
f. (U) Civil Considerations
g. (U) Attachments and Detachments
h. (U) Assumptions

**2. (U) MISSION (S-3, XO - from analysis)**

**3. (U) EXECUTION.**
a. (U) Concept of movement. (S-3)
b. (U) Tasks to subordinate units. (S-3)
c. (U) Detailed timings. (S-3)
d. (U) Coordinating instructions. (S-3)
  (1) (U) Order of march.
  (2) (U) Routes.
  (3) (U) Density.
  (4) (U) Speed. (Include catch-up speed)
  (5) (U) Method of movement.
  (6) (U) Defense on move.
  (7) (U) Start, release, or other critical points.
  (8) (U) Convoy control.
  (9) (U) Harbor areas and/or Convoy Collection Points (CCPs).
  (10) (U) Instruction for halts – long term ('RED AIR Actions) and short term .
  (11) (U) Lighting.
  (12) (U) Air support.

**4. (U) SERVICE SUPPORT (S-1 / S-4)**
a. (U) Traffic control. (Performed by MPs or coordinated Host Nation Police)
b. (U) Recovery.
c. (U) Medical.
d. (U) Petroleum, oils, and lubricants.
e. (U) Water.

**5. (U) COMMAND AND SIGNAL (XO/S-3 or S-6)**
    a.   (U) Command. (XO)
        (1) (U) Location of commander and chain of command.
        (2) (U) Location of key individuals or particular vehicles.
    b.   (U) Signal. (S-3 or S-6)

**ACKNOWLEDGE:**

                             MENTER
                             LTC

**OFFICIAL:**
COLE

**ANNEXES: (As required)**

**DISTRIBUTION:**

———————
(Classification)

## 9.9 FRAGMENTARY (FRAGO) ORDER FORMAT

<u>(Classification)</u>
(Change from oral orders, if any) (Optional)

Copy ____ of ____ copies
123$^{rd}$ Sus Bde
(Place of issue)
(Date-time-group of signature)
(Message reference number)

**FRAGMENTARY ORDER** _____

**References: (Mandatory) reference the order being modified.**

**Time Zone Used Throughout the Order: (Optional)**

1.  **(U) SITUATION**. (Mandatory) Include changes to the existing order.

2.  **(U) MISSION. (Mandatory) List the new mission.**

3.  **(U) EXECUTION**.
    Intent: (Cdr) (Optional)
    a.  (U) Concept of operations. (SPO) (Mandatory)
    b.  (U) Tasks to subordinate units. (Mandatory)
    c.  (U) Coordinating instructions. (Mandatory) Include statement, "Current overlay remains in effect".

4.  **(U) SERVICE SUPPORT** (S-1 /S-4) (Optional) (Include changes)

5.  **(U) COMMAND AND SIGNAL** (XO/S-3) (Optional) (Include changes)

**ACKNOWLEDGE:** (Mandatory)

                                                  MENTER
                                                  COL

**OFFICIAL:**
COLE

ANNEXES: (Optional)
DISTRIBUTION: (Optional)

_____
(Classification)

## CHAPTER 10

# TIME ANALYSIS

★★★

1. Backwards plan the available time. Use 1/3 – 2/3 rule. XO owns the time schedule and must enforce it ruthlessly. Two versions are provided for unit use.

|  | **DTG** | **H-HR** |
|---|---|---|
| **DTG MSN RECEIVED FROM HIGHER** | _____ |  |
| **CURRENT DTG** | _____ |  |
| **EXECUTE MSN NLT DTG** | _____ |  |
| **TIME ALLOWED FOR STAFF PREP (1/3)** | _____ |  |
| **TIME ALLOWED FOR SUB STAFF PREP (2/3)** | _____ |  |
| **INFORMATION EXCHANGED W/CDR** | _____ |  |
| **WARNING ORDER #1 DISSEMINATED** | _____ |  |

---

### 1/3 TIME BEGINS

---

| **MISSION ANALYSIS BRIEFING**<br>**(CDR'S PLANNING GUIDANCE)** | _____ |
|---|---|
| **WARNING ORDER #2 DISSEMINATED** | _____ |

**COURSE OF ACTION BRIEFING** _____

**WAR GAMING** _____

**DECISION BRIEFING** _____

**WARNING ORDER #3 DISSEMINATED** _____

**ORDERS BRIEFING** _____

**ORDER DISSEMINATED NLT DTG** _____

---

### 1/3 TIME ENDS

---

**STAFF CONTINUES PLANNING/COORDINATION**

**SUBORDINATES BACK BRIEF CDR** _____

## Staff Time Schedule

| EVENT | TIME | STATUS |
|---|---|---|
| Receive mission | | |
| Situation update brief (mission analysis format) | | |
| Issue Warning Order #1 | | |
| Conduct Mission Analysis<br>    - Prepare Cartoon of AO<br>    - Complete MA Worksheets / Asset<br>      Availability analysis<br>    - Complete SITEMP (MPCOA/MDCOA)<br>    - Draft RFI's and CCIR | | |
| Conduct MA Worksheet scrub | | |
| Rehearsal - mission analysis brief | | |
| Mission analysis brief | | |

| | | |
|---|---|---|
| Receive Cdr's guidance and intent | | |
| Issue Warning Order #2 | | |
| Develop focused course of action | | |
| Course of action analysis | | |
| Initial wargame | | |
| Staff estimates (personnel, intelligence, CSS, support operations – formats) | | |
| (Course of action comparison) as needed | | |
| Rehearsal – Decision brief | | |
| Decision brief | | |
| Issue Warning Order #3 | | |
| Wargame with Cdr | | |
| Order preparation<br>   - OPORD Slides Turn in<br>   - OPORD Products Turn in | | |
| Rehearsal – operation order brief | | |
| Issue operation order | | |
| Company commanders confirmation briefs | | |
| Company commanders backbriefs | | |
| Rehearsals | | |

## 10.1 ORDERS TIMELINE

| EVENT | TIME | LOCATION | REMARKS |
|---|---|---|---|
| **Mission Received** | | | |
| Mission Analysis (MA) working group | | | |
| Battlestaff MA product turn in | | | |
| S-2 and S-3 MA initial review | | | |
| Battlestaff MA product turn in | | | |
| Battlestaff MA final product check | | | |
| S-2 and S-3 MA final review | | | |
| MA final print | | | |
| MA Rehearsal | | | |
| **Mission Analysis Brief to CDR** | | | |
| COA development working group | | | |
| Battlestaff COA development product turn in | | | |
| S-3 COA review | | | |
| COA brief rehearsal | | | |
| **COA Briefing to CDR** | | | |
| Analysis war gaming session | | | |
| Battlestaff COA Decision Brief product turn in | | | |
| S-3 COA Decision Brief initial review | | | |
| Battlestaff COA Decision final product check | | | |
| S-2, S-3, and SPO War Game final review | | | |
| COA Decision Brief final print | | | |
| COA Decision Brief rehearsal | | | |
| **Decision Briefing to CDR** | | | |

| | | | |
|---|---|---|---|
| Battlestaff OPLAN/OPORD product turn in | | | |
| S-3 OPLAN/OPORD initial review | | | |
| Battlestaff OPLAN product turn in | | | |
| Battlestaff OPLAN/OPORD final product check | | | |
| S-3 OPLAN/OPORD final review | | | |
| S-3 Orders Briefing review | | | |
| Orders Briefing rehearsal | | | |
| **Orders Briefing to CDR** | | | |
| OPLAN/OPORD change working group | | | |
| OPLAN/OPORD product review | | | |
| OPLAN/OPORD issue rehearsal | | | |
| **OPLAN/OPORD issue** | | | |

## 10.2 OPERATIONAL TIMELINE SAMPLE FORMAT

### Operational Timeline (BSB Sample)

| Phase | | | | |
|---|---|---|---|---|
| **D-Day** | **Date** | | | |
| **Time** | **0001-0600** | **0601-1200** | **1201-1800** | **1801-2400** |
| **H-Hour** | | | | |
| **Air Tasking Order** | | | | |
| **Weather** | | | | |
| **Enemy Activity** | | | | |
| **BDE Activity** | | | | |
| **BDE Resupply/RO** | | | | |
| **BSB Resupply/RO** | | | | |
| **Move** | | | | |
| **Medical** | | | | |
| **BSB Defense** | | | | |
| **BROC/BDOC** | | | | |
| **C2** | | | | |
| **Risk Management** | | | | |

*CHAPTER 11*

# BACKBRIEFS AND REHEARSALS

*"An order than can be misunderstood, will be misunderstood"*
*Field Marshal Helmut von Moltke,*
*Chief of the Prussian General Staff*
*Battle of Sedan, September 1870*

1. **Background.** The Military Decision Making Process does not come to an end at the conclusion of the OPORD/OPLAN brief as many staffs believed in the past. At the very least, the Sustainment Unit commander may require subordinate leaders to immediately provide him with a "Confirmation Brief" followed a short time later with an OPLAN /OPORD "Backbrief." Once the subordinate commander has confirmed his/her mission with the Sustainment Unit commander, a rehearsal is set to ensure in everyone's mind that the plan is well understood by all players involved and that it provides one last review of the unit's Sustainment Synchronization and Decision Support Matrix.

2. **Post OPORD/OPLAN Briefs.**

   a. **Confirmation Brief.** (Ref FM 5-0, Para 4-33). Immediately after receiving the OPORD/OPLAN, subordinate leaders brief their commander on the order they just received, focusing on their understanding of the commander's intent (particularly those key tasks identified by him outside specific taskings found within Para 3b). Subordinate leaders will also go over tasks as assigned, their purposes, and the relationship of their tasks to those of other elements conducting the operation. (One example is the assembly and dispatch of a Forward Logistics Element whose creation requires more than one unit to create). They repeat any important coordinating measures specified in the order. The confirmation brief is normally used with other types of rehearsal.

**b.** **Backbrief.** (Ref FM 5-0, Para I-7, I-8). The backbrief differs from a confirmation brief in that subordinate leaders are given time to complete their plan. Backbriefs require the fewest resources and are often the only option under time-constrained conditions.

Subordinate leaders explain their actions from start to finish of the mission. Backbriefs are performed sequentially, with all leaders going over their tasks. When time is available, backbriefs may be combined with other types of rehearsals. Doing this lets all element leaders coordinate their plans before performing more elaborate drills. If possible, backbriefs are performed overlooking subordinates' AOs, after they have the chance to develop their own plans and make the necessary reconnaissance or unit taskings. A sample backbrief is provided in 11.1 below.

## 11.1 Sample Backbrief Format

1. Higher Unit's Purpose
2. Higher Unit's Intent
3. Constraints/Restraints/Limitations
4. Intelligence Overview
5. Specified, Implied, Essential Tasks
6. Unit's Mission Statement
7. Unit Commander's Intent (Purpose, Key Tasks, End State)

8. Task Organization for Support
9. Concept of the Operation/Concept of Support (by phase or event)
10. Rules of Engagement
11. Minimum force requirements/Convoy Security needs
12. Time Schedule
13. Critical Execution checklist items

If time does not permit for a full Back Brief, an abbreviated Back Brief may be given, consisting of the following steps:

1. Higher Unit's Commander's intent.
2. Unit's Mission Statement
3. Unit Commander's Intent (Purpose, Key Tasks, End State)
4. Concept of the Operation/Concept of Support (by phase or event)
5. Minimum force requirements/Convoy Security needs
6. Time Schedule
7. Critical Execution checklist items

**11.2 Rehearsals**. Per Para 5-56, ATTP 5-0.1, rehearsals are defined as:

> .... *a session in which a staff or unit practices expected actions to improve performance during execution. Rehearsing key combat (sustainment) actions before execution allows participants to become familiar with the operation and to translate the relatively dry recitation of the tactical plan into visual impression. This impression helps them orient themselves to their environment and other units when executing the operation. Moreover, the repetition of combat tasks during the rehearsal leaves a lasting mental picture of the sequence of key actions within the operation. This appendix contains guidelines for conducting rehearsals. It describes rehearsal types and techniques. It lists responsibilities of those involved.*

Rehearsals allow staff officers, subordinate commanders, and other leaders to practice executing the course of action (COA) the commander chose at the end of the military decision-making process (MDMP). Rehearsals are *the commander's tool* to ensure all subordinate leaders understand the plan and are "in sync" so to speak with it. Commander's use rehearsals to ensure staffs and subordinates understand their intent and the concept of operations/concept of support. Rehearsals also synchronize operations at times and places critical to successful mission accomplishment.

For units to be effective and efficient in conducting sustainment operations, unit rehearsals need to occur as a matter of habit. All commands at every level should routinely train and practice a variety of rehearsal techniques and types.

The key ingredient to conducting successful rehearsals is time. The time required for a rehearsal varies with the complexity of the task to rehearse, the type and technique of rehearsal, and the level of participation. Successful rehearsals are conducted at the lowest possible level, using the most thorough technique possible, given the time available. Under time-constrained conditions, staffs conduct reduced rehearsals. These focus on critical events determined by reverse planning.

During offensive operations, staffs address the following actions in order: the objective, passage of lines, and movement to the objective—then other phases of the operation. During defensive operations, staffs address counter reconnaissance, battle handover, and commitment of counterattack forces or the striking force—then other phases of the operation. Each unit has different critical events, based on its readiness and the unit commander's assessment.

Whenever possible, rehearsals are based on a completed operation order (OPORD). A contingency plan may be rehearsed to prepare for an anticipated deployment. The rehearsal is a coordination event, not an analysis. It is not a substitute for the war game. War games are preformed during the MDMP to analyze several COAs and determine the optimal one. Rehearsals are conducted during preparation to practice executing the COA that the commander chose at the end of the MDMP. Commanders avoid making major changes to OPORDs during rehearsals. They make only those changes essential to mission success.

## 11. 3 REHEARSAL TYPES

Each rehearsal type achieves a different result and has a specific place in the preparation time line. The five types of rehearsals are (in order to shortness/availability of time):

* Net Rehearsal
* Map Rehearsal
* Sketch Map Rehearsal
* Terrain Model Rehearsal
* Reduced Force Rehearsal
* Full Dress Rehearsal

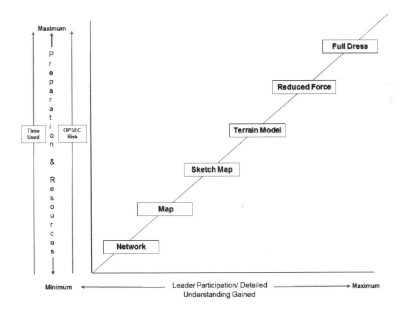

*From Figure I-1, FM 5-0. Rehearsal Techniques Relative to Time, Resources OPSEC Participation, and Understanding*

a.  **Network**. This type of rehearsal is conducted utilizing either a unit Local Area Network (LAN) or Wide Area Network (WAN). This technique works best with units who have clear SOPs and functional/ working communications. Critical portion of the plan are talked through by Commanders and staffs using a sequence provided by the owning commander. This type of rehearsal requires all unit information systems (INFOSYS) owned by the unit as well as a copy of the OPORD/OPLAN with overlays in order to execute their portion of the plan.

b.  **Map**. A map rehearsal as the name indicates, utilizes a map and appropriate overlay (either sustainment or operational) of the same used to plan the operation. Generally this technique is easiest to set up and conduct provided all units involved are operation within the same echelon and scale of map. If paper maps are unavailable, projection off an MCS or BCS[3] workstation screen will suffice.

c.  **Sketch Map**. The sketch map rehearsal technique can be used by commanders nearly anywhere regardless of daylight or weather conditions. Map sketches are drawn large enough for all participants to view and demonstrate required logistical/sustainment actions and movements using markers or "sticky" pad 'Post-it' notes.

d.  **Terrain Model**. Also known as the "sand table" rehearsal, this technique requires far less resources and time than the Reduced Force or Full Dress rehearsals. Commanders use an accurately constructed terrain model to assist subordinate leaders to visualize the terrain as well as understand the Commander's intent, vision, and the concept of the operation/support at hand. Ideally if practical, the terrain model should be placed in an area nearby that overlooks the actual terrain the unit is conducting support operations.

e. **Reduced Force**. If mission requirements only allow for key leaders to be present, then a reduced-force rehearsal is called for, with leader involvement is usually decided by the commander. Typically, this type rehearsal is simpler, utilizing fewer resources and time that that called for in the full-dress rehearsal or used as a preparation for a full-dress rehearsal if time permits. This is generally the most popular rehearsal to conduct if time permits for the assembly of a terrain model for participates to role play.

f. **Full Dress**. The most time consuming, detailed, yet most effective of the all the rehearsals available is the Full Dress rehearsal. Ideal for companies and below, commanders begin to trade off OPSEC and time management/availability the higher the echelon using this technique and must consider the time resource needs of their subordinates when considering this option. Traffic management and vehicular parking within the immediate area the rehearsal is conducted is also a consideration in order to maintain OPSEC. The rehearsal area must be identified, secured, and maintained prior to and throughout this option.

## 11.4. Rehearsal Execution.

a. Regardless of the type of rehearsal conducted, sustainment participants should bring the following tools with them:

(1) Sus Bde/CSSB Sustainment Execution Matrix and Concept of Support for their organization and the next higher.

(2) BSB Sustainment Execution Matrix and Concept of Support for their organization and the next higher.

(3) A functional detailed plan for their part of the overall operation.

(4) An ability to "act out" their portion of the plan by phase.

      (5)   Confirmation of their task organization and their customer task organization. Ex: CSSB (by company/detachment) and the task organization of the customer they are tasked to support (Support Brigade or Brigade Combat Team).

   b.   Order of the Brief.

For a CSSB, the following participants either speak or are on standby for questions:

| SPEAKING ROLES | INITIAL NONSPEAKERS |
|---|---|
| BDE/BN XO | MOVEMENT CONTROL TEAM REP |
| BDE/BN S3 | MP PLT LDR (IF AVAILABLE) |
| BDE/BN S2 | TCF/SECFOR CDR (IF AVAILABLE) |
| BDE/BN S1 | CSSB CO COMMANDERS |
| BDE/BN S4 | CHAPLAIN (IF AVAILABLE) |
| BDE/BN S6 | |
| BN/CO XO'S | |
| SPO OFFICER | |
| MED BDE REP/SPT BDE MED CO CDR | |
| COMMENTS BY CMD XO/BDE/BN COMMANDER | |

   c.   Speaker Roles and Responsibilities.

     (1)   XO
* Appoints the scribe
* Conducts role call
* Provides Cdr's guidance for Sustainment Rehearsal

     (2)   S3 Operations
* Provides overview of terrain model
* Provides boundaries and locations of friendly forces
* States Task Organization
* Friendly situation

* Mission, Concept of Operation, and Commander's Intent
* Speaks and covers each phase and events that conclude that phase
* Protection of Sustainment assets and LSA/FOB ISR
* Unit & FLE/FLB moves, CRSP and/or Trailer Transfer Points (TTPs) establishments

(3) S2 Intelligence
* Provides and overview of enemy situation
* Displays enemy symbols on terrain model
* Focuses on all enemy threats to Sustainment operations and Areas of Concern to Sustainment operators
* Portrays civilian & refugee impacts within the area of operations and their possible impact to Sustainment operations
* Reviews Commander's Critical Intelligence Requirements (CCIR)

(4) S4 Sustainment and Logistics
* Provides an overview of *"the Sustainment unit"* logistics posture
* Provides internal support unit locations
* Provides an understanding of infrastructure and alternative support (HNS)
* Identifies priorities of support
* Provides a snap shot of the Units Concept of Support (Para 4a)

(5) S1 Human Resources
* Provides personnel status by unit
* Medical support available to support sustainment operations

(6)   Support Operations (SPO)
*   Provide and overview of AOR logistics and Concept of Support (Annex I)
*   Covers all support/sustainment actions and muscle moves for each phase (MSOs, SROs, CROs, CRSP establishment, FLE echelonment, etc)
*   Priorities of support
*   Locations of all sustainment units in LSA/FOB/ FLE/FLB and Unit AO
*   Status of on hand stocks (critical). Recommend this be done in pallets, gallons, short tons, etc. Use the term "Days of Supply" (or DOS) only if everyone has a clear understanding what this entails.
*   Throughtput (ATHP, CL IV, V, Fuel, CL IX) schedules

In Brigade Combat Team/Support Brigade Sustainment Rehearsals, the following is added:

(7)   BCT/BN/TF XO
*   Coverage of maneuver actions during each phase of the operation

(8)   Each Supported Unit S-4
*   Coverage of unit logistics for each phase
*   Current unit logistical assets available
*   Unit location of:
    Battalion Aid Stations (BAS), Casualty Collection Points (CCP) and AXP
    Unit Maintenance Collection Points (UMCP)
    Combat Trains – Task Force/Combined Arms Support Areas and FSC locs
    Maneuver/Maneuver Support Unit locations

d.  Conduct of the Rehearsal. Like Combined Arms Rehearsals, Sustainment rehearsals are usually conducted as a *Before, During, and After* Operations Phase.

  (1)  BEFORE PHASE: Consists of all required Sustainment Bde conducted MROs, BCT/Task Force/Support Brigade movements from current locations to TAAs, Attack Positions conducted prior to LD (or defend time). Sustainment Bde/CSSB positioning of CRSPs, FLEs, TTPs are also identified here.

    (a)  BCT/TF/Support Brigade XOs successfully lay out:
      -  Terrain
      -  Route Security and SEC FOR support utilized
      -  Enroute requirements such as RO, Recovery, CASEVAC, WARLOCK employment

    (b)  Sustainment Brigade/CSSB/BSB Support Ops
      -  Posturing
      -  Pre-positioning
      -  Movement of sustainment units and resulting support impact (i.e. "blackouts")   •

  (2)  DURING PHASE: This phase should reflect the same mission phases as the OPORD. Key topics of concern within this phase include water, fuel and ammunition resupply/replenishment operations (RO), casualty treatment and evacuation (via ground & air), and maintenance recovery.

    (a)  Unit XOs/Slice Units/BSB:
      -  Layout every functional area
      -  Continue to physically depict locations
      -  Hasty displacement plans
      -  Alternate communication, retrans plans and digital connectivity

- Use of aerial resupply (if required)
- Response to threats/civilian actions
- Medical evacuation (both by ground and air)
- Security measures employed enroute/ Warlock on/off time & locations

(b) All participates should cover the movement of critical sustainment nodes that fall within their area of concern in order to ensure full visualization of the operating environment.

For example: a Sustainment Brigade is conducting a BCT/ BSB SRO.

Sus Bde SPO identifies (or confirms previous support mission tasker) BCT OCL/MCL requirements and delivery location, HNS, or contractor involvement.

MCT Rep confirms movement DTG and MSR utilized. If possible, MSR status identified/confirmed

CSSB SPO identifies distro/trans element (size, type trucks and composition) load out and PCI times.

S-3 discusses SECFOR requirements and link up sites

(c) After a particular phase or a key important movement aspect of a rehearsal is completed, the rehearsal director (usually the Unit Commander or his Deputy/XO) will require a back brief by key functional operators to confirm customer to sustainment unit linkage.

Example: Unit MEDIVAC/CASEVAC Operations. Walk through medical evacuation from the point of injury to the Battalion Aid Station and on to the Brigade Support Medical Company (or in the case of a Support Brigade, to the Support Brigade Medical Company, SBMC) – across all phases – emphasizing the connectivity of the Ambulance Exchange Point (AXP) and potential unit replenishment operations. It is vitally important that players must "*visualize*" the operation from all aspects.

One final note – all players must clearly articulate all triggers related to the movement of logistics assets across the battlefield. This is why you spend so much time developing a Sustainment Synchronization Matrix during the Wargaming Phase of the Military Decision Making Process. Share the knowledge with everyone present.

(3)   AFTER PHASE: This phase focuses on continuing to logistically shape the conduct of operation for future actions/activities. THERE ARE ALWAYS MISSIONS TO CONDUCT TOMORROW!!! ALWAYS THINK A MINIMUM OF THREE DAYS (72 HRS) IN ADVANCE.

Participants should discuss:

LOGISTICAL ACTIONS ON THE OBJECTIVE-
-   RECOVERY OF COMBAT SYSTEMS
-   CLEARING CASUALTIES
-   PRE-POSITIONING CLASS IV AND OTHER COMMODITIES

OTHER TOPICS TO ADDRESS -
-   ROUTES
-   SECURITY
-   TRAFFIC CONTROL
-   REPORTING TIMELINES

*CHAPTER 12*

# THE 'RUNNING' ESTIMATE & STAFF ESTIMATES

### ★★★

**12.1 The 'Running' Estimate**. As depicted in Chapter 6, ATTP 5-0.1, a *running estimate* is the continuous assessment of the current situation used to determine if the current operation is proceeding according to the commander's intent and if planned future operations are supportable (FM 5-0). The commander and each staff section maintain a running estimate. In their running estimates, the commander and each staff section continuously consider the effects of new information and update the following:

- Facts.
- Assumptions.
- Friendly force status.
- Enemy activities and capabilities.
- Civil considerations.
- Conclusions and recommendations.

Estimates are not just for staffs. Commanders also develop a running commander's estimates to consolidate their understanding and visualization of an operation. The commander's running estimate summarizes the problem and integrates information and knowledge of the staff's and subordinate commanders' running estimates.

Is a Running Estimate required for each staff section? The short answer is yes, especially if that section has a critical bearing on the pending operation. Overall, each staff section builds and maintains running estimates. The running estimate helps the staff to track and record pertinent information as well as to provide recommendations to commanders. Running estimates represent the analysis and expert opinion of each staff section by functional area. Staffs maintain running estimates throughout the operations process to assist commanders in the exercise of mission command.

Each staff section and command post functional cell maintains a running estimate focused on how their specific areas of expertise are postured to support future operations. Because an estimate may be needed at any time, running estimates must be developed, revised, updated, and maintained continuously while in garrison and during operations. As a rule of thumb, if it requires more than 15 minutes to update a staff estimate, it is not considered a current 'running' estimate.

## 12.1. Staff Estimate Make Up.

1.  Mission Receipt/Analysis, facts and assumptions, and the situation analysis (of the area of operation, area of interest, and enemy, friendly, and support requirements) furnish the structure for the staff estimate. The running estimate consists of significant facts, events, and conclusions based on analyzed data. A generic running estimate is provided below in Figure 12.1. Failure to make estimates can lead to errors and omissions when developing, analyzing, and comparing COAs.

2.  Essential Qualities of Running Estimates:

    a.  Comprehensive estimates consider both the quantifiable and the intangible aspects of military operations.

    b.  Must be as thorough as time and circumstances permit. The commander and staff must constantly collect, process, and evaluate information. Updates are made:

(1)   When the commander and staff recognizes new facts.

(2)   When they replace assumptions with facts or find their assumptions invalid.

(3)   When they receive changes to the mission or when changes are indicated.

c.   Estimates for the current operation can often provide a basis for estimates for future missions.

d.   Estimates must visualize the future and support the commander's battlefield visualization.

*Figure 12.1 – A 'generic' base running estimate*

---

**1. SITUATION AND CONSIDERATIONS.**
   **a. Area of Interest.** Identify and describe those factors of the area of interest that affect functional area considerations.
   **b. Characteristics of the Area of Operations.**
      **(1) Terrain.** State how terrain affects staff functional area's capabilities.
      **(2) Weather.** State how weather affects staff functional area's capabilities.
      **(3) Enemy Forces.** Describe enemy disposition, composition, strength, and systems within a functional area as well as enemy capabilities and possible courses of action (COAs) with respect to their effects on a functional area.
      **(4) Friendly Forces.** List current functional area resources in terms of equipment, personnel, and systems. Identify additional resources available for the functional area located at higher, adjacent, or other units. List those capabilities from other military and civilian partners that maybe available to provide support within the functional area. Compare requirements to current capabilities and suggest solutions for satisfying discrepancies.
      **(5) Civilian Considerations.** Describe civil considerations that may affect the functional area to include possible support needed by civil authorities from the functional area as well as possible interference from civil aspects.
   **c. Assumptions.** List all assumptions that affect the functional area.
**2. MISSION.** Show the restated mission resulting from mission analysis.
**3. COURSES OF ACTION.**
   **a.** List friendly COAs that were war-gamed.
   **b.** List enemy actions or COAs that were templated that impact the functional area.
   **c.** List the evaluation criteria identified during COA analysis. All staffs use the same criteria.
**4. ANALYSIS.** Analyze each COA using the evaluation criteria from COA analysis. Review enemy actions that impact the functional area as they relate to COAs. Identify issues, risks, and deficiencies these enemy actions may create with respect to the functional area.
**5. COMPARISON.** Compare COAs. Rank order COAs for each key consideration. Use a decision matrix to aid the comparison process.
**6. RECOMMENDATIONS AND CONCLUSIONS.**
   **a.** Recommend the most supportable COAs from the perspective of the functional area.
   **b.** Prioritize and list issues, deficiencies, and risks and make recommendations on how to mitigate

---

## 12.3. Types of Running Estimates:

### a. Commander's Estimate. (See 12.4)

(1) The commander's estimate, like the operations estimate, is an analysis of all the factors that could affect a mission.

(2) Estimate analysis includes risk assessment, force protection, and effective utilization of all resources. The estimate also includes visualizing all reasonable COAs and how each COA would affect friendly forces.

(3) The commander's estimate and operations estimate generally follow the same format. However, the commander's estimate deals more with assessing the intangibles of training, leadership, and morale, and it results in a decision.

### b. Operations Estimate

(1) The S-3 prepares the operations estimate, which considers all elements that can influence the unit's current operation and feasible future courses of action. It results in a recommendation to the commander.

(2) To prepare the estimate, the S-3 must understand:

(a) The commander's intent (one and two levels up).
(b) The risk assessment.
(c) The current task organization (two echelons below).
(d) The unit's status, such as locations, combat capabilities, and current mission.

(e)  The availability and capabilities of higher and joint assets.
(f)  Other information, such as location, status, and mission of flank and supporting units.

c.  **Personnel Estimate (See 12.5)**

(1)  The S-1 prepares the personnel estimate, which is an analysis of how all human resources and personnel factors impact soldier and unit effectiveness before, during, and after the mission. It includes a current overall personnel status of the organization, its subordinate units, and any attached or supporting elements. It includes assessment of the following factors:
(a)  Medical evacuation and hospitalization.
(b)  Unit strength maintenance.
(c)  Replacements.
(d)  Soldiers' readiness.
(e)  Organizational climate.
(f)  Cohesion.
(g)  Discipline, law, and order.

(2)  The estimate predicts losses (where and when they could occur) and when, where, and if such losses cause the culmination of an operation. It contains the recommendations and conclusions about the feasibility of supporting major operations and tactical missions.

d.  **Intelligence Estimate. (See 12.6)** The S-2 or S-2 Intel NCO prepares the intelligence estimate. All examine the area of interest to identify intelligence collection needs.

e.  **Sustainment (Logistics) Estimate. (See 12.7)** The SPO prepares the logistics estimate, which provides an accurate and current assessment of the CSS situation sustainment unit external support mission, its subordinate units, and any attached or supporting elements. It is an estimate of how service support factors can affect mission accomplishment. This estimate includes how the functional areas of supply, transportation, services, maintenance, labor, facilities, and construction affect various COAs. It contains any inputted S-4 recommendations and conclusions about the feasibility of supporting tactical missions.

f. **SPO Support Ops Estimates. (See 12.8)** The SPO prepares an estimate regarding the supported customer's posture within their functional area, focused on the anticipated requirements, known and projected capabilities and identified shortfalls. Estimates include recommendations for overcoming shortfalls.

g. **Signal Estimate.** The S-6 (Signal Officer) prepares the communications estimate in relation in to the situation and his functional responsibilities.

h. **Special Staff Estimates.** Each special staff officer creates his own staff estimate in relation to the situation and his functional responsibilities.

## Staff Estimate Considerations Checklist

In preparing Staff (Running) Estimates, Planning Staff should review the following items to ensure all are taken into consideration under the Analysis, Comparison and Recommendation/ Conclusions paragraphs.

1. The five questions logistics planners and operators should always be able to answer are:

- **Where are we on the battlefield?**
- **Why are we here?**
- **How do we support from here?**
- **How do we get support from here?**
- **When, to where, and in what sequence do we displace to ensure continuous operations?**

2.  The following Running Estimate preparation methodology is based on a requirement, capability, shortfall, analysis, and solution model. This methodology would commence after the staff received the mission and continues through redeployment. Bottom line, it is a continuous process used in each step of the MDMP and refined whenever new information is received.

3.  To put this methodology into context, there must be some continuity between the tactical decision making process and the logistic planning process. Each of the model's categories (requirements, capabilities, shortfall, analysis, and solutions) must have any associated, necessary, and valid assumptions stated up front.

## REQUIREMENTS

1.  What method is used to determine logistics requirements? [For example: personnel density, equipment density, weather planning factors, operating tempo (OPTEMPO), combination, etc.]

2.  What is the source of the requirements determination calculations? [For example: The Logistics Estimate Worksheet (LEW), Operations Logistics Planner (OPLOGPLN), The *Modular G1/G4 Battle Book*, historical data, etc.]

3.  What is your customer list for this requirement? Will it change during the operation?
4.  Identify implied logistics tasks based on the tactical plan. What are the ramifications of river crossings, pauses, deep attacks, etc.?

5.  Is there a CBRNE/WMD threat?

6.  What do you need?

7.  How long will you need it?

8.  Where do you need it?

9.  What do you need to put it there? [For example, fuel bladders/bags, rough-terrain container handlers (RTCHs), forklifts, cranes, etc.]

10. How will you get it there?

11. When do you need it there? How long will it take to get it there?

12. How soon will it be available to move there? Where is it coming from?

13. What do you need to do with it before moving it where you need it? (For example, does it have to be containerized, broken down, segregated, separated, disassembled, configured, or reconfigured before movement?)

    — How long will that take?
    — What are the requirements for that?

14. Does it have to move again after it gets there? (For example, is it a GS-GS transaction? GS-DS? DS-DS? DS-user?) Who will move it from there?

15. What are the competing demands for this requirement?

16. What is required to offload it when it gets there?

17. Does anything need to be done with it once it gets there? (For example, does it have to be unpacked, assembled, etc.?)

18. What has to be done to move it once it is there?

19. Does this requirement have special employment considerations? (For example, require a large, level area of land or a fresh water source; be located near an MSR; need refrigeration; require dedicated transportation; etc.)

20. How often will the commodity, supply, or service be required? How often must it be replenished?

21. Does the requirement have preparatory activities? [For example, engineers to berm a bag farm, airfield matting for forward arming and refueling points (FARPs), road and pad construction for an ASA]

22. What is the expected duration of the required preparation?

23. How do you request the preparation and who approves it? (For example, engineer work has to be approved through channels.)

24. What support is required for the preparatory activities?

## CAPABILITIES

1. What are the units available that have the capability to fulfill the requirement?

2. What is the basis of allocation for the unit that has the necessary capability? (For example, is its basis of allocation one per corps or division, or is it based on supported populations or expected equipment densities?)

3. Is more than one unit required to provide the capability? [A few examples: the Petroleum, Oils, and Lubricants (POL) Supply Company is usually employed with the medium truck company (POL). Typically, a Water Purification and Distribution Company pairs up with a Field Service Company (SCLR & MA)]

4. What are the overall receipt, storage, and issue requirements for my area of support for this particular commodity, supply, or service?

5. Are receipts and issues exclusive capabilities? (For example, can a unit receive, store, *and* issue so much of a particular commodity, or can it only receive *or* store *or* issue *or* rewarehouse so much of a particular commodity?)

6. Will this capability be used to weight the battle logistically?

7. What is the total short ton (STON)/gallon/pallet/other distribution capability by mode? Line haul? Local haul? Other? With today's delivery/distribution systems, focus on pallets!

8. What distribution planning factors were used (DOS, gallons, STONs, *pallets*)?

9. How many locations require this capability?

10. Are any units with this capability already committed?

11. Are any units with this capability due in? When?

12. Do units depend on other units to function? (For example, to perform its mission, some mode transportation units must bring cargo to a cargo transfer company.)

13. Can a unit deploy elements (sections or platoons) to place the capability where it is required?

14. Does the unit have unique management/employment considerations?

## COMPARISON/SHORTFALL

1. If there is no shortfall, go to the *analysis* portion of this methodology.

2. Which requirements exceed capabilities?

3. For requirements that exceed capabilities, is it overall or in a particular area, region, or time?

4. How much is the shortfall in terms of units of measurement (pallets, STONs, gallons, square feet)?

5. What does the shortfall equate to in terms of days of supply?

6. At what point in the battle is the requirement expected to exceed the capability?

7. What is the type of shortfall? Is it a supply availability shortfall, a resource [equipment, materials handling equipment (MHE), personnel, facilities, man-hours, etc.] shortfall, or a distribution shortfall?

## ANALYSIS

The analysis process has to occur for all support operations even if there is no shortfall. The sustainment planner is required to determine how to support the operation.

1. What is the earliest the support operation can begin?

2. What is the latest the support operation can begin?

3. Is it better to be early or late?

4. What is the purpose of the support? (For example, is the purpose to build stocks at GS, to sustain a force for a given period of time at DS, or to resupply a user?)

5. Will support be provided from a fixed location or from a forward logistics element?

6. What is the significance of the shortfall?

7. What is the potential impact of the shortfall?

8. What is the expected duration of the shortfall?

9. What is the cause of the shortfall (battle loss, time-phased force deployment sequence, etc.)?

10. If the shortfall is a *supply availability* shortfall, consider the following:

a. Is the shortfall only at this level or is at higher levels as well?

b. Is it a result of higher commands' efforts and support priorities?

c. Is the supply available at other echelons and, if so, where?

d. How long will it take to get here?

e. Is there an acceptable alternative, a substitute, or an alternative source of supply?

11. If the shortfall is a *resource shortfall* (equipment, MHE, personnel, facilities, man-hours, etc.), consider the following:

a. Can similar resources be diverted or obtained from somewhere else

b. Is HNS a viable alternative? Contractor support?

c. How specialized is the shortfall resource? (For example, it is easier to train a mortuary affairs specialist than it is to train a doctor. It is easier to find an automotive mechanic than it is an M1 fire control specialist.)

d. Can a secondary or related military occupational specialty (MOS) be used?

e. Does a sister service, contractor or coalition partner have the capability?

12. If the shortfall is a *distribution shortfall,* consider the following:

a. Is the shortfall due to a lack of assets or to a time-distance problem?

b. Does the shortfall capability require special handling or any special distribution requirements?

    c.   Are there any alternative distribution modes?

    d.   What are the alternative mode requirements? (For example, a pipeline requires continuous pump and hose/pipeline maintenance, engineer support to lay the pipeline, etc.)

    e.   Are host nation distribution assets available?

    f.   Are sister service/coalition assets available?

    g.   Are they compatible? (For example, European and SWA host nation fuel tankers are metric and require a coupler adapter to interface US tankers or bags.)

    h.   Are there any airfields, field landing strips, or helipads near the requirement?

13.   How will logistics capability be echeloned forward? Which units will be tasked to establish forward logistics bases?

## SOLUTIONS

1.   Determine the most workable solutions based on analysis.

2.   Integrate with other support operations and commodities.

**12.4 Commander's Guidance Worksheet.**

| OPORD # | Unit HQs | DTG | Cdr's Signature |
|---|---|---|---|

1.   Commander's Intent
    a.   Broader purpose

    b.   Key tasks

    c.   Endstate

2.   Decisive points/ actions:

3.   COAs to consider (where/ when/ how to mass to accomplish mission and intent)
    a.   Friendly

    b.   Enemy

4.   How we must posture for next phase (logistically/ geographically)

5.   Recon guidance

6.   Deception guidance (if applicable)

7.   Priorities for:
    a.   Human Resource

    b.   Supply (Fuel, Arm)

    c.   Maintenance

    d.   Transportation

    e.   Field Service

    f.   Combat Health Service

    g.   Force protection/ security measures to be implemented

    h.   EOD, Religious, and Fin Svc

8.   Risk (areas acceptable)

9.   CCIR
    a.   EEFI

    b.   FFIR

    c.   PIR

10.   Decisions I see myself making:

11.   Time plan (confirm/ readjust proposed timeline)

12.   Type order

13.   Type Rehearsal

## 12.5 Personnel Estimate

### Personnel Estimate

The S-1 prepares the personnel estimate, which is an analysis of how all human resources and personnel factors impact soldier and unit effectiveness before, during, and after the mission. It is includes a current overall personnel status of the organization, its subordinate units, and any attached or supporting elements. Personnel status includes assessments of the following factors, medical evacuation and hospitalization, unit strength maintenance, replacements, soldier's readiness, organizational climate, cohesion, and discipline, law and order. The personnel estimate predicts losses (where and when losses could occur) and when, where, and if such loses cause the culmination of an operation. It contains the feasibility of supporting major operational and tactical missions.

-----------------

(Classification)

Headquarters
Place
Date, time and zone
Msg ref no.

PERSONNEL (PERS) ESTIMATE NO____

References: Map, charts, or other documents.

Time Zone Used Throughout the Estimate:

1.  **MISSION**: This paragraph lists the command's restated mission.

2.  **THE SITUATION AND CONSIDERATIONS:**

    a.  Intelligence Situation. This paragraph contains information from the intelligence officer. As the personnel officer, include a brief summary when the details are appropriate and there is a written estimate. Refer to the appropriate intelligence document or use an annex of the estimate. Include:

(1)  Characteristics of the area of operations.

(2)  Enemy strength and dispositions.

(3)  Enemy capabilities. Include enemy and non-enemy sponsored terrorist activities–

　　(a)  Affecting the mission

　　(b)  Affecting personnel activities.

b.  Tactical Situation. Information for this paragraph comes from the commander's planning guidance and from the S-3. Include –

(1)  Present disposition of major tactical elements.

(2)  Possible courses of actions. List all given courses of action.

(3)  Projected operations, if known. List projected operations and other planning factors required for coordinating and integrating staff estimates.

c.  Sustainment Situation. To list the Sustainment situation –

(1)  Present dispositions of sustainment units and installations that affect the personnel situation.

(2)  Show any projected developments within the sustainment WFFA field that might influence personnel operations.

d.  Civil-Military Operations Situation. Information for this subparagraph comes from the CMO officer at the Sus Bde (for CSSBs)/Div or Bde (for BSBs). Such information should help you:

(1)  Present dispositions of civil affairs units and installations that affect the personnel situation.

(2)  Show any projected developments within the CMO field that might influence personnel operations.

e. Troop Preparedness Situation. Show the status in this subparagraph under the appropriate subheadings. Subparagraphs include-

(1) Unit strength. Indicate authorized, assigned, and attached strengths. Include the effects of deployability, losses (combat or non-combat), critical MOS's and skill shortages, projections (gains and losses), and any other situations affecting strength.

(2) Other personnel. Indicate personnel, other than unit soldiers, whose presence affects the unit mission. Include EPW's, augmentees (non-US forces), civilian internees and detainees, DA civilians, and others, depending on local circumstances.

(3) Soldier personal readiness. Indicate those elements of quality of life and personnel administration and management which provide services, facilities, and policies affecting soldier personal readiness.

(a) Soldier services. In this paragraph include –

(1) Administrative services (pay, orders, evaluation reports, awards, reenlistment, eliminations, separations, promotions, assignments, transfers, personal affairs, leaves, and passes).

(2) Health services (field medical support, disease, mental health, and other services).

(3) Health care (medical, dental, entitlements, eligibility, and physical fitness).

(4) Support services (transportation, commissary, PX, clothing, laundry, legal, spiritual, law and order).

(5) Personnel development (education and professional development).

(6) Community relations.

          (7)    Moral support activities (Army community services, libraries, community centers, clubs, movies, and post office).

          (8)    Family member assistance planning.

   (b)   Duty conditions, Include –
          (1)    Work facilities (location and quality).
          (2)    Work requirements (impact of frequency and length of field duty and rotation between remote and non-remote duty locations).
          (3)    Equipment (adequacy).

   (c)   Other.

(4)   Human potential. Indicate factors affecting the stability and human potential of individual soldiers, teams, and crews to accomplish the mission. Consider, but do not limit yourself to, such factors as turbulence and turnover, experience, personal problems, and individual stress, status of crews, and MOS mismatch with the unit.

(5)   Organizational climate. Indicate factors affecting personnel readiness. Include-
   (a)   Communications effectiveness with the chain of command.
   (b)   Performance and discipline standards.
   (c)   Incentives.
   (d)   Drug and alcohol abuse standards.
   (e)   Counseling.
   (f)   Human relations.
   (g)   Supervision.
   (h)   Planning
   (i)   Ethics

        (j)   Organization stress.

        (k)   Other.

    (6)   Commitment. Indicate the relative strength of the soldier's identification and involvement with the unit. Also note their:

        (a)   Morale.

        (b)   Motivations.

        (c)   Confidence.

        (d)   Trust.

    (7)   Cohesion. Indicate factors which unite and commit soldiers to accomplish the mission such as:

        (a)   Esprit.

        (b)   Teamwork.

  f.   Assumptions. Until specific planning guidance from the commander becomes available, you may need assumptions for initiating planning or preparing the estimate. Modify assumptions as factual data becomes available.

**3.   ANALYSIS OF COURSE OF ACTION**: For each COA, analyze personnel factors affecting each subheading in paragraph 2e indicating problem areas, trends, and deficiencies which might affect troop preparedness.

**4.   COMPARISON OF COURSES OF ACTION**:

  a.   Evaluate deficiencies from a personnel standpoint. List advantages and disadvantages, if any, to accomplishing the mission.

  b.   Discuss the advantages and disadvantages of each COA under consideration. Include methods for overcoming deficiencies or modifications required in each COA.

## 5. CONCLUSION:

a. Indicate whether you have personnel to support the mission (paragraph 1).

b. Indicate which COAs you can best support from the personnel viewpoint.

c. List the major personnel deficiencies which the commander must consider. Include specific recommendations concerning methods of eliminating or reducing the effect of these deficiencies.

/s/_____
(Personnel Officer S-1)

ANNEXES: (as required)

_____
(Classification)

## 12.6 Intelligence Estimate

_____

(Classification)

Headquarters
Place
Date, time and zone
Msg ref no.

**INTELLIGENCE (INTEL) ESTIMATE NO____**

**References**: Map, charts, or other documents.

**Time Zone Used Throughout the Estimate**:

1. **MISSION**: This paragraph lists the command's restated mission.

2. **THE SITUATION AND CONSIDERATIONS**:

   a. Characteristics of area of operation.
      (1) Weather. How will different military aspects of weather affect the intelligence area of concern and its resources?
      (2) Terrain. How will terrain affect the intelligence area of concern and its resources?
      (3) Other pertinent facts. Analyze political, economical, sociological, psychological, and environmental infrastructure, as they relate to the area.

   b. Enemy forces. Enemy dispositions, composition, strength, capabilities, and COAs as they affect intelligence.

   c. Friendly forces.
      (1) Friendly courses of actions.

    (2)   Current status of intelligence resources within the responsibility of the S-3.

    (3)   Current status of other resources that affect the S-3.

    (4)   Comparison of requirements versus capabilities and recommended solutions.

    (5)   Key considerations (evaluation criteria) for COA supportability.

  d.   Assumptions.

**3.**   **ANALYSIS**: Analyze each COA using key considerations (evaluation criteria) to determine advantages and disadvantages.

**4.**   **COMPARISON**: Compare COAs using key considerations (evaluation criteria). Rank order COAs for each key consideration. A decision matrix should visually support comparison.

**5.**   **RECOMMENDATION AND CONCLUSIONS:**

  a.   Recommended COA based on the comparison (most supportable from specific staff perspective).

  b.   Issues, deficiencies, and risks with recommendations to reduce their impacts.

/s/_____

(S-2 Officer)

ANNEXES: (as required)

12.7 Sustainment Estimate

The S-4 prepares the Sustainment estimate, which provides an accurate and current assessment of the sustainment situation of the organization, its subordinate units, and any attached or supporting elements. The logistics estimate is an analysis of how service support factors can affect mission accomplishment. It contains the S-4's conclusions and recommendations about the feasibility of supporting major operational and tactical mission. This estimate includes how the functional areas of supply, transportation, services, and maintenance, labor, facilities, and construction affect various COAs.

---

(Classification)

Headquarters
Place
Date, time and zone
Msg ref no.

SUSTAINMENT ESTIMATE NO____

**References: Map, charts, or other documents.**

**Time Zone Used Throughout the Estimate:**

1. **MISSION**: This paragraph lists the command's restated mission.

2. **THE SITUATION AND CONSIDERATIONS:**

   a. Intelligence Situation. This paragraph contains information from the intelligence officer. As the S-4 officer, include a brief summary when the details are appropriate and there is a written estimate. Refer to the appropriate intelligence document or use an annex of the estimate. Include:

(1) Characteristics of the area of operations. Describe the general characteristics of the area of operations. Emphasize any specific aspects which might affect the sutainment effort.

(2) Enemy strength and dispositions.

(3) Enemy capabilities. Include:

    (a) Any activities affecting the mission. Keep information general, but include both enemy and non-enemy sponsored terrorist activities.

    (b) Any activities affecting sustainment activities. Give detailed information oriented toward possible effects of logistics operations. Include what you know about the enemy air assault and airborne capabilities, TACAIR, artillery, CBRNE capabilities, guerrilla operations, and stay-behind or by-passed enemy forces.

b. Tactical Situation. Information from this paragraph comes from the commander's planning guidance and from the S-3. Subparagraphs should be general and concise statements of tactical intentions. The S-4 should include:

(1) Present disposition of major tactical elements. (Also put this information on the Sustainment overlay annex/LCOP, if appropriate).

(2) Possible courses of action. Lit all given courses of action. (These courses of action are carried forward through the remainder of the estimate).

(3) Projected operations. If known, list projected operations and other planning factors needed for coordinating and integrating staff estimates.

c. Personnel Situation. Include information you obtain from the personnel officer. Include total strength, unit strength, and factors for casualties, replacements, hospital returnees, etc.

    (1)    Present dispositions of personnel and administration units and installations which would affect the Sustainment/CSS situation.

    (2)    Show any projected developments within the personnel field likely to influence sustainment operations.

d.    Civil- Military situation. This paragraph details information from the civil-military officer The S-4 should include:

    (1)    Present disposition of CMO units and installations affecting logistics operations.

    (2)    Projected developments with the CMO field likely to influence sustainment operations.

e.    Sustainment Situation. This subparagraph should reflect the current status. In the case of detailed information at higher levels of command, a summary may appear under the subheadings with reference to an annex to the estimate. You may use an overlay to show all sustainment units and installations, current and proposed. Include current status, capability, and any enhanced or reduced capability caused by attached, detached, or supporting units.

    (1)    Maintenance. Provide a general statement about the present capability [such as repair time factors, posture of maintenance units, some references to Class VII and Class IX status if it affects maintenance capability, status of Class VII end items (such as repair parts, vans, wreckers) that may affect maintenance, etc.].

    (2)    Supply. Provide overall status of controlled items and POL allocations, including pertinent comments on resupply availability, etc. Provide information under subheadings of classes supply, list them in the most meaningful measure (days of supply, total line items, equipment shortages – Class VII) by unit.

(3)  Services. Provide present status, include both capabilities and problems.

(4)  Transportation. Provide present capabilities of mode-operating units to support transportation requirements. Detail adequacy of routes, facilities, and terminals to support distribution requirements. Discuss capability of movement control and in-transit visibility of movements and to assure sustained flow. Address time and distance factors which influence the capability to provide support at the right place and time. Consider factors such as facilities and terminals, airlift/drop, and in-transit visibility.

(5)  Labor. Provide present situation, status, restrictions on use of civilians, etc..

(6)  Facilities and construction. Provide availability of host nation facilities to serve as headquarters and support facilities. Provide status of construction to upgrade existing facilities and create facilities where needed.

(7)  Health service support. Provide present status of medical treatment and evacuation resources, projected location of patient-collecting points, and ambulance exchange points (AXP's), status of health service logistics (including blood, medical regulating, and any anticipated increase in casualty rates or EPW) work loads.

(8)  EPW operations. Provide facilities, construction, and sustainment functions.

(9)  Other.

f.  Assumptions. Until the commander provides specific planning guidance, you may need assumptions for initiating planning or for preparing the estimate. Modify assumptions as factual data becomes available.

NOTE: As you proceed with the estimate process, keep in mind the sustainment (CSS) concept is intended to support the mission

2. **ANALYSIS OF COURSES OF ACTION:** Analyze all sustainment factors for each subheading (paragraph 2e) for each course of action indicating problems and deficiencies. This paragraph, and any subparagraphs, should contain narrative analysis statements explaining mathematical and applied logic. (Mathematical calculations you perform to assess status of any class of supply, maintenance attrition rates, tonnage lift capacity, and so forth, are solely a means to obtain information for full analysis.) The result of your analysis for subheadings for each course of action should provide both sustainment and tactical impact.

   a. Sufficiency of Area. Determine if the area under control will be adequate for sustainment operations. Will it be cleared of enemy units? Will other units be sharing the same area (units passing through one another)? Will boundaries remain unchanged? Etc.

   b. Material and Services. Include all that apply:

      (1) Maintenance.
      (2) Supply.
      (3) Services.
      (4) Transportation.
      (5) Labor.
      (6) Facilities.
      (7) Contract services
      (8) Other

## 3. COMPARISON OF COURSES OF ACTION:

a.  Evaluate Sustainment deficiencies. List any advantages and disadvantages to accomplish the mission

b.  Discuss the advantages and disadvantages of each course of action you consider. Include methods of overcoming deficiencies or modifications each course of action required.

## 4. CONCLUSIONS:

a.  Indicate which course or courses of action is sustainable - sustainment can best support. If all are sustainable, focus on levels of efficiency and effectiveness.

b.  List the major Sustainment deficiencies and shortfalls the commander must consider. Include specific recommendations concerning the methods of eliminating or reducing the effect of these deficiencies. Note – not everyone needs to be supported equally. Use the derived Concept of Support to cross allocate or redistribute commodities/services. For example, if there is an identified shortfall of a specific type of artillery ammunition (such as D544 DPICM), then weight the main effort/decisive operations, minimizing to the safest extent possible the shaping/supporting efforts.

/s/_____

(S-4 Officer)

ANNEXES: (as required)

## 12.8 Support Operations Mission Analysis Checklist

An effective checklist tool for SPOs, but note it does not cover everything. Make sure requirements are integrated. (Example: Identify the amount of Class V to be moved and stored. The Trans section then determines assets needed to move it. S&S section then identifies the fuel needed based on the anticipated mileage. Maint. Section identifies anticipated class IX and repair activities based on vehicle usage. S-2 identifies availability of and/or any security requirements.

| 1. | GENERAL REQUIREMENTS – ALL STAFF | |
|---|---|---|
| **Tasked** | **Item** | Status |
| | Understand Commanders Mission (Next two higher echelons) | |
| | Understand Commanders Intent (Next two higher echelons) | |
| | Review Area of Operations | |
| | Understand Concept of Operations from Higher | |
| | Review Task Organization | |
| | Identify Specified Tasks | |
| | Identify Implied Tasks | |
| | Identify Essential Tasks | |
| | Review Available Assets | |
| | Identify Any Attachments/Detachments | |
| | Determine Any Limitations | |
| | Identify Any Risks | |
| | Determine Critical Facts | |
| | Determine Critical Assumptions (OPLAN Only) | |
| | Review/Determine Time Line (1/3 - 2/3 rule) | |
| | Determine Current Status | |
| | Determine Projected Status by D-Day/Execution | |

| | | |
|---|---|---|
| | Determine Critical Shortages (Effects/Impacts on Operations) | |
| | Predict Critical Shortages by Phases of Operations | |
| | Determine Resupply Rate and Method | |
| | Determine if Host Nation Support is Available | |
| | Determine Higher Supporting Units | |
| | Determine Resupply Unit Locations | |
| | Determine Any Supply Constraints | |
| | Determine Any Shortfalls/Warstoppers | |
| | Determine Any Contracting Support Required | |
| **2.** | **SERVICE SUPPORT - GENERAL (ALL)** | |
| **Tasked** | **Item** | **Status** |
| | Facts: Determine status of: CLASS I, II, III(P), IV, VI, VII, X, and maps | |
| | Determine any critical shortages | |
| | ASSUMPTIONS: Determine resupply rates | |
| | Determine availability of host nation support | |
| | CONCLUSION: Determine projected SUPPLY status on d-day | |
| | Review projected distribution system | |
| **3a.** | **SERVICE SUPPORT - FIELD SERVICES** | **Status** |
| | Facts: Determine status of field services (FS) field feeding, laundry & bath support, clothing repair, & water purification | |
| | Identify total number of soldiers to be supported | |
| | Identify critical equipment and supply shortages | |
| | Assumptions: Determine any host nation support available | |
| | Conclusions: Determine FS status on D-day and throughput operations | |
| | Other: Determine location of FS support units | |

| | | |
|---|---|---|
| | Identify supplies to support FS operations | |
| | Determine transportation / time requirements to move FS units | |
| **3b.** | **SERVICE SUPPORT - FUELING** | |
| **Tasked** | **Item** | **Status** |
| | Facts: Determine current status of bulk carriers/ storage assets | |
| | Determine current supply status in terms of DOS and O/H gallons | |
| | Review bulk fuel distribution system | |
| | Identify any critical shortages of fuel or fuel support equipment | |
| | Assumptions: Determine amount of fuel required to support daily operations | |
| | Determine resupply rates | |
| | Determine host nation support available | |
| | Conclusions: Determine projected status of Class III at D-day and during phases of operation | |
| | Other: Identify any enroute movement requirements | |
| | Identify any RO/ FARP missions | |
| | Determine location of fuel resupply units | |
| | Identify fuel testing (lab) support | |

| | | |
|---|---|---|
| Solving fuel shortfalls (1) set priorities; (2) increase tanker trips per day; (3) request assistance from higher | | |
| **3c.** | **SERVICE SUPPORT - ARMING** | |
| **Tasked** | **Item** | **Status** |
| | Facts: Determine current Class V status | |
| | Review current distribution system | |
| | Identify known restrictions | |
| | Identify Class V critical shortages | |

| | | |
|---|---|---|
| | Assumptions: Determine resupply rates | |
| | Determine any host nation support available | |
| | Conclusion: Determine projected supply status on D-Day | |
| | Other: Identify projected location of ammunition units/ supply points | |
| | Identify any lift problems | |
| | Identify emergency resupply procedures | |
| | Identify any required EOD support | |
| | Forecast requirements | |
| | Determine/ review CCL requirements | |

Solving ammunition shortfalls: (1) sub-allocate to subordinates; (2) establish restrictions to firing; (3) pre-draw/ cache critical items; (4) request an increase in CSR

| 4. | MAINTENANCE - FIXING | |
|---|---|---|
| **Tasked** | **Item** | **Status** |
| | Facts: Determine current equipment maintenance status (FMC, NMC) | |
| | Determine Class IX status/ critical status | |
| | Identify maintenance and evacuation priorities | |
| | Establish maintenance repair timelines | |
| | Determine controlled substitution/ cannibalization procedures | |
| | Assumptions: determine any host nation support available | |
| | Determine projected equipment losses | |
| | Conclusions: Determine projected maintenance status on D-Day | |
| | Other: Identify critical weapons systems status | |
| | Review MST employment plan | |
| | Review distribution system for Classes VII and IX | |
| | Determine location of higher level maintenance units | |

| Improving material readiness rates: (1) Prioritize by unit and by equipment; (2) Re-look time guidelines; (3) Delegate authority to controlled exchange and cannibalization | | |
|---|---|---|
| **5.** | **TRANSPORTATION - MOVING** | |
| **Tasked** | **Item** | **Status** |
| | Facts: Determine current readiness status of transportation assets | |
| | Determine status of critical LOCs/ MSRs | |
| | Determine any critical transportation shortages | |
| | Assumptions: Determine any host nation support available | |
| | Conclusions: Analyze projected transportation assets status on D-Day | |
| | Determine projected status on LOCs and MSRs on D-Day | |
| | Other: Determine transportation requirements | |
| | Determine movement and route use priorities | |
| | Analyze transportation network (ports, airfield, roads, waterways, railroads) | |
| | Determine locations of cargo transfer points | |
| | Determine transportation control requirements/ first destination, points, traffic control points, etc.) | |
| **6.** | **HEALTH SYSTEM SUPPORT (HSS)** | |
| **Tasked** | **Item** | **Status** |
| | Determine HSS mission statement | |
| | Determine Enemy Situation (strength and disposition, combat efficiency, capabilities, logistic situation, state of health, weapons) | |
| | Determine Friendly Situation (strength and disposition, combat efficiency, present and projected operations, logistic situation, rear area protection plan, weapons) | |
| | Determine Characteristics of the Area of Operations (terrain, weather and climate, dislocated civilian population and EPWs, flora and fauna, disease, local resources, NBC and DE weapons) | |

| | | |
|---|---|---|
| | Determine Strengths to be Supported ( U.S. Army, U.S. Navy, U.S. Marines, U.S. Air Force, U.S. Coast Guard; DoD Civilians; Allied forces; Coalition forces; EPWs; U.S. National Contract Personnel; Indigenous civilians and Third Country personnel; detainees; internees; others) | |
| | Determine Health of the Command (acclimation of troops, presence of disease, status of immunizations, status of nutrition, clothing and equipment, fatigue, morale, status of training, other) | |
| | Determine Special Factors (items of special importance in the particular operation to be supported such as unique conditions to be encountered in CBRNE/DE warfare or the impact of patients suffering from combat stress will have on the HSS system) | |
| | Determine patient estimates (indicate rates and numbers by type of unit)—number of patients anticipated, distribution within the AO, evacuation time, areas of patient density, possible MASCALs, lines of patient drift and evacuation) | |
| | Determine Support Requirements (patient evacuation and medical regulation, hospitalization, health service logistics—to include blood management, medical laboratory services, dental services, veterinary services, preventive medicine services, combat stress control services, area medical support, C4I (command, control, communications, computers, intelligence), others as appropriate) | |
| | Identify Resources Available (organic medical units and personnel, attached medical units and personnel, supporting medical units, civil public health capability and resources, EPW medical personnel, health service logistics, medical troop ceiling) | |
| | Determine courses of action (as a result of the above considerations and analysis, determine and list all logical COAs which will support the commander's plan and accomplish the HSS mission—consider all SOPs, policies, and procedures in effect)—courses of action are expressed in terms of what, when, where, how, and why. | |
| | Determine if the HSS mission can/ cannot be supported. | |

| | Determine which medical COA can best be supported from the HSS standpoint. | |
|---|---|---|
| | Identify the limitations and deficiencies in the preferred COA that must be brought to the commander's attention. | |
| | Identify factors adversely affecting the health of the command. | |

## 12.9 Asset Availability Worksheet

### Asset Availability Worksheet

1. Identify system capabilities not individual. Match up personnel with a complete system (i.e. Driver, Assistant Driver, Prime mover and mission trailer).

2. Identify capabilities in consistent and appropriate terms and state them (i.e. 30% local haul of four 60 km round trips, 60% long haul of two 180 km round trips, 10% maintenance or single lift capability of XXX). Identify manning, maintenance, trafficability, etc. as issues.

| UNIT | SYSTEM | CAPABILITIES | ISSUES (STATUS, LOCATION, etc) |
|---|---|---|---|
| | | | |
| | | | |
| | | | |
| | | | |
| | | | |
| | | | |
| | | | |
| | | | |
| | | | |
| | | | |
| | | | |
| | | | |
| | | | |
| | | | |
| | | | |
| | | | |
| | | | |
| | | | |
| | | | |
| | | | |
| | | | |
| | | | |

*CHAPTER 13*

# COMMANDER'S GUIDANCE GUIDELINES

This is a generic list of information commander's consider as they develop their guidance. The commander does not have to address every item. It should be tailored to meet specific needs and the commander will issue guidance on only those items appropriate to a particular mission.

**Intelligence:**
1. Enemy COAs to consider during the COA development and COA analysis phase of the planning process. This may be the enemy's most probable COA, most dangerous COA, or a combination of the two.
2. Enemy's critical decision points and vulnerabilities.
3. PIR (CCIR)
4. Targeting guidance
5. High-Value targets
6. Defining of the enemy commander's mission
7. Defining of the enemy commander's methods
8. Desired enemy perception of friendly forces
9. Intelligence focus for reconnaissance and security effort
10. Reconnaissance and surveillance guidance
11. Specific terrain and weather factors to consider
12. Use of organic assets: gun trucks, electronic warfare devices/systems, attached aviation.

## Maneuver:

1. Initial intent
   - Purpose of operation
   - Method (phases/sequences)
   - Desired end state
2. Concept of operations:
   - Decisive point
   - Battlefield organization (close, deep, rear)
   - Task/purpose
   - Resources to be used for each
3. COA development guidance
   - Critical events
   - Number of COAs to be developed
   - COAs to consider or not consider and formations to consider
   - Shaping the battlefield
   - Defeat mechanism
   - Main and supporting effort
     * Task organization
     * Where/what risk to accept
     * Task/purpose of subordinate units
   - Reserve guidance (composition, mission, priorities, command and control measures)
   - Reconnaissance or counter reconnaissance guidance
   - Composition
   - Command and control measures
   - FFIR

4. Reconnaissance and surveillance guidance and priorities
5. OPSEC considerations

## Maneuver Support and Survivability:

1. Priority of effort and support
2. Mobility:
   - Breaching/bridging guidance
   - Employing assets guidance

3.  Countermobility:
    -   Obstacle effects/emplacement guidance
    -   FASCAM use and duration
4.  Survivability: Assets available to dig survivability positions
5.  CBRNE defense operations:
    -   Chemical reconnaissance assets
    -   MOPP posture
    -   Decontamination guidance
    -   Masking and unmasking guidance
    -   Employment of smoke
    -   Detection, reporting, marking
6.  Management of engineer supplies and materiel
7.  Environmental guidance

**Air Defense:**
1.  Protection priorities
2.  Positioning guidance
3.  Weapons control status for specific events

**Inform and Influence Activities (IIA):**
1.  Military deception guidance:
    -   Amount and types of resources to commit to the deception plan
    -   Intent for exploiting the enemy actions
    -   EEFI (CCIR)
2.  OPSEC considerations:
    -   Identification of actions that can be observed by the enemy
    -   Determination of indicators from which enemy intelligence systems can gain critical information
    -   Selection of measures to reduce vulnerabilities
3.  Electronic warfare (EW) considerations:
    -   Measures for electronic protect (EP)
    -   Support needed for electronic warfare support (ES)
    -   Methods of electronic attack (EA)

4. Physical destruction considerations:
   - Planned indirect fire support targets to support C2W plan
   - Maneuver actions to suppress, neutralize, and destroy enemy
   - Air defense measures to nullify enemy aircraft
5. PSYOPS considerations:
   - Priority of effort for attached PSYOPS forces
   - Allocation of organic and/or supporting resources to support PSYOPS efforts (field artillery, close air support, unmanned aerial vehicles, security elements)
6. Public affairs (PA) considerations:
   - Effective publications that are dependent on credibility
   - Early deployment of public affairs personnel
   - Information security practiced at the source
7. Themes and Messages
   - Specific Themes that support the operation
   - Medium(s) to employ to convey messages

## Sustainment:
1. Commander's guidance for sustainment:
   - Sustainment priorities in terms of manning, fueling, fixing, arming, moving, and sustaining
2. Location of sustainment assets
3. MEDEVAC treatment and evacuation guidance
4. Classes of supply:
   - Anticipated requirements and pre-stockage of Class III, IV, and V
5. Controlled supply rates
6. Guidance on construction and provision of facilities and installations

## Command and Control:
1. Rules of engagement
2. CP position guidance

3. Position of commander
4. Integration of retransmission assets or other communications equipment
5. LNO guidance
6. Force protection measures
7. Time-line guidance
8. Type of order and rehearsal
9. Specific signal guidance

**Design**
1. Decision on employment of 'Design'
2. Size/composition of Design Team

# MISSION ANALYSIS BRIEFING FORMAT

### ★★★

## MISSION ANALYSIS BRIEFING

| **SUBJECT** | *BRIEFER* |
|---|---|
| 1.  Opening comments | CDR |
| 2.  Introduction (participants, purpose and desired conclusion) | XO |
| 3.  Roll Call, time plan for MA Brief (enforced by XO) | XO |
| 4.  Map overview of Brigade/Division AO, Friendly situation | S-3 |
| 5.  Mission and commander's intent (two levels up) | S-3 |
| 6.  Mission, commander's intent, concept of the operation, and deception plan or objectives (one level up) | S-3 |
| 7.  Review of commander's initial guidance | S-3 |
| 8.  Enemy situation with impact on logistics (deep, close, rear) Initial IPB products<br>  a.   Area of Operation/Interest | S-2, Intel NCO |

      b.   Avenues of approach
      c.   Weather/Terrain Analysis (affects of
           weather and key/decisive terrain)
      d.   Enemy intent and objectives
      e.   Enemy order of battle
      f.   Enemy capabilities
      g.   Enemy vulnerabilities
      h.   Enemy COAs: (graphically represented
           on two separate handouts)
           (1)   Most likely
           (2)   Most dangerous
      i.   Friendly intelligence capabilities
          (other than organic)

| | | |
|---|---|---|
| 9. | Specified, implied and essential tasks | S-3 |
| 10. | Constraints and restraints on the operation | S-3 |
| 11. | Forces available (2 levels down/by type unit; include Avn sorties) | S-3 |
| 12. | Overview of CSS battlefield (LOC's, MSR's, airfields, rail, ports, other CSS infrastructure) | SPO |
| 13. | Task Org for support (incl. Sustainment attachments/augmentation) | S-3/SPO |
| 14. | Overview of supported unit support concept (para. 4 OPORD) | SPO |
| 15. | Transportation requirements, capabilities and shortfalls with proposed recommendations | S4 |
| *16.* | *HSS requirements, capabilities and shortfalls with proposed recommendations (BSB)* | *C-Med Cdr* |

| | | |
|---|---|---|
| *17.* | *HSS augmentation and evac platforms (BSB)* | *C-Med Cdr* |
| 18. | Results of requirements, capabilities and shortfalls analysis | SPO |
| 19. | DS sustainment stocks required (min 3 DOS at CSSB/Sus Bde) | SPO |
| 20. | CL III distribution plan | SPO |
| 21. | CL V storage, transfer and distribution plan | SPO |
| 22. | Results of material damage and combat power prior to LD estimates | SPO |
| 23. | Support concept prior to higher HQ staff analysis | SPO |
| 24. | Critical personnel and equipment shortfalls with impact on mission | S-1, S-4 |
| 25. | Hazards and Initial Risk Assessment | S-3 |
| 26. | Recommended initial CCIR | S-3 |
| 27. | Recommended time lines (planning, preparation, execution) | XO |
| 28. | Recommended mission statement | XO |
| 29. | Approves support concept and mission statement | CDR |
| 30. | Commander's intent | CDR |
| 31. | Commander's planning guidance | CDR |

# COURSE OF ACTION BRIEFING FORMAT

★★★

**COURSE OF ACTION BRIEFING**

| **SUBJECT** | *BRIEFER* |
|---|---|
| 1. Introduction (Purpose and desired conclusion) | XO |
| 2. Update Status (RFIs and CCIR) | XO |
| 3. Intelligence<br>   a. Updated IPB (weather and terrain)<br>   b. Possible enemy COAs (Event Template) | S-2, Intel NCO |
| 4. Mission Statement | S-3 |
| 5. Update of personnel and equipment (chart or projection) | S-1/S-4 |
| 4. Proposed COAs, in order (prepare handouts)<br>   a. Array of forces, logistics & medical support (sketch)<br>   b. Scheme of support statement (before, during, and after operations)<br>   c. Course of Action rational for each COA<br>     (1) Considerations affected by possible enemy COA(s), logistics assets Available, missions assigned, or timeline imposed. | SPO/S-3<br><br>SPO/S-3<br>SPO/S-3 |

      (2)   Why units are arrayed as shown on sketches

      (3)   Priorities of support, phasing, C2, and availability of assets

      (4)   Why selected control measures used

  d.   Discuss risk and end state of each COA      SPO/S-3

5.   Commander's guidance for war gaming      CDR

6.   Time and Location for War gaming      XO

*CHAPTER 16*

# DECISION BRIEFING FORMAT

★★★

**DECISION BRIEFING**

| **SUBJECT** | *BRIEFER* |
|---|---|
| 1. Introduction (purpose and desired conclusion) | XO |
| 2. Mission Statement/Intent of HHQs | S-3 |
| 3. Status of Friendly Forces | S-3 |
|     a. TASKO changes | |
|     b. Relative combat power ratios (friendly/enemy) | |
|     c. Unit locations (own and adjacent) | |
| 4. Updated terrain analysis | S-2/Intel NCO |
| 5. Facts updated (changes/additions only) | S-3/OPS NCO |
| 6. Enemy COAs (most likely/most dangerous) (flip slides) | S-2/Intel NCO |
| 7. Friendly COAs, in sequence (against "Most Likely" COA) ("Most Dangerous" COAs become branch CONPLANs) | S-3 |
| 8. Overall COA comparison with weighted comparisons | S-3 |

9.  COA comparisons (War fighting
    Functional Area specific criteria)
    a.  Movement & Maneuver                          S-3
    b.  Command and Control                          S-3
    c.  Fires                                        S-3
    d.  Protection (ADA, Survivability, CBRNE)       S-3
    e.  Intelligence                                 S-2/Intel NCO
    g.  Sustainment                                  SPO/S-4/S-1
        (1)  Logistics                               SPO/S-4
        (2)  Personnel                               S1
        (3)  CMO                                     S1

10. Recommended COA                                  S-3/XO

11. Decision                                         CDR

12. Intent Statement (for re-approval/modification)  CDR

13. Time and Location for Orders Briefing: _____XO

*CHAPTER 17*

# ORDERS BRIEFING FORMAT

## ★★★

## ORDERS BRIEFING

| SUBJECT | BRIEFER |
|---|---|
| **1. INTRODUCTION** | XO |

- Classification
- Purpose of briefing
- What do we need at the conclusion of the briefing

| | |
|---|---|
| **2. PRELIMINARY DATA** | S-3 |

- Classification of OPLAN/OPORD
- Header Data
- OPLAN/OPORD Number
- References
- Time Zone

| | |
|---|---|
| **3. TASKO** | S-3 |

- Area of Operations/Area of Interest Overview (permanently posted)
- *Brigade Overview (permanently posted) (BSB only)*
- *Corps/Division Overview (permanently posted) (Sus Bde/CSSB only)*
- Sustainment Bde detailed TASKO (permanently posted) (Sus Bde/CSSB)

4. **SITUATION**                                    S-3
   - Terrain & Weather Data
   - Enemy Forces (TASKO) (permanently posted)
   - Friendly Forces
   - Attachments/Detachments
   - Assumptions (OPLAN Only)

5. **MISSION**                                       S-3
   - CORPS/TSC/ESC Mission (permanently posted)
   - DIVISION Mission (if applicable – Sus Bde) (permanently posted)
   - BRIGADE Mission (permanently posted) (BSB only)
   - SUSTAINMENT BRIGADE (permanently posted for CSSB)

6. **EXECUTION**                                     S-3
   - HHQ's Intent (permanently posted)
   - SUSTAINMENT BDE CDR'S Intent
     (permanently posted) (CSSB)
   - DIVISION Concept of Operations (BSB)
   - BDE CDR's Intent and Concept of Operations
   - Movement of Sustainment units (all Phases)    SPO
   - FLE's, CRSP, TTPs, CSCs other special Log events

   - General Concept of Support (all Phases)        SPO
     Material and Services (by Phase)
     Priority of Support
     Priority of Movement (fwd & rear)
     Special events in any Phase
   - Concept of Support for each commodity          S P O
     (all Phases)
     Method of supply for each class
     Stockage for each class
     Operations of next higher supplying Div
     Control of command regulated items
     Critical / special activities
     Schedules

- Transportation              S-4/MCT (if avail)
  MSR's - primary, alternate, dirty (or SPO Trans if avail)
  Traffic circulation / control plan
  Priorities of support / movement
  Schedules / Taskings

- Maintenance (Air and Ground for       S-4
  each subparagraph)
     Approving authority for controlled (or SPO Maint if avail)
      exchange/cannibalization
  Control of command regulated CL IX
  Priority of maintenance
  Location of facilities and collection points
  Repair time limits at each maint level
  Evac procedures

- Medical Concept of Support     S-1, Bde Surgeon
  Collection, evacuation, treatment (C-Med Cdr if BCT)
  of US, Allied, EPW, Civilian
  sick, injured, wounded - facilities, evac routes
  CHS logistics (incl blood) - stockage
  objectives, next higher spt
  Combat stress control, preventive med,
  dental, optical, veterinary

- BSB/LSA/FOB defense plan           S-3
- CCIR (PIR, EEFI, FFIR)             S-3
- Tasks to organic units              S-3
- Tasks to attached units
- Tasks to other supporting units

7. **SERVICE SUPPORT** (Internal support unit logistics)
   - Internal Concept of Support         S-4
   - Personnel, Religious, Legal         S-1

8. **COMMAND AND SIGNAL**         S-6/S-3

# PLANS UPDATE TO CDR FORMAT (OR COMMANDER'S UPDATE BRIEF — CUB)

★★★

**PURPOSE**: Update CDR on Plans/Contingencies for next 24 hours.

| SUBJECT | BRIEFER |
|---|---|
| - General Support Changes Next 24 Hrs | S-3/SPO |
| - Decision Points that could require Command Group decision next 24 Hrs | XO/S-3 |
| - Synchronization Matrix for next 24 Hrs | XO/S-3/SPO |
| - Contingency Plans in development Status Nature of Plan | S-3 |

# ORDERS BREAKDOWN FOR STAFF ANALYSIS

General. When the unit receives an OPORD from higher head-quarters, the order is broken down and distributed per the below chart. It is not always possible or realistic to copy, dissemi-nate, and read the entire OPORD from a higher headquarters. However, there are portions of the plan that must be read by various staff sections and key information must be disseminated to all staff and unit commanders. A complete copy of the Base OPORD will be given to BC, XO, CSM, 1 ea (S-1, S-4, HHC), 2 ea (S-2/3, SPO). A complete copy of all annexes will be made for the BC and XO. All other annexes are copied and distributed in the numbers listed below.

| ANNEX | *TITLE* | *COPIES (Total)* | BC (Master Copy) | XO | SPO | S-1 | S-2 &3 | S-4 | CSM |
|-------|---------|------------------|------------------|-----|-----|-----|--------|-----|-----|
| A. | Task Organization | 7 | X | X | X | X | X (P) | X | X |
| B. | Intelligence | 3 | X | X | | | X (P) | | |
| C. | Operations Overlay | 5 | X | X | X | | X (P) | X | |
| D. | Fires | 3 | X | X | | | X (P) | | |
| E. | Protection | 4 | X | X | | | X (P) | | X |
| F. | Sustainment | 7 | X | X | X | X (P) | X | X (P) | X |
| G. | Engineer | 3 | X | X | | | X (P) | | |

| | | | | | | | | | |
|---|---|---|---|---|---|---|---|---|---|
| H. | Signal | 3 | X | X | | | X (P) | | |
| I. | Not Used | | | | | | | | |
| J. | Public Affairs | 3 | X | X | | X (P) | | | |
| K | Civil Affairs Operations | 6 | X | X | X | X (P) | X | X | |
| L. | Recon & Surveillance | 3 | X | X | | | X (P) | | |
| M. | Assessment | 3 | X | X | | | X (P) | | |
| N. | Space Operations | 3 | X | X | | | X (P) | | |
| O. | Not Used | | | | | | | | |
| P. | Host Nation Support | 3 | X | X | X (P) | | X | | |
| Q. | Spare | | | | | | | | |
| R | Reports | 7 | X | X | X | X | X (P) | X | X |
| S. | Special Technical Operations | 3 | X | X | | | X (P) | | |
| T. | Spare | | | | | | | | |
| U. | Inspector General | 4 | X | X | X (P) | | | | X |
| V. | Interagency Coordination | 3 | X | X | X (P) | | | | |
| W, X, Y. | Spare | | | | | | | | |
| Z. | Distribution | | X | X | | X (P) | X | | |

(P) Primary responsibility

NOTE: This chart illustrates the orders breakdown in an unconstrained environment. In a constrained environment, risk is assumed by reading only those products that time permits. All staff sections must read all of the base order.

# CHAPTER 20

# SET UP OF THE PLANS VAN/ROOM

## ★★★

**The following maps are posted:**
- 1:250,000 with Corps operations overlay.
- 1:50,000 Brigade Planning map with current operational and support graphics
- 1:100,000 S-3 Planning map with current operational and support graphics.
- 1:100,000 S-3 Planning map with enemy FS range fans, Mobility Corridors and Avenues of Approach down to Battalion level.

**The following charts will be posted:**
- Mission and Intent Statements for appropriate BCT, Division & Sustainment Bde
- Enemy intermediate and subsequent objectives
- OPLAN/OPORD Status Chart.
- CONTINGENCY PLAN Status Chart.
- HVT List (developed by Bde S-2 using Mission Analysis)
- HPT List
- Battlefield Framework worksheet.
- Synchronization Matrix. (developed during War Gaming)
- DST
- Task Organization.
- Time Analysis Chart.
- Posted FRAGOs/INTSUMs/WOs/etc.
- Commander's Planning Guidance.

- Status board for assets requested from higher
- Relative Combat Power chart.
- Current Target Synchronization Matrix (BCT)
- Planning assumptions.
- Graphical Control Measures for division-level planning.
- WFFA Chart

**Tools to be available in Van**:
- Butcher Pad and Easel (with extra pads).
- Graphics Templates.
- 2 DVNTs (one attached to fax machine).
- Personal Computer and Laser Printer (PC Programs: MS Word, MS Excel, MS PowerPoint, Form Tool).
- Screen for viewing overheads.
- Alcohol and Non-Permanent markers (Broad, Medium, & Fine) in all colors.
- Tube-type markers of various colors (for butcher pad)
- Current operational graphics cartoons (paper and transparency versions)
- MCOO, DST.
- Screening criteria (offensive and defensive) for Decision Briefing.

# OPERATIONAL ENVIRONMENT FRAMEWORK

**AREA OF INFLUENCE.** A geographical area wherein a commander is directly capable of influencing operations by maneuver or fire support systems normally under the commander's command or control. (JP 3-16)

**AREA OF INTEREST (AOI).** Area of concern to the commander, including the area of influence, areas adjacent thereto, and extending into enemy territory to the objectives of current or planned operations. This area also includes areas occupied by enemy forces that could jeopardize the accomplishment of the mission.

AOI is based on the ability of the threat to project power or move forces into the AO. Also consider the geographical locations of other activities or characteristics of the environment that might influence COAs or command decisions. Consider also any anticipated future missions or "be prepared" and "on order" missions identified during mission analysis, and determine their effect on the limits of the AI. An additional consideration would be to divide the AI into several components, such as a ground AI, an air AI, or a political AI. Such a division accommodates the types of information relevant in each AI as well as their usually different geographical limits. (See FMs 3-0 (Para 6-72), JP 2-03, JP 3-16)

**AREA OF OPERATIONS (AO)** A geographical area, including the airspace above, usually defined by lateral, forward, and rear boundaries assigned to a commander, by a joint force higher commander, in which he has responsibility and the authority to conduct military operations. A thorough knowledge of the characteristics of this area leads to its effective use. Generally, because this is the area where the command will conduct its operations, the evaluation of the battlefield's effects is more thorough and detailed within the AO than within the Area of Interest (AOI). An area of operations should not be substantially larger than the unit's area of influence. The limits of the AO are normally the boundaries specified in the OPORD or contingency plan (CONPLAN) from higher headquarters that define the command's mission. (See FM 3-0 (C1) Para 6-68)

**AREA OF RESPONSIBILITY (AOR).** The geographic area associated with a combatant command within which a combatant commander has authority to plan and conduct operations. (See FMs 3-0, FM 5-0, and JP 0-2

*CHAPTER 22*

# WARFIGHTING FUNCTIONAL AREA (WFFA)

## ★★★

### WARFIGHTING FINCTIOAL AREAS

1. **INTELLIGENCE**
2. **MOVEMENT & MANEUVER**
3. **FIRES**
4. **PROTECTION**
5. **SUSTAINMENT**
6. **MISSION COMMAND**

### TACTICAL SUSTAINMENT FUNCTIONS
See Support Concept Matrix

1. SUPPLY - CL I, CL II, CL III (B/P)CL IV, CL V, CL VI, CL VIII support

2. HUMAN RESOURCES – All Personnel management, CAO, OPMS/EPMS

3. MAINTENANCE - all maintenance management, CL VII, CL IX,

4. TRANSPORTATION - all ground, air, water transportation management, traffic control, routes, security

5.  FIELD SERVICES – Shower, Clothing Repair, Laundry, Mortuary Affairs

6.  HEALTH SYSTEMS SUPPORT - all Medical and CL VIII

7.  EOD – Explosive Ordnance Disposal

8.  FINANCIAL MANAGEMENT SERVICES – pay issues and financial dispersement operations

9.  RELIGIOUS & LEGAL SUPPORT.

# COMMANDER'S CRITICAL INFORMATION REQUIREMENTS (CCIR) GUIDANCE

★★★

**1. General.** Commanders determine their CCIRs and consider the nominations of the staff. CCIRs are situation dependent and specified by the commander for each operation. Commanders continuously review the CCIRs during the planning process and adjust them as situations change. The initial CCIRs developed during mission analysis normally focus on decisions the commander needs to make to focus planning. Once the commander selects a COA, the CCIRs shift to information the commander needs in order to make decisions during preparation and execution. Commanders designate CCIRs to inform the staff and subordinates what they deem essential for making decisions. The fewer the CCIRs, the better the staff can focus its efforts and allocate sufficient resources for collecting them.

CCIRs are published within Para 3.j (2), Coordinating Instructions, of the Operations Plan (OPLAN) or Operations Order (OPORD). The S-3 is responsible for staff input and formulation of recommended CCIR for sustainment unit Cdr approval. From the time of receipt of a mission, there is always a lack of information available to planners. A system of developing information needs and requesting this information and monitoring responses from higher or lateral headquarters, must be in place immediately – supervised by the S-3 or SPO sections.

a. XO manages CCIR as directed by CDR and provides them to all staff sections.

b. Each staff section nominates CCIR's to the XO for inclusion in the final list.

c. Total number of PIR's should be **limited to ten or less and should be tied to any decisions identified within the organization's Decision Support Template/Matrix that the Commander will need to make**.

d. CCIR's should be limited to the information needed by the CDR to visualize the battlefield and thereby make critical decisions, especially those that either determine or validate a specific COA. Only that which is important to mission accomplishment should be in the CCIR's.

e. CCIR's are time sensitive. They are based on a specific time and space to drive identified decisions at designated decision points.

f. CCIR's generate RFI's to the support brigade/BCT or higher intelligence gathering systems and create the tasks for the Unit's R&S plan. These sources, together with internal status reports, answer the CCIR's.

g. CCIR's are composed of PIR's, and FFIR's as detailed in the CCRI Template. In addition to nominating CCIRs to the commander, the staff also identifies and nominates essential elements of friendly information (EEFIs). Although EEFIs are not CCIRs, they have the same priority as CCIRs and require approval by the commander. An EEFI establishes an element of information to protect rather than one to collect. EEFIs identify those elements of friendly force information that, if compromised, would jeopardize mission success. Like CCIRs, EEFIs change as an operation progresses.

## 2. CCIR

Helps the commander:
- Manage information to ensure they get a complete picture of the battlefield
- Create, confirm, or modify a COA
- Verify and update their assessment of current operations and their estimate of future operations and requirements
- Readily recognize when execution or adjustment of support operations may be necessary
- Assess the unit's ability to accomplish its mission in accordance with the higher commander's intent

### 3. PRIORITY INFORMATION REQUIREMENTS (PIR)

(How I see the enemy and current/future support operations). PIR is what the commander wants or needs to know about the enemy, changes to the AO, Task Organization, support requirements, or future support operations. For a Sustainment unit, these include (as a minimum) the following:

- Changes to missions
- Changes to task organization
- Changes in readiness (personnel, equipment, and systems)
- Enemy actions in AO

### 4. FRIENDLY FORCES INFORMATION REQUIREMENTS (FFIR)

(How the enemy sees me). FFIR allows the commander to determine the combat capabilities of their unit. These are not routine reports, but items that are critical enough that they are reported immediately over the command channel when their status changes. For a Sustainment unit, these include (as a minimum) the following:

- Status of forces in base and/or base cluster
- Status of units in AO

## 5. *ESSENTIAL ELEMENTS OF FRIENDLY INFORMATION (EEFI)

(What do I not want the enemy to know about me). EEFI allows the commander to determine how the enemy sees the friendly unit. For a BSB/CSSB, these include (as a minimum) the following:

- Location of assigned units
- Traffic patterns
- Location of BSAs, LSA, Sus Bdes, CRSPs, CSCs, TCPs, etc.
- Location of base or base cluster units

* Per ATTP 5-0.1, EEFI is no long a part of the Commander's CCIR

### CCIR TEMPLATE

1. **How I See the Enemy (Priority Intelligence Requirements (PIR))**
   - Most probable enemy COA
   - Artillery/Rockets/Mortars (capabilities, location, range fans)
   - Air Insertion
   - Objectives
   - Use of Terrain
   - Formations in depth

**EXAMPLE**
   - Location of SPF units/teams operating in the area
   - Reporting any units in CBRNE posture.
   - Convoy ambushes
   - First enemy contact
   - Blocked or cut MSR

2.  **How the Enemy Sees Me (Essential Elements of Friendly Information (EEFI))**
    -   My most probable Spt Ops Concept COA
    -   Location of sustainment facilities, stockage & fuel locations and activities.
    -   MSR's
    -   Supply stockages

    **EXAMPLES**
    -   Location of March Unit Commanders during convoy movements
    -   Location of BSB or LSA ATHPs
    -   Location of the BCT/BSB TOC
    -   Location of the BCT alternate TOC
    -   Location of the BSB BMSC

3.  **How I See Myself (Friendly Force Information Requirements (FFIR))**
    -   Time distance factors in Area of Operations
    -   Supported unit sustainment statuses
    -   Supported unit tactical situation
    -   MSR status
    -   Supporting unit statuses

    **EXAMPLES**
    -   Any traffic accidents reducing long convoy route mobility
    -   Any non BCT elements operating in the BCT's area
    -   Loss of 5K tankers
    -   Loss of PLS systems
    -   Loss of wheeled or tracked ambulances
    -   PERSAT below 75% for the BSB/CSSB
    -   Captured FBCB2-BFT device

# GENERAL PLANNING CONSIDERATIONS

★★★

1. Avoid predictability.
2. Use appropriate doctrinal terms.
3. Integrate reconnaissance into the battlefield framework.
4. BRT/CAV must be augmented if given a covering force mission.
5. Effective counter-reconnaissance is necessary forward of a main defensive area (MBA).
6. Make timely decisions to transition between phases. The target time (decision to contact) for transition from attack to defense is 24 hours, with 12 hours being the minimum to coordinate and emplace BCT obstacle plan. The correct identification of triggers for such a transition is essential.
7. Preparatory to transition to defense select the ground necessary for both the covering force and MBA and continue to attack, if necessary, to secure it.
8. Be clear about the nature of an area defense (focused on terrain) or a mobile defense (focused on the enemy).
9. The maneuver force(s) reserve, if committed, becomes the main effort.
10. Reserves should not be used piecemeal.
11. Reserve deployment options should be illustrated on a DST.
12. There is no requirement for an uncommitted TCF; it may be used for rear area counter-reconnaissance or other supplementary tasks.

13. Orders given in an OPORD/OPLAN base document should not be repeated in an annex.
14. The DST and Synchronization Matrix are decision aids for the Commander rather than components of the OPORD/OPLAN.
15. Maintain continuity of purpose throughout the OPORD/OPLAN.
16. Do not become overly focused on current and/or close operations to the detriment of future and/or deep operations.
17. Read subordinates' OPORDs/OPLANs.
18. Endeavor to destroy the enemy's will to win by the maintenance of tempo, effective reconnaissance, and attack by fire.
19. If a security zone is utilized, it should be 15-20 km deep and incorporate significant obstacles covered by fire.
20. A counter attacking enemy force should be attrited and fixed or delayed by obstacles and observed fire.
21. Artillery assets, particularly MLRS, need to be protected from local attack.

*CHAPTER 25*

# NOTES FOR PREPARATION OF OPLANS/OPORDS

1.  Staff sections with responsibility for annexes, appendices, tabs, and enclosures published separately from the plan/order are responsible for preparation, coordination, and staffing. Distribution remains the responsibility of the S-1. **RECOMMEND USING STANDARD FONT TIMES NEW ROMAN, 12 PITCH**.

2.  Margins and spacing. Left, right, top, and bottom margins are 1 inch. Within the document, left justification will be used and the page numbers will be centered at the bottom of the page.

3.  Heading. The heading shown below is the standard for all brigade/division Plans/Orders. The heading will be typed at the top right of the first page of the basic plan/order, conforming to the margin requirements indicated above.

    Example:       Copy Number ___ of ___ Copies
    Headquarters, 123 BSB, 1ˢᵗ BCT *(or Headquarters, 52nd Sus Bde))*
    Smallville, OH 12345-6789
    (DTG)
    (MRN)

4.  Unless otherwise indicted, all pages will be indicated as (UNCLASSIFIED) at the top of each page and under the page number.

5.   References. The basic plan/order and each annex will list only those references applicable to that element. References listed in the basic plan/order need not be repeated in subsequent annexes, appendices, tabs, or enclosures.

6.   Paragraphing.

   a.   When there is only one paragraph to any one element, that paragraph is un-numbered. When a paragraph is subdivided, it must have at least two sub-divisions. The tabs are 0.25 inches and the space is doubled between paragraphs. Subsequent lines of text for each paragraph may be flush left or equally indented at the option of the chief of staff or executive officer, as long as consistency is maintained throughout the order.

   b.   When paragraphs are sub-divided, they will be numbered and lettered as follows:

   1., a., (1), (a), 1., a.

   c.   Each progressive sub-division of a paragraph will be formatted as follows: (double space)

   1. Upper and Lower Case - BOLD.

      a. Upper and Lower Case and Underlined.

         (1) Upper and Lower Case.

            (a) Upper and Lower Case.

               1. Upper and Lower Case.

                  a. Upper and Lower Case.

                  b. Las subdivision is 0.25" indented from its parent.

7. Page numbering:

    a. Pages preceding the basic plan/order are numbered using lower case Roman Numeral (i.e., i, ii).

    b. Pages of the basic plan/order are numbered with Arabic Numbers (i.e., 1, 2, 3).

    c. Pages of annexes, appendices, tabs, and enclosures are numbered as follows:

        (1) Annex A, page 1 is number A-1.

        (2) Annex A, Appendix 1, page 2 is numbered A-1-2.

        (3) Annex A, Appendix 1, Tab A, page 2 is numbered A-1-A-2.

        (4) Annex A, Appendix 1, Tab A, Exhibit 1, page 2 is numbered A-1-A-1-2.

8. Capitalization and Punctuation.

    a. Names of geographic locations are capitalized (BALTIMORE).

    b. Paragraph titles are capitalized and underlined (SOLID CAPITALS).

    c. Full capitalization should be used on proper names (Task Force BRAVO, OBJECTIVE NAIL, AXIS RED, etc.).

    d. All title designations are in upper and lower case with the initial capitals (Task Force).

    e. Whenever reference is made to a specific annex within the plan/order, use the following format:

(1)   Capital letters will be used when identifying the title of annex referred to, i.e., IAW annex C (OPERATIONS).

(2)   When referring to appendices, tabs, or enclosures, the title will be in upper and lower case, i.e., Appendix 12 (Fire Support) to Annex C (OPERATIONS).

(3)   Do not use the word "See" when referring to an annex, appendix, enclosure, or tab.

9.   Abbreviations.

a.   Use abbreviations as authorized in AR 310-50. Be consistent. Do not use acronyms and abbreviations not found in FM 1-02 or JP 1-02.

b.   Spell out the entire acronym or abbreviation and place the acronym or abbreviation between parentheses at first use in the document. After this first use, use the acronym or abbreviation throughout the document.

10.   The final draft must be proof-read for punctuation, grammar, and spelling.

11.   Ensure your staff principal concurs with your input to preclude controversies and delays during staffing of the final plan/order.

12.   Ensure what is written is in consonance with the higher headquarters plan/order.

## Blast from the Past

# "An order that can be misunderstood will be misunderstood."

**Field Marshal Helmuth Von Moltke, Chief of the Prussian General Staff Battle of Sedan, Sep 1870**

# MOVEMENT RATES

### ✩✩✩

| UNOPPOSED RATE OF MOVEMENT | DAY | NIGHT |
|---|---|---|
| NON-RESTRICTIVE TERRAIN | 24 kmph | 24 kmph (w/lights) |
| RESTRICTIVE | 16 kmph | 8 kmph (black out) |
| SEVERELY RESTRICTIVE | 1 kmph | 1/2 kmph |

| AGAINST PREPARED DEFENSE (24+ hrs) OPPOSED RATE OF MOVEMENT* | Non-Restrictive | Restrictive | Severely Restrictive |
|---|---|---|---|
| Intense resistance (1:1) | .6 | .5 | .15 |
| Very Hvy (2:1) | .9 | .6 | .3 |
| Heavy (3:1) | 1.2 | .75 | .5 |
| Medium (4:1) | 1.4 | 1 | .5 |
| Light (5:1) | 1.5 | 1.1 | .6 |

| Negligible (6+:1) | 1.7+ | 1.3+ | .6+ |

*Bdes and below in kmph against **prepared defense**. Rates reduced by 1/2 at night. If there is surprise, multiply by (5) for complete surprise, (3) for substantial surprise, or (1.3) for minor surprise. Effects of surprise last 3 days (reduce effect by 1/3 on day 2 and by 2/3 on day 3)

## AGAINST HASTY DEFENSE (2-12 hrs)

| OPPOSED RATE OF MOVEMENT* | Non-Restrictive | Restrictive | Severely Restrictive |
|---|---|---|---|
| Intense resistance (1:1) | 1 | .8 | .4 |
| Very Hvy (2:1) | 1.5 | 1 | .6 |
| Heavy (3:1) | 2 | 1.3 | .8 |
| Medium (4:1) | 2.4 | 1.75 | .9 |
| Light (5:1) | 2.6 | 2 | 1 |
| Negligible (6+:1) | 3.0+ | 2.3+ | 1.1+ |

*Bdes and below in kmph against **prepared defense**. Rates reduced by 1/2 at night. If there is surprise, multiply by (5) for complete surprise, (3) for substantial surprise, or (1.3) for minor surprise. Effects of surprise last 3 days (reduce effect by 1/3 on day 2 and by 2/3 on day 3)

# TASK ORGANIZATIONS

★★★

## DIVISION LEVEL

Task Forces (Bde Size)
Named TFs (alphabetic order)
Named TFs (alphanumeric order)
Brigade Combat Teams
   (alphanumeric order)
Fires Brigade (FIB)
   Aviation Brigade (CAB)
   TFs of Bn size
   Named TFs (alphabetic order)
Numbered TFs (alphanumeric
   order)
Maneuver Enhancement Brigade (MEB)
Battlefield Surveillance
   Brigade (BSFB)*
Division Special Troops
   Battalion (DSTB)
DMAIN

CP1

Band
* now known as 'Reconnaissance
   and Surveillance'

## BRIGADE LEVEL

Task Forces of Bn size
   Named TFs (alphabetic

   Named TFs (alphanu-
   meric order)

Battalions

   Infantry
   Air Assault
   Airborne
Combined Arms
RSTA/Cavalry

Separate ground
   maneuver battalions
   companies or both

Named Teams (alphabetic
   order)
Numbered Teams (alpha-
   numeric order)
Fires Battalion
Aviation Battalion

Engineer Battalion

## SUSTAINMENT BDE
BN (BSTB)
BSTB
CSSB
TRANS BN
POL Supply BN
MVMT CNT BN (MCB)
  MCT
ORDNANCE AMMO BN
EOD BN

TERMINAL OPERATING BN

Brigade Special Troops

ADA
Chemical
Engineer
Military Intelligence
Military Police
Network Signal/Support

Brigade Support
  Battalion
  Distro Co
  Fwd Maint Co
  Medical Co
  Fwd Spt Co's

## CSSB
Quartermaster Supply Co (QSC)
Quartermaster Co (Mortuary
  Affairs or "MA")
POL Supply Co (GS)
Service Co (FSC)
Petroleum, Pipeline Terminal
  Operating Co
Truck Co (POL)
Truck Co (PLS)
Provider Co
Truck Co (LT/MED)
Material Support Co
Truck Co (MDM)
Truck Co (HET)
Cargo Transfer Co (CTC)
Support Maintenance Co (SMC)
Component Repair Co (CRC)
Human Resource Co (Postal, R5)
Finance Co

Ammo Co (Modular)
Water Purification &
  Distribution Co
Quartermaster Field

Quartermaster Heavy
  Aerial Supply Co
Aerial Delivery Co
Quartermaster Force

Quartermaster Heavy

# COMMAND RELATIONSHIP DEFINITIONS

At the theater level, when Army forces operate outside the US, they are assigned under a "Joint Forces Command or "JFC". A JFC is a combatant commander, sub unified commander, or a joint task force commander (JTF) commander authorized to exercise COCOM or operational control (OPCON) over a joint force. Combatant commanders provide strategic direction and operational focus to forces by developing strategy, planning campaigns, organizing the theater, and establishing command relationships.

1. **ORGANIC.** An element assigned to and forming an essential part of a military organization.

2. **ASSIGNED.** Units or personnel placed in an organization where such placement is relatively permanent and/or where such organization controls, administers, and provides logistic support to units or personnel for the primary function, or greater portion of the functions, of the unit or personnel.

3. **ATTACHED.** Units or personnel temporarily placed in an organization. Subject to limitations imposed by the attachment order, the commander of the formation, unit, or organization receiving the attachment will exercise the same degree of command and control as he does over units and personnel organic to his command (parent organization retains responsibility for transfer/promotion of personnel).

4. **OPERATIONAL CONTROL (OPCON). (NATO)** Authority delegated to a commander to...
   - Direct forces assigned so he may accomplish specific missions or tasks usually limited by function, time, or location
   - Deploy units concerned.
   - Retain or assign tactical control of those units.

   OPCON does not include authority to assign separate employment of components of the units concerned, nor does it include service support control or matters of administration, discipline, internal organization, or unit training.

5. **COMBATANT COMMAND (COCOM). (DOD)** The non-transferable command authority exercised only by combatant commanders unless the NCA direct otherwise. Combatant commanders exercise it over assigned forces. COCOM provides full authority to organize and employ commands and forces to accomplish mission, they exercise COCOM through subordinate commands, to include sub-unified commands, service component commands, functional component commands, and JTFs.

6. **OPERATIONAL COMMAND (OPCOM). (NATO)** OPCOM is inherent in COCOM. The authority granted to a commander to assign missions or tasks to subordinate commanders, to deploy units, to reassign forces, and to retain or delegate operational and/or tactical control as necessary. OPCON may be exercised at any echelon at or below the level of the combatant command. It can be delegated or transferred. It does not include responsibility for administration or logistics.

7. **TACTICAL COMMAND (TACOM). (NATO)** The authority delegated to a commander to assign tasks to forces under his command for the accomplishment of the mission assigned by a higher authority.

8. **TACTICAL CONTROL (TACON). (NATO)** TACON is authority normally limited to the detailed and specific local direction of movement and maneuver of forces to accomplish a task. It allows commanders below combatant command level to apply force and direct the tactical use of CSS assets but does not provide authority to change organizational structure or direct administrative or logistical support. TACON is often the command relationship established between forces of different nations in a multinational force. It may be appropriate when tactical level Army units are placed under another service headquarters. Army commanders make one Army force TACON to another when they want to withhold authority to change the subordinate force organizational structure and leave responsibility for administrative support or CSS with the parent unit of the subordinate force.

| IF RELATIONSHIP IS: | | INHERENT RESPONSIBILITIES ARE: | | | | | | | |
| --- | --- | --- | --- | --- | --- | --- | --- | --- | --- |
| | | Has Command Relationship with: | May Be Task Organized by: | Receives CSS from: | Assigned Position or AO By: | Provides Liaison To: | Establishes/ Maintains Communications with: | Has Priorities Established by: | Gaining Unit Can Impose Further Command or Support Relationship of: |
| COMMAND | Attached | Gaining unit | Gaining unit | Gaining unit | Gaining unit | As required by gaining unit | Unit to which attached | Gaining unit | Attached; OPCON; TACON; GS; GSR; R; DS |
| | OPCON | Gaining unit | Parent unit and gaining unit; gaining unit may pass OPCON to lower HQ. Note 1 | Parent unit | Gaining unit | As required by gaining unit | As required by gaining unit and parent unit | Gaining unit | OPCON; TACON; GS; GSR; R; DS |
| | TACON | Gaining unit | Parent unit | Parent unit | Gaining unit | As required by gaining unit | As required by gaining unit and parent unit | Gaining unit | GS; GSR; R; DS |
| | Assigned | Parent unit | Parent unit | Parent unit | Gaining unit | As required by parent unit | As required by parent unit | Parent unit | Not Applicable |
| SUPPORT | Direct Support (DS) | Parent unit | Parent unit | Parent unit | Supported unit | Supported unit | Parent unit; Supported unit | Supported unit | Note 2 |
| | Reinforcing (R) | Parent unit | Parent unit | Parent unit | Reinforced unit | Reinforced unit | Parent unit; reinforced unit | Reinforced unit: then parent unit | Not Applicable |
| | General Support Reinforcing (GSR) | Parent unit | Parent unit | Parent unit | Parent unit | Reinforced unit and as required by parent unit | Reinforced unit and as required by parent unit | Parent unit; then reinforced unit | Not Applicable |
| | General Support (GS) | Parent unit | Parent unit | Parent unit | Parent unit | As required by parent unit | As required by parent unit | Parent unit | Not Applicable |

NOTE 1. In NATO, the gaining unit may not task organize a multinational unit (see TACON).
NOTE 2. Commanders of units in DS may further assign support relationships between their subordinate units and elements of the supported unit after coordination with the supported commander.

*CHAPTER 29*

# SUSTAINMENT BATTLE STAFF DUTY DESCRIPTIONS

## ★★★

### 29.1 The Sustainment Brigade BATTLESTAFF

1. **Battlestaff** is a non-doctrinal term that describes the group of officers, NCOs, and soldiers that participate in the Sustainment Bde/CSSB planning process. This group expands as the mission and situation dictates, though there are constraints on its general size due to space limitations.

2. **S-1.** The S-1 is overall responsible for any and all related personnel issues for the Sustainment Brigade during tactical operations. Upon receiving the mission, the S-1 gives current friendly unit strength estimates, critical shortages, and available external personnel support. Throughout the planning process, the S-1 is also the staff proponent for the Sustainment Brigade Chaplain, Surgeon, and in certain circumstances Safety. Beginning with Mission Analysis, the S-1 builds the personnel estimate, creating an all encompassing casualty estimation and casualty evacuation during war gaming. Simultaneously, based on availability from higher headquarters, the S-1 estimates replacement numbers, and in conjunction with S-4, and the XO, determines the priority of fill to the units. In COA development and COA decision brief, the S-1 makes recommendations to the command based on

personnel supportability, i.e. casualty estimations, casualty evacuation, and the ability to maintain unit replacement flow. The S-1 develops the personnel and administration portions of Sustainment Brigade OPLANS and collects and compiles the following appendices: Personnel, Legal, Religious Support, Medical Support, and Safety. As a member of the Sustainment Brigade staff, and the tactical Battle Staff, the S-1 is the tactical POC for all personnel issues in the organization.

> **References:**   ADP/ADRP 3-0 Unified Land Operation
> FM 1-0 Human Resources Support
> FMI 1-0.01 S-1 Operations
> FMI 1-0.02 Theater-Level Human Resource
>   Support
> ADP/ADRP 5-0 The Operations Process
> UNIT TACSOP

> **Participates:** All Battlestaff planning sessions.

> **Brief:** As required at: Mission Analysis, COA Decision Brief, Orders Brief

3. **S-2.** The S-2 supports the Battle Staff's command estimate process. Support consists of monitoring the current situation, war gaming as the enemy commander, coordinating and synchronizing the IPB effort, conducting parallel planning with higher, adjacent, and subordinate headquarters, and providing intelligence input to all plans, orders, and fragos. Responsible for the following OPLAN/OPORD/FRAGO input: Enemy Forces, Intelligence, Electronic Warfare, Deception, Coordinating Instructions, ANNEX B (Intelligence), ANNEX P (C2W), and input to the Decision Support Matrix and Synchronization Matrix.

**References:**  ADP/ADRP 3-0 Unified Land Operation
ADP/ADRP 5-0 The Operations Process
FM 2-0 Intelligence
FM 2-01.3 Intelligence Preparation of the
Battlefield (IPB)
FMI 2-01.301 Specific Tactics, Techniques, &
Procedures and Applications for IPB
FMI 2-91.6 Solider Surveillance &
Reconnaissance
FM 3-55.1 Information Collection
FM 34-8-2 Intelligence Officers Handbook,
May 98
FM 34-81 Weather Support for Army Tactical
Operations, Aug 89
FM 5-33 Terrain Analysis, Jul 90

**Participates:** All Battle Staff planning sessions and all briefings from MA through Orders Briefing.

**Briefs:** Provides briefing input to all briefings from MA though Orders issue. In addition to briefing slides/input, products include:

| | |
|---|---|
| Image maps | Hydrology overlay |
| Slope image overlay | MCOO overlay |
| Elevation image overlay | Key Terrain overlay |
| Line of Communication overlay | Avenue of Approach overlay |
| Enemy Situation overlay | Intelligence |
| Synchronization Matrix | |
| Enemy Event Template | Enemy COAs |
| NAI Overlay | Collection Plan |
| Intelligence Priorities | |

4. **S-3.** The S-3 is responsible for the supervision, development and maintenance of all plans for the Sustainment Brigade.

The S-3 leads the Battle Staff through the Military Decision Making Process and supervises development of briefings and written orders. During war gaming, the S-3 supervises the conduct of the war game and arbitrates disputes. The S-3 performs other duties as assigned by the XO. Responsible for the following input to the Sustainment Brigade OPLAN/OPORD: Friendly Forces, Attachments and Detachments, Assumptions (OPLAN only), Mission, Intent, Tasks to Subordinate Units, Coordinating Instructions, Command and Signal, ANNEX A (Task Organization), ANNEX C (Operations Overlay), ANNEX Q (OPSEC), and ANNEX S (Deception).

**References:**   FM 3-06 Series
ADP/ADRP 3-0 Unified Land Operations
FM 3-07 Stability Opns and Support Opns
ADP/ADRP 5-0 The Operations Process
ATTP 5-0.1 Commander and Staff Officer
  Guide
ADP/ADRP 6-0 Mission Command
FM 1-02 Operational Terms and Graphics,
  Sep 04
TACSOP, SUSTAINMENT BRIGADE
  TACSOP

**Participates:** Mission Analysis, COA Development, War Gaming, OPLAN review and production.

**Brief:** Mission Analysis, COA Briefing, Decision Brief, Warning Orders, Contingency Plans

5. **PLANS OFFICER (Sustainment Bde/CSSB only).** As required, the Plans Officer assists the S-3 in the execution of his duties and the production of the order. Normally, the Plans Officer will assist in the following tasks: Fighting friendly forces during the war game, assisting the S-3 producing portions of

the order. He is directly responsible to write and proofread OPLANs/ OPORDs before release, manages task organization, writes FRAGOs, briefs subordinate commands, and takes briefings from higher commands. Primary responsible individual for LSA defense plans. Performs other duties as assigned by the S-3.

**References:** Same as for S-3

**Participate:** In all of the Sustainment Brigade and higher headquarters related planning activities and responsibilities and War Gaming.

**Brief:** None. (Be prepared to brief in absence of S-3)

6. **S-4 .** S-4 is responsible for all aspects of tactical maintenance, supply, transportation and services planning for contingency missions and training exercises. Responsible for integrating and synchronizing combat service support considerations internal to Sustainment Brigade with other battlefield operating systems in the development of estimates, plans, and orders. Monitors current operations to endure sustainment systems continually support the Sus Bde forces. Maintains liaison with higher, supporting, and supported organizations to rapidly and effectively transfer logistical planning and operational information between affected units. Provides continuous coordination with and technical assistance to the Battle Staff and Sus Bde units on all multifunctional internal Sus Bde logistical matters. Recommends priorities for allocating resources. Determines the adequacy of and recommends priorities for employing logistics support units. Provides input to Sus Bde OPLANs/OPORDS: Service Support Para, and ANNEX F (Sustainment).

**References:**

FM 3-06 Series
ADP/ADRP 3-0 Unified Land Operations
ADP 4-0 Sustainment
ATP 4-93 The Sustainment Brigade
ADP/ADRP 5-0 The Operations Process
ATTP 5-0.1 Commander and Staff Officer
  Guide
FM 1-02 Operations, Terms and Graphics,
  Modular G1-G4 Battlebook
OPLOGPLNR Software, Logistics Estimator,
  Log Est Worksheet (LEW)
SUSTAINMENT BRIGADE TACSOP

**Participate:** Mission Analysis, COA Development, War Gaming, OPLAN/OPORD production, Logistics Estimate, Synch Matrix Development, Movement Rehearsals, Sustainment Rehearsals, and Decision Support Matrix (DSM) Development.

**Brief:** Mission Analysis (internal sustainment – man, arm, fix, sustain, and move the force), Decision Brief, and Orders Brief.

7. **MOVEMENT CONTROL OFFICER (ATTACHED).** Develops guidance, plans and policies for the Division's transportation requirements for highway, rail, air, sea transportation and military ocean terminal services. Plans, coordinates, and monitors the Division's transportation assets to meet movement requirements. Prepares the transportation/mobility appendices for Division support plans/orders. Plans and coordinates with higher and adjacent headquarters/agencies for transportation services in support of strategic deployments. Provides continuous coordination with and technical assistance to the General Staff, brigades, and subordinate units on all transportation logistic matters. Provides staff supervision for all Division movements.

**References:**

FM 3-06 Series
ADP/ADRP 3-0 Unified Land Operations
ADP 4-0 Sustainment
ATP 4-93 The Sustainment Brigade
ADP/ADRP 5-0 The Operations Process
ATTP 5-0.1 Commander and Staff Officer
  Guide
FM 1-02 Operations, Terms and Graphics,
Modular G1-G4 Battlebook
OPLOGPLNR Software, Logistics Estimator,
  Log Est Worksheet (LEW)
SUSTAINMENT BRIGADE TACSOP
MTMCTEA Ref 94-700-2
FMI 3-35 Army Deployment & Redeployment,
  Jun 07
FM 4-01.011 Unit Movement Opns, Oct 02
FM 4-01.30 Movement Control, Sep 03
FM 55-1 Transportation Operations, Oct 95
FM 55-15 Transportation Reference Data,
  Oct 97

**Participate:** Mission Analysis, COA Development, Movement Rehearsals, War-Gaming, Sustainment Rehearsal

**Brief:** By exception only

8. **Sustainment Brigade S-6 (Signal Officer).** Determine any specific or implied communications tasks from higher headquarters. Develop Signal staff estimate. Identify all non-doctrinal communications requirements. Coordinate sufficient communications assets to support all forces available to the Sus Bde. Identify all communications restrictions to the Battle Staff. Ensure that any course of action developed is communications supportable. Provide command and control evaluation

to course of action selection. Prepare all signal and distribution annexes to Sus Bde OPLANs/OPORDs. Provide information exchange with the Signal Battalion S3 for concurrent planning. Responsible for ISSO. ISSO responsibilities are as follows: Responsible for tactical distribution and CP reproduction for the Sus Bde. Manages the Sus Bde Communications Security (COMSEC) distribution, accountability, and destruction within the Sus Bde. Prepares ANNEX H (Signal) to Sus Bde OPLANs/OPORDs.

> **References:**  ADP/ADRP 3-0 Unified Land Operations
> ADP/ADRP 5-0 The Operations Process
> ATTP 5-0.1 Commander and Staff Officer
> Guide
> FM 6-02 Series manuals
> FMI 6-02.45 Signal Support to Theater
> Operations
> FM 1-02 Operations, Terms and Graphics

**Participates:** Mission Analysis, COA Development, COA Analysis, War Gaming, and OPLAN/OPORD Development/ Production.

**Brief:** OPLAN/OPORD para 5 Command and Signal; other by exception

9. **CHEMICAL OFFICER.** The Sus Bde CBRNE Chemical Officer is overall responsible for any and all related NBC issues for the Sus Bde during tactical operations. Upon receiving the mission, the Sus Bde CBRNE/Chemical Officer provides information on the Sus Bde's MOPP and radiation exposure status, currently assigned chemical units, availability of external chemical support, and a summary of recent and present enemy CBRNE events that may indicate future actions. Along with the S-2, he develops possible enemy courses of action,

determines enemy capabilities, and recommends PIR/IR and NAIs as related to CBRNE operations. During Mission Analysis, the Sus Bde CBRNE/Chemical Officer provides constraints from higher headquarters on the use of nuclear weapons and acceptable risks, riot control agents, and herbicides. He also identifies any terrain restrictions relevant to unit dispersion, decontamination, and smoke operations. In the development and analysis of each COA, he makes recommendations on each COA in regards to the principles of NBC defense, contamination avoidance, protection, and decontamination. He continuously analyzes the vulnerability of friendly dispositions to CBRNE strikes and makes recommendations and coordination with the S-4, supported unit Chem Off, G5, AC2, and ADA on the supportability and feasibility of decontamination and smoke operations. As a member of the Brigade's Special Staff, and the Battle Staff, the Brigade CBRNE/Chemical Officer is the tactical POC for all CBRNE issues in the Brigade, and is in constant communication with the CBRNE personnel manning the Main CP, CP1 and Major Subordinate Commands. Collects and compiles the CBRN paragraph (Annex E 'Protection', Para 3a(6)) to Brigade's OPLANs/OPORDs.

**References:**   FM 1-02 Operations, Terms and Graphics,
FM 3-11.3 Multiservice TTPs for CBRNE
Containment, Feb 06
FM 3-11.4 Multiservice TTPs for CBRNE
Protection
FM 3-11.5 Multiservice TTPs for CBRNE
Decontamination
FM 3-50 Smoke Operations, Dec 90
FM 3-101 Chemical Staffs and Units, Nov 93
FM 3-11 Multiservice TTPs for NBC Defense
Ops, Mar 03

**Participate:** All Battle Staff Planning Sessions and War Gaming

**Brief:** None

## 28.2 CSSB/BSB BATTLESTAFF

### 1. <u>Battalion Commander (BC)</u>

a. Dual-hatted as Senior Tactical Commander of Brigade Support Area (BSA) (BSB only).

b. Approves Warning Orders (WARNOs).

c. Approves restated mission. –

d. Provides initial guidance and initial Commander's Intent (written if time available).

e. Approves courses of action (COAs).

f. Decides on a COA.

g. Approves Commander's Critical Information Requirements (CCIR) list.

h. Provides final Commander's Intent.

i. Approves final operations plans and orders (OPLANs/ OPORDs).

j. Approves fragmentary orders (FRAGO5).

k. Approves command priorities for internal support.

**2. Battalion Executive Officer (XO).** In addition to commanding in the Battalion Commander's absence:

    a.   Serves as Command Post (CP) OIC.

    b.   Implements BCs directives and supervises MDMP. Ensures staff unity of effort and coordination.

    c.   Rehearses the staff for all staff briefings, rehearsals, and battle update briefs (BUBs).

**3. S2 & S3 (Operations and Intelligence Officers).**

    a.   BSB-BSA INTEGRATION. Serves as plans and orders officer-in- charge (OIC). Responsible principally for planning of BSB deployment flow of personnel and equipment from home station through staging base(s) into the area of operations (AO).

         *   "WFFA" - Responsible for coordinating and synchronizing the following war fighting functional area for the BSB and BSA:
- Air Defense Artillery (ADA)
- Countermobility-Mobility-Survivability (CM-M-S) Engineer Support
- Fire Support (FS)
- Intelligence (Intel)
- Command and Control (C2).

         *   Also supervises & coordinates:
- Terrain/Land management
- Tenant unit perimeter defense integration
- Military police support
- Tactical combat force (TCF) integration -
- BSA quick reaction force (QRF)

- Perimeter and area of influence defense planning
- Communications
- Operations, physical, logistics, and signal security (OPSEC. PHYSEC, LOGSEC, & SIGSEC).
- Tactical movements (convoys, displacements and occupation plan).
- Sustainment Engineering

b.  Serves Officer-in-Charge (OIC) of BSA Movement Plans Cell.

c.  Performs time-available analysis in concert with (ICW) XO for each step in the planning process (adhering to "1/3-2/3 rule" - 1/3 of time available given to Bn staff, and 2/3 to subordinate elements).

d.  Issues coordinated WARNOs when approved by BC.

e.  Maintains Battalion tactical map overlays/situation map of Brigade and Division and friendly and enemy situation.

f.  Prepares and maintains battalion consolidated reports matrix showing reports requirements, time due-in and -out, and when they arrived and were sent.

g.  With other staff input, formulates the recommended Commander's Critical Information Requirements (CCIR).

h.  Maintains status of answers to CCIR/ISSUES. Significant Activities and detailed Daily Staff Journal Duty Officer's Log (DA Form 1594) for the battalion.

i.  Drafts, coordinates, and consolidates staff input for OPORDs, OPLANs and FRAGOs:

(1) Drafts Map Sheets, References, Time Zone. Used, and Task Organization sections.

(2) ICW Spt Ops Section, drafts Para 1, Situation, and any associated annexes.

(3) ICW Spt Ops Section, drafts restated mission and Para 2, Mission.

(4) ICW Spt Ops Section, drafts Para 3, Execution, and any associated annexes. Ensures Commanders Intent is incorporated.

(5) Includes the S4 and S1 input for Para 4, Service Support, and any associated annexes.

(6) Drafts Para 5. Command and Signal

## 4. Support Plans Operations Officer. (SPO)

**a.** **BSB**. Principally responsible for taking BCT estimated requirements (from the Bde S4) and recommending to the Battalion Commander how the BCT is best supported by available capabilities.

**CSSB.** Principally responsible for taking Sustainment Bde replenishment operations (RO) mission taskings and recommending to the Battalion Commander how the CSSB can best execute with available assets and capabilities

(1) Applies sustainment capabilities in synchronization with forecasted Bde requirements to ensure the right amount is provided at the right place at the right time.

(2)   Provides input to S-3 for determination of specified tasks to unit subordinate elements in OPLAN/OPORD or FRAGO in Para 3.b. Tasks to Subordinate Elements.

(3)   Provides input to S-3 on concept of operation and mission statement for WARNOs. OPLANs/OPORDs and FRAGOs.

(4)   Prepares and maintains the sustainment map overlay/LCOP and current status of BSB/CSSB DS assets for reporting and CCIR.

(5)   Recommends liaison personnel and locations to Bn Cdr. Normally a 24-hour requirement at HHQ Main Command Post and/or Sustainment Brigade HQ.

(6)   Principal coordinator, parallel planner, and battalion liaison for BCT (Sus Bde) planning sessions, higher echelon support, host nation support (HNS) and/or commercially contracted support to the HHQ or on an area support basis.

b.   **BSA – BSB**. Recommends to BCT S3 where to position locations of the BSA, Logistics Release Points (LRPs) and Forward Logistics Elements (FLE). Coordinates CAB/IN/RSTA/Fires Battalion Support Areas ICW with Bn S-4s. Assures these positions are on posted to BCT graphics. Provides representative to BSA Movements Plans Cell.

**CSSB**. Recommends to the Bn Cdr/Sus Bde SPO/S-3 where to position locations of any projected CRSPs, TTPs, CSCs, "Mini-Marts", and Forward Logistics Elements (FLE). Assures these positions are on posted to HHQ and supported unit graphics. Provides representative to Sus Bde Movements Coordination Cell.

## 5. S1 (Personnel and Administration Officer).

a. Principally responsible for unit personnel and administration status and planning to include coordinating medical support, preventive medicine, Enemy Prisoners of War (EPW) collection, stress management, legal, financial, and civil-affairs ("S5") matters. Prepares personnel estimate.

b. Principally responsible for personnel status to assist S-3 in determining relative combat power. Develops unit casualty collection points (CCPs) and FPW/Displaced Civilian (DCs) plans. Serves as the unit Public Affairs Officer (PAO).

c. In conjunction with the S4, drafts personnel and administration portions of Para 4, Service Support, and any associated annexes.

## 6. S4 (Logistics Officer).

a. Principally responsible for the internal supply, transportation, and service support to the unit's assigned or attached units. Monitors unit field sanitation, Plans for BSA/LSA/FOB damage control, Prepares logistics estimate, Supervises and coordinates the "Sustainment" WFF internal to the unit ICW S1 and BMT.

b. Within the BSA/LSA/FOB:

(1) Serves as key member of the unit's Movements Plans Cell/Movement Coordination Cell (MCC). Authority to control of all convoy/vehicle movements and monitors checkpoints, release points,

start points, and BSA/LSA/FOB exit and entrance gates.

(2)   Prepares unit feeding plan to include provisions for EPWs, DCs. and Mortuary Affairs Collection point (MACP) site.

(3)   Prepares Traffic Control Plan for the BSA/FOB.

*CHAPTER 30*

# INFORMATION UPDATE

★★★

| SUBJECT | BRIEFER |
|---|---|
| 1. **INTRODUCTION** | **XO** |

- Purpose of the Briefing
- What is required at the conclusion of the Briefing

| | |
|---|---|
| 2. **MISSION** | **S-3** |
| 3. **TASKO** | **S-3** |
| 4. **ENEMY SITUATION** | **S-2/Intel NCO** |

A - COMPOSITION
B - DISPOSITION
C - COMBAT POWER
D - STRENGTHS
E - WEAKNESSES/VULNERABILITIES
F - CAPABILITIES

| | |
|---|---|
| 5. **WEATHER** | **S-2/Intel NCO** |
| 6. **TERRAIN** | **S-2/Intel NCO** |
| 7. **SIGNIFICANT EVENTS SINCE LAST UPDATE** | **S-2/Intel NCO** |
| 8. **FRIENDLY SITUATION** | **S-3** |

A - MAIN EFFORT

B - PRIORITY OF FIRES

C - BRIEF DESCRIPTION OF RESULTS
   OF OPERATIONS

D - BATTALIONS IN CONTACT

E - BATTALIONS NOT IN CONTACT

F - RESERVES

G - CURRENT FLOT/LOCATION OF
   LEAD ELEMENTS

H - SIGNIFICANT EVENTS SINCE LAST
   UPDATE

I - PROBLEMS (FRIENDLY)

J - OPPORTUNITIES (FRIENDLY)

K - KNOWN STATUS OF FLANKING
   UNITS

## 9. SUSTAINMENT/CSS CONSIDERATIONS  SPO/S-1/S-4

A - CRITICAL EVENTS SINCE LAST
   UPDATE

B - PROBLEMS

C - OPPORTUNITIES

## 10. DETERMINATION OF NEED FOR       XO
## MORE DETAILED ANALYSIS

Note: This briefing will be conducted at predetermined times as directed by the XO or CDR. The specific intent of this briefing is to update the CDR as soon as possible after his arrival back at unit TOC during tactical or field operations.

Note: Upon receipt of a new mission/order from higher HQs, the CDR may request an initial facts brief/update.

## CHAPTER 31

# LOGISTICS AUTOMATION REFERENCE

### ★★★

| ACRONYMS | NAME | FUNCTIONS |
|----------|------|-----------|
| **BCS3** | Battle Command Sustainment Support System | Interfaces with GCCS-A; Interfaces with Sustainment STAMIS(s); Sustainment information for tactical/Sustainment Commanders; Collect and analyze technical CSS data; Near real-time sustainment information. |
| **DAMMS-R** | Department of the Army Movement Management System-Redesign Primarily used at Installation level | Movements Management; Transportation Management; Transportation Resources; Management at Division Through Theater |
| **SAAS** | Standard Army Ammunition System | Class V Management; Total Asset Visibility; Inventory Accountability; Material Management Activities |
| **MTS** | Movement Tracking System | Near Rear Time tracking of sustainment assets on the battlefield with encrypted text messaging; designed to provide command and control over distributed assets supporting and conducting theater operations |

| SARSS (All Versions) | Standard Army Retail Supply System | Supply Mgt; Stock Control; Receipt/Storage; Requisition/ Issue; War reserve; Material Rebuild; Major Item Acquisition; Catalog Processing; Demand/ Document History |
|---|---|---|
| ILAP | Integrated Logistics Analysis Program | Produce Information Management Reports Combining Data from several Standard Systems |
| SDS | Standard Depot System | Industrial Log System; Industrial Ops/Ammo/ AMC; Installation Mgt Standard System; Seamless Info. Processing; Processing Transactions while creating Mgt. Info. |
| SAMS I / II / TDA | Standard Army Maintenance System– Installation/Table of Distribution and Allowances | Shop Production; Maint. Control Records; Shop Supplies; Order Repair Parts; Equipment. Performance Report; Selected Maint; Equip. readiness; Engineering Data; Life – Cycle Mgt |
| PBUSE | Standard Property Book System–Redesign | Property/Accountability Reporting; Unit Hand Receipts; SSA Equip. Request /Receipt Interface; Authorization Asset Control; Serial Number Tracking; CBS-X, Reqval |
| MC4 | Theater Army Medical Management Information System | Med. Supply; Med Maint; Med. Assemblage Management; Track Patients |
| TCAIMS-II | Transportation Coordinator Automated Information Management System | Selected Trans. Functions; Unit Equipment/Pers. Deployment |

| **CTASC** | Corps/Theater Automated Data Processing Service Center | Information systems that satisfy tactical information requirements under wartime conditions. CTASC uses SARSS-O to process and monitor the flow of logistics data and to support Class II, III(P), IV, VII, and IX supply actions. |
|-----------|--------------------------------------------------------|----------------------------------------------------------------------------------------------------------------------------------------------------------------------------------------------------------------------------------------------------------|
| **SAMS-E** | Standard Army Maintenance System – Enhanced | Motor Pool Ops; Flight Line Ops; BN S-4 Ops; Process PLL; Army Maint. Mgt; SARSS/SAMS Interface; Request Supplies; Forecast Basic Loads; Hand Receipt Asset Visibility; Unit Load Planning; Bulk POL Mgt; Facility Mgt; Produce Flight Packs; Track Aircraft Readiness; Maintain Historical Data; Order Repair Parts |

CHAPTER 32

# QUICK REFERENCE DATA

The data listed in the following enclosures provide quick reference data and planning factors. This data must be modified based on METT-TC and equipment availability (026 Report).

## 32.1 Logistical Planning Data

1. Transportation

| Nomen | Model | LIN | Useable cargo area Length | Width | Pallets (40" X 48") | 463L Pallet |
|---|---|---|---|---|---|---|
| LMTV | M1078 | T60081 | 147 | 88 | 6 | 1 |
| HEMTT | M977 | T59278 | 216 | 90 | 8 | 2 |
| MTV | M1083 | T61908 | 168 | 88 | 6 | 1 |
| Trailer, 22 1/2 Ton | M871 | S70027 | 350 | 88 | 14 | 3 |
| Trailer, 34 Ton | M872 | S70159 | 485 | 93 | 20 | 4 |
| PLS | M1075 | T40999 | 227 | 90 | 8 | 2 |

2. Medical

| Unit type | Assets |
|---|---|
| BSB – HBCT | 4 ea M997 ambulance (wheel) |
| | 6 ea M113 ambulance (track) |
| BSB – Stryker | 10 ea M997 ambulance |
| BSB - IBCT | 10 ea M997 ambulance |

| | |
|---|---|
| CAB/RSTA | 10 ea M113 ambulance |
| IN BN/Recon Sqdn | 10 ea M997 ambulance |
| IN BN (Stryker) | 8 ea Stryker Evac Vehicles |
| Fires BN (all) | 3 ea M997 ambulance |

3. Tactical Unit Fuel Distribution Capacity

### *Forward Support Company (FSC)

| Type Unit | #/Type Veh. | Mobile Gallons Avail |
|---|---|---|
| IN BN | 3 x M978 | 6,750 |
| CAB | 12 x M978 | 27,000 |
| Fires (H) | 5 x M978 | 11,250 |
| Fires (I) | 3 x M978 | 6,750 |
| Recon Sqdn (H) | 4 x M978 | 9,000 |
| Recon Sqdn (I) | 3 x M978 | 6,750 |

* Note: Stryker Brigades (SBCTs) do not possess FSCs at this time
Useable holding capacity of the M978 is 2250 gal

### Distribution Company, Brigade Support Battalions.

| Type Unit | #/Type Veh. | Mobile Gallons Avail |
|---|---|---|
| HBCT | 14 x M978 | 31,500 |
| | 15 x M969 (5K) | 72,000 |
| IBCT | 11 x M978 | 24,750 |
| | 4 x M969 (5K) | 19,200 |
| SBCT | 14 x M978 | 31,500 |
| | 14 x FARE** | 42,000 |

**FARE is ground equipment; however, drums are able to be slingloaded.
Useable holding capacity of the M969 is 4800 gal

## TOTAL BRIGADE FUEL HOLDING CAPABILITY (IN GAL)

|  | BSB | FSCs | UNIT | TOTAL |
|---|---|---|---|---|
| HBCT | 103,500 (33%) | 74,250 (24%) | 134,611 (43%) | 312,361 |
| IBCT | 43,950 | 27,000 | TBD | TBD |
| SBCT | 31,500 (33%) | 42,000 (44%) (FARE) | 22,596 (23%) | 96,096 |

4. SUSTAINMENT BRIGADE/CSSB FUEL HOLDING UNIT CAP.

   a. <u>POL SUPPORT PLT (50K)</u>

     (1)   Store *600,000* gallons at one location or *300,000* gallons each at two locations.

     (2)   Can receive and issue up to 200,000 gallons of bulk petroleum per day.

     (3)   The Area Support Section can store up to *120,000* gallons of bulk petroleum at one location and *60,000* gallons at each of two locations. It can receive and /or issue in any combination up to *120,000* gallons daily.

     (4)   The distribution section can distribute *48,750* gallons of fuel daily based on 75% availability of fuel dispensing vehicles at two trips per day.

     (5)   Can establish and operate two hot refueling points using two FARE systems for transitory aircraft operating in their area.

   b. <u>POL SUPPORT PLT (210K)</u>

     (1)   Store up to *1,680,000* gallons at one location or *840,000* gallons each of two locations.

     (2)   Can receive and issue up to *300,000* gallons of bulk petroleum per day.

(3)   The Area Support Section can store up to *120,000* gallons of bulk petroleum at one location and *60,000* gallons at each of two locations.

(4)   It can receive and/or issues in any combination up to *120,000* gallons daily.

(5)   The distribution section can distribute *48,750* gallons of fuel daily based on 75% availability of fuel dispensing vehicles at two trips per day.

(6)   It can also establish and operate two hot refueling points using two FARE systems for transitory aircraft operating in their area.

## 6. WATER GENERATION

a.   Requirements, Appendix b, FM 10-52

| AREA | SUSTAIN | MIN |
|---|---|---|
| Temperate area | 6.1 gal/man/day | 3.4 g/m/d |
| Tropical area | 7.7 " | 5.0 g/m/d |
| Arctic area | 6.6 " | 3.9 g/m/d |
| Arid area | 7.9 " | 5.2 g/m/d |

b.   Sustainment unit capabilities:

(1)   BSB equipped with 1 TWPS: 30,000 gal/day (20 hr operation/fresh water source)
" " 2 LWS (Lightweight Water Pur): 5,000 gal/day (20 hr opn/fresh)
Total BSB Water Production: *35,000* gal/day

(2)   Water Purification & Distribution Company,

(a)   Production: 6 ea 3K ROWPU: *360,000* gal/day (20 hr/day/fresh source)
3 ROWPU/PLT x 2 PLTs

(b)  Storage: Water storage for *168,000* gal. Distribution Plt can provide storage of *168,000* gals at one location or *80,000* gals at two locations.

(c)  Distribution: Can distribute up to *66,000* gal of water/day base on 75% equipment availability and two trips/day

c.  Doctrinal notes (Ref Figure 32-1)

(1)  Water is provided through supply point distribution and transported by units via the 900 gallon hippo trailer. In an arid environment, where insufficient water sources are available, any additional water is provided by corps.

(2)  Sustainment Bde medium truck companies may augment Water Purification & Distribution Companies in distributing water using 5,000 gallon semi trailers, or using 4,750 or 3,000 gallon Semi Mobile Fabric Tanks (SMFT) on semi trailers.

(3)  Sustainment Bdes/CSSBs use SMFTs to haul water to Support Brigades without operational water purification sources to Spt Bdes/BCTs who have shut down their ROWPUs as a result of tactical operations. FAWPSS are used for remote locations. FAWPSS and full 500 gallon drums can be loaded on vehicles, towed short distances, or sling loaded by aircraft.

# Modular Water Support

*Figure 32-1 Modular Water Distribution within Corps AOR*

7.  Planning Factor Rates in Pounds Per Man Per Day (PMD) (References: CDRSC ST 101-6, S-1/S-4 Battle Book)

Class II(less CDE)     2.091 PMD Southwest Asia
                       3.367 PMD Northeast Asia

to include Chemical Defense Equipment add:
  NATO   +2.205 PMD
  SWA    +3.270 PMD
  NEA    +4.038 PMD

Class III (p)     .51 PMD
Class IV          8.50 PMD (4.0 barrier mat & 4.5 base const)
Class VI (after D+60)2.06 PMD temperate
                  3.40 PMD tropical/arid

Class VIII        1.03 PMD Southwest Asia
Class IX         2.5 PMD

## 32.2 Personnel Loss Estimates.

### a.   Short Term Loss Estimates (Up to 5 days)

(1) Table 4-17. Distribution of Battle Losses by Branch.

|            |        |
|------------|--------|
| Infantry   | 62.0%  |
| Artillery  | 3.6%   |
| Armor      | 23.1%  |
| Engineers  | 3.3%   |
| All Others | 8.0%   |

### b.   Unit on contact (% Loss)

|                                                    | Battle Loss | Non-Battle Loss | Total |
|----------------------------------------------------|-------------|-----------------|-------|
| Covering & Security Force Action ATTACK            | 0.9         | 0.3             | 1.2   |
| Meeting Engagement                                 | 2.4         | 0.3             | 2.7   |
| Of a position 1$^{st}$ day                         | 3.8         | 0.3             | 4.1   |
| Succeeding days                                    | 1.9         | 0.3             | 2.2   |
| Of a fortified zone 1$^{st}$ day                   | 6.3         | 0.3             | 6.6   |
| Succeeding days                                    | 3.2         | 0.3             | 3.5   |
| Defense:                                           |             |                 |       |
| Meeting Engagement                                 | 1.5         | 0.3             | 1.8   |
| Of a position 1$^{st}$ day                         | 1.9         | 0.3             | 2.2   |
| Succeeding days                                    | 1.0         | 0.3             | 1.3   |
| Of a sector 1$^{st}$ day                           | 3.2         | 0.3             | 1.9   |
| Succeeding days                                    | 1.6         | 0.3             | 1.9   |
| Inactive situation (In contact, neither attacking) | 0.7         | 0.3             | 1 . 6 |
| Pursuit                                            | 1.3         | 0.3             | 1.6   |
| Retirement and delaying action                     | 0.7         | 0.3             | 1.0   |

## 32.3 CHEMICAL PLANNING FACTORS

* FOG OIL CONSUMPTION RATE FOR SMOKE GENERATION:
  ONE (1) GAL DRUM/GENERATOR/MISSION HOUR

* WATER CONSUMPTION FOR OPERATIONAL DECON:
  100-150 GALS/WHEEL VEHICLE
  150-200 GALS/ARMORED OR LARGER VEHICLE

(UNIT LEVEL VEHICLE WASHDOWN 1-3 MINUTES/ VEHICLE)

* WATER CONSUMPTION FOR THOROUGH DECON:
  400-500 GALS/VEHICLE
  (1 CHEMICAL DECON PLT CAN DECON 12 VEHICLE/ HOUR)

* DEGREDATION EFFECT OF MOPP 4:
  MULTIPLY TASK TIME BY 1.5 TO 2.5

HISTORICAL PLANNING RATES FOR THE ARRAY OF FRIENDLY FORCES:

| FRIENDLY MISSION | FRIENDLY:ENEMY | NOTES |
|---|---|---|
| DELAY | 1:6 | |
| DEFEND | 1:3 | Prepared and Fortified |
| DEFEND | 1:2.5 | Hasty |
| ATTACK | 3:1 | Prepared and Fortified |
| ATTACK | 2.5:1 | Hasty Position |
| COUNTERATTACK | 1:1 | Flank |

## 32.4 AVIATION REFERENCE DATA

### AERIAL RESUPPLY - GENERAL

Aerial resupply operations are extremely important in both heavy and light divisions. Units can use aerial resupply to reduce the impact of time/distance factors on logistical operations. Detailed planning and execution are necessary to effectively utilize air assets for logistical operations. Proper training for ground support personnel at the Landing Zone/Pickup Zone and the Drop Zone is critical to mission success.

### AERIAL RESUPPLY

Aerial resupply is a method of delivering supplies and equipment from an aircraft to ground elements. Airdrop support units are organic to the separate airborne brigade and to the airborne division which rely heavily on air lines of communication for logistics support. Armored, infantry, and mechanized divisions have no organic support. They rely on corps units or teams for airdrop support.

Aerial resupply is accomplished using airland and airdrop techniques. The air dropping of supplies is a joint effort involving the Army and the Air Force. Air Force aircraft are used most often. Air Force assets are used for airdrop, and airland resupply operations. Army helicopters may drop supplies, but are most often used to sling load supplies.

1. Selecting the Drop/Landing (DZ/LZ) Zone. The selection of a usable drop/landing zone is extremely important. Logistical and tactical considerations are analyzed to ensure the DZ/LZ is correctly placed to support the mission. The area must be accessible to the aircraft that will use the site. The unit requesting an aerial resupply mission (preplanned, immediate, or emergency) coordinates with the support operations officer and is responsible for selecting, securing, preparing, and marking the

drop/landing area, and providing qualified ground guides and unloading teams to expedite aircraft turnaround time.

As a general rule, a DZ/LZ must provide for 30 meters separation between utility aircraft and 40 meters between cargo aircraft. Obstructions such as tree stumps, bushes, or man-made objects that could damage the aircraft or the load must be removed before operations can begin. The number of expected aircraft, weather, and light conditions at the time of delivery are also considered in the planning process. If night resupply is scheduled, a larger area is normally needed. The surface should be solid enough to prevent an aircraft or load from bogging down. Excessive slope may preclude helicopter landing. The avenue of approach and departure should be over the lowest obstacle in the direction of the prevailing winds.

Weather conditions often determine the size of the landing zone. Generally, hot and humid conditions at a landing site will decrease the lift capabilities of helicopters. Therefore, a large area with a longer approach and/or departure route is required for fully loaded helicopters.

2. Coordination Procedures For Aerial Supply. The unit request goes to the battalion S-4, through the supporting support battalion's support operations section to the MCO in a division environment. The MCO coordinates movement of supplies with the MSB and the FSB support operations sections. If the MCO determines that air resupply is appropriate, the request is passed through the DTO to the G-3. The G-3 operations section allocates helicopters. The G-4 ensures the CSS role for helicopters is considered concurrently with the tactical mission. The priorities for helicopter resupply should be addressed in the division OPORD and used by the MCO. Emergency requests are concurrently passed through both the logistics and operations channels to the brigade S-3 and division G-3. The G-3 operations section approves emergency requests and tasks the aviation brigade to perform the mission.

At the same time, the G-4 coordinates with the SUSTAINMENT BRIGADE support operations branch who coordinates with the RSS, MSB or FSB support operations section to prepare the shipment. A liaison officer from the Aviation Brigade S-3 Air, normally a pathfinder, coordinates with the MCO and support operations section. Throughput of aerial resupply to the using unit is the preferred method of delivery. Regardless of whether the mission is preplanned or emergency, if division helicopters cannot perform it for any reason, the request goes from the division TOC to the corps TOC. The diagram below shows the flow of a preplanned airdrop request.

AIRDROP REQUEST

Aerial resupply is divided into two categories, rotary wing and fixed wing. Rotary wing resupply is normally performed with Army aviation assets. Fixed wing resupply is primarily performed with Air Force assets and requires additional planning and coordination.

## ROTARY WING RESUPPLY

Rotary wing aircraft use two methods of delivery - internal load and external load (slingload). The majority of rotary wing resupply will be conducted using UH-60 Blackhawk, CH-47 Chinook, or UH-1 Huey Helicopter. Average expected endurance is between 2 and 2.5 hours.

### Aircraft capabilities and Characteristics

| Type Aircraft | Weapon System | Max number of rounds | Max effective range | Max external payload | Max internal payload | Ave/Max speed (knots) (KPH) (MPH) | Fuel capacity (pounds) (gallons) | Average fuel consumption (pounds) (gallons) |
|---|---|---|---|---|---|---|---|---|
| **AH-64** | 30mm chain gun | 1200 | 3000 | | | 120/185 222/342 138/214 | 2405 370 | 810 179 |
| | 2.75 rkt | 76 (4, 19 shot pods) | 9000 indirect | | | | | |
| | Hellfire | 16 | 7000+ | | | | | |
| **OH-58D** | 50-cal MG | 500 | 2000 | | | 80/120 148/222 92/138 | 780 112 | 225 43 |
| | 2.75 rkt | 14 (2, 7 shot pods) | 9000 indirect | | | | | |
| | Hellfire | 4 | 7000+ | | | | | |
| | Stinger | 4 | 5000 | | | | | |
| **UH-60** | | | | 9000 | 3360 | 120/193 222/356 138/222 | 2360 362 | 960 181 |
| **CH-47D** | | | | 26,000 | 20,206 | 125/165 232/306 144/190 | 6695 1030 | 2600 522 |

| Type | Max Load (External) | # of Hooks | Usable Length | Usable Width | Usable Height |
|---|---|---|---|---|---|
| UH-1 | 4000 lbs. | 1 | 39 in. | 50 in. | 50 in. |
| UH-60 | 8000 lbs. | 1 | 110 in. | 72 in. | 54 in. |
| CH-47 | 10k - 26k | 3* | 366 in. | 90 in. | 78 in. |

*  Depending on model, may have one center hook and one hook forward and aft

Sling Load Operations:

Ground crew teamwork and proficiency are the most important part of sling load operations. All units should have an ongoing training program to keep ground crews current on unit equipment and train new ground crew personnel. The size of the crew may vary depending on the situation. Generally, three people make up the crew: the signal man, the hook up man, and an assistant. Each crew member will need a separate issue of equipment to perform their mission. Sample Ground Crew Equipment Listing:

| | |
|---|---|
| Goggles | 4240-00-052-3376 |
| Snap Ring Pliers | 5120-00-023-0049 |
| Flashlight w/wand | 6230-00-163-1856 |
| Static Discharge Probe | 1670-01-194-0926 |

External Load Carrying Devices

- Sling Sets: There are two types currently in use; the 10,000 and 25,000 pound capacity set.

| VISIBLE DIFFERENCES BETWEEN THE 10,000 AND 25,000 POUND CAPACITY SLING SETS | | |
|---|---|---|
| ITEM | 10,000 lb. CAPACITY | 25,000 lb. CAPACITY |
| Sling Rope Color | Olive Drab | Black |
| Sling Rope Diameter | 7/8 in | 1 1/4 in |
| Clevis Color | Dull Gray Aluminum | Gold Steel |
| Number of Chain Links | 111 | 88 |
| Weight | 52 lbs. | 114 lbs. |

- Pallet Slings. Pallet slings have a carrying capacity of 4000 pounds. Two types of slings are in use: The MK 100 and MK 86.

| DIFFERENCES BETWEEN THE MK 86 AND MK 100 PALLET SLINGS | | | |
|---|---|---|---|
| Type | Color of Coded Tubing | Load Height 40 x 48 in pallet | Weight |
| MK 86 MK 100 | Black Yellow | 29 to 40 in. 48 to 70 in. | 13 lbs. 15 lbs. |

- Cargo Nets. There are two types currently in use; the 5,000 and 10,000 pound capacity net.

| VISIBLE DIFFERENCES BETWEEN THE 5,000 AND 10,000 POUND CAPACITY CARGO NETS | | |
|---|---|---|
| ITEM | 5,000 lb. CAPACITY | 10,000 lb. CAPACITY |
| Net Color | Olive Drab | Black |
| Material | Nylon Cord | Nylon mesh Cord |
| Load Zone Size | 5 ft. sq. | 6 ft. sq. |
| Weight | 58 lbs. | 96 lbs. |

- A-22 Cargo Bag. The bag is an adjustable cotton duck cloth and webbing container consisting of a sling assembly, cover, and four suspension webs. The bag can transport 2000 lbs. of cargo. It can be rigged with or without the cover.

Return of Air Items. Units must develop a detailed plan to return all air items (sling sets, nets and bags) to their supporting unit. The supporting unit will not be able to sustain aerial resupply operations without an effective plan to return these items.

## AERIAL RESUPPLY - FIXED WING

Fixed wing aircraft use a variety of methods to deliver supplies- Combat Off Load (COL), Containerized Delivery System (CDS), Door Bundles and Low Velocity Air Drop (LVAD).

Combat off load requires an operational and secure airfield/field landing strip, material handling equipment is not required to unload palletized supplies. However it should be available to move supplies of the runway or parking area. Fuel storage containers need to be available when using the Aerial Bulk Fuel Delivery System (ABFDS) or "Bladder Birds".

The CDS is the primary method of fixed wing resupply to combat units. Rigger units "rig" the supplies using A-22 containers. Max planning weight is 2000 lbs.

Door Bundles are used to resupply small elements, such as Special Operations Forces (SOF) and Long Range Reconnaissance Detachments (LRSD). Rigger units "rig" the supplies using A-21 containers.

The LVAD (Heavy Drop) uses aerial delivery platforms to deliver Maneuver, Maneuver Support, and Sustainment assets to the battle area. Rigger support and sufficient preparation time is critical to ensure a successful operation.

Parachute rigger units are necessary to configure/pack CDS, Door Bundles and LVAD loads. A rigger detachment can "rig" 50 short tons/day and a rigger company can "rig" 200 short tons/day of all classes of supply. The amounts can increase significantly if rigging involves only like items, i.e. Class I MREs only.

## Cargo Aircraft Capabilities and Dimensions

| Type | Cargo Compartment | | | # 463L Pallets | Fuel | CDS Bundles | PAX |
|------|--------|--------|--------|------|------|------|------|
| | Length | Height | Width | | | | |
| C-130 | 492 in. | 108 in | 120 in | 6 | 6k | 16 | 90 |
| C-141B | 1120 in. | 110 in. | 123 in. | 13 | 9k | 40 | 200 |
| C-17 | 986 in. | *162 in. | 216 in. | 18 | N/A | 40 | **102 |
| C-5A | 1452 in. | 162 | 228 in. | 36 | N/A | N/A | ***73 |
| KC-10 | 1508 in | 96 in **** | 218 in **** | 25 | N/A | N/A | 69 |

\* 162 in. aft of wing and 147.5 in. under wing
\*\* Potential for 84 additional seats
\*\*\* Contingency for 255 seats in cargo compartment
\*\*\*\* Some restrictions due to fuselage profile

*CHAPTER 33*

# SUSTAINMENT ASSETS

★★★

## 33.1 TRANSPORTATION – VEHICLE TYPES

**FMTV**

TRK CARGO, LMTV: M1078

TRK CARGO, LMTV: M1078
w/CANVAS CARGO TOP

TRK CARGO, LMTV: M1078
w/S-280 SHELTER

LMTV VAN: M1079

TRAILER, CGO, LMTV DROPSIDE:
M1082

TRK CARGO, MTV: M1083

TRK CARGO, MTV: M1083
w/CANVAS CARGO TOP

TRK CARGO, MTV: M1083
w/S-280 SHELTER

TRK CARGO, MTV: M1083
w/HEIGHT REDUCEABLE SHELTER

TRK CARGO, MTV w/MHE: M1084

TRK CARGO, MTV, LWB : M1085

## FMTV

TRK CARGO, MTV, LWB: M1085
w/CANVAS CARGO TOP

TRK CARGO, MTV, LWB: M1085
w/S-280 SHELTER

TRK CARGO, MTV, LWB w/MHE: M1086

TRK, VAN EXPANSIBLE, MTV: M1087

TRK TRACTOR, MTV: M1088

TRK WRECKER, MTV: M1089

TRK 5 TON DUMP, MTV: M1090

TRK TANK POL, MTV, 1500 GAL:
M1091

TRAILER, CGO, MTV DROPSIDE:
M1095

## HEMTT'S

TRUCK, CGO, HEMTT: M977

TRUCK, CGO, HEMTT, w/MHE (LT CRANE):
M977 TRUCK, CGO, HEMTT
w/MHE (MED CRANE): M985

TRUCK, ELECT POWER PLANT , HEMTT:
M977EPP

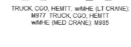

TRUCK, TANK FUEL SERVICEING, HEMTT,
2500 GAL: M978

TRUCK, POTABLE WATER SERVICEING, HEMTT,
M978

TRUCK, TRACTOR, HEMTT: M983

**HEMTT'S**

TRUCK, WRECKER, HEMTT: M984A1

TRUCK, GUIDED MISSILE TRANSPORTER,
HEMTT: M985GMT

TRUCK, HEMTT-LHS: M977 (XM-1120)

TRUCK, CGO, HEMTT- LHS
w/ 20 FT CONTAINER

TRUCK, CGO, HEMTT- LHS
w/MECC

TRUCK, CGO, HEMTT- LHS
w/FRS (NOTIONAL)

**M939 SERIES 5 TON VEHICLES**

TRUCK, CARGO, 5 TON: M923

M931 TRACTOR w/5000 GAL TANKER

TRUCK, CARGO, 5 TON: M923
w/CANVAS

M931 TRACTOR w/M871 (30FT FLAT BED TRAILER)

TRUCK, VAN EXPANSIBLE, 5 TON
6x6: M934

M931 TRACTOR w/M871 (30FT STAKE BED TRAILER)

TRUCK, TRACTOR, 5TON: M931

M931 TRACTOR w/M871 (30FT TRAILER) & 20 FT CONTAINER

**M915 SERIES TRUCK, TRACTOR, LINEHAUL**

TRUCK, TRACTOR, LINEHAUL: M915

M915 TRACTOR w/M872 (40FT FLAT BED TRAILER)

M915 TRACTOR w/7500 GAL TANKER

M915 TRACTOR w/M872 (40 FT STAKE BED TRAILER)

M915 TRACTOR w/M872 TRAILER & 40 FT CONTAINER

**HET**

TRUCK, TRACTOR, HEAVY EQUIPMENT TRANSPORT (HET): M1070

TRUCK, TRACTOR, HET w/M1000 TRAILER

TRUCK, TRACTOR,HET w/M1000 TRAILER & M1A1 ABRAMS MAIN BATTLE TANK

## MISCELLANEOUS ITEMS

FORKLIFT 4K

FORKLIFT 6K

FORKLIFT, 10K

MOBILE EXPANDIBLE CONTAINER
CONFIG. (MECC)

FORKLIFT, EXTENDED REACH
50K

CONTAINER 20FT

CONTAINER 40FT

ARMORED SECURITY VEHICLE
(ASV)

INTERIM ARMORED VEHICLE
(IAV) (WHEELED)  (NOTIONAL)

CUCV: M1008A1

CUCV: M1009

## CHAPTER 34

# MILITARY SYMBOLS GUIDE

## MILITARY SYMBOLS: UNIT TYPE

| Symbol | Label | Symbol | Label | Symbol | Label |
|---|---|---|---|---|---|
| AG | Adjutant Gen. | | (CHEM. cont) *Recon.* | MI | Military Intelligence |
| Air Force (surveillance) / Army | Aerial Obser. | SMOKE | *Smoke* | MP | Military Police |
| US / NATO | Airborne | CA | Civil Affairs | | Motorized |
| Y | AIR ASSAULT | DPU | Data Process. | | Mountain |
| V | *(no air)* | D | Dental | X | Ordinance |
| | Air Cavalry | | Engineer | | Petroleum |
| | Air Defense | EW | Elec. Warfare | | PSYOPS |
| | AMPHIBIOUS | • | Fld. Artillery | | Quartermaster |
| | *Engineer* | | Finance | RGR | Ranger |
| | Antiarmor | | INFANTRY | RHU | Replacement |
| | Armor | | *Light* | | Rocket ARTY |
| | Armored CAV | | *Mechanized* | SVC | Service |
| | ARMY AVIATION *(rotary)* | | *BIFV mount.* | | Signal |
| | *(fixed)* | | *" dismount.* | | Sound Ranging |
| | Attack Heli. | | *Motorized* | SF | Special Forces |
| | Bridging | L | Labor | | SUPPLY |
| | Cavalry/recon. | | Maintenance | | *" & Maint.* |
| | CHEMICAL (NBC) | | Medical | | *" & Trans.* |
| DECON | *Decon* | MET | Meteorological | SPT | Support |

385

# MILITARY SYMBOLS: SIZE & MARKING/INSTALLATION ROLE IND

## UNIT SIZE

The size of units and installations is shown by placing the appropriate size indicator directly above the basic symbol.

| US Description | STANAG 2019 Description | Symbol |
|---|---|---|
| Squad/crew | Smallest unit/UK section | |
| Section or unit larger than a squad but smaller than a platoon | Unit larger than a US squad/UK section but smaller than a platoon equivalent | |
| Platoon or detachment | Platoon/troop equivalent | |
| Company, battery, or troop | Company/battery/squadron equivalent | |
| Battalion or squadron | Battalion equivalent | |
| Group or regiment | Regiment/group equivalent | |
| Brigade | Brigade equivalent | |
| Division | Division | |
| Corps | Corps | |
| Army | Army | |
| | Army group/front | |
| Battalion task force | | |
| Company team | | |

## MARKING SYMBOLS

size of unit

unit designation

higher echelons of command

branch or duty performed

other information (DTG)

Unit Symbols:
Friendly    Enemy

## COLLECTING POINTS

| | |
|---|---|
| CAN | Canibalization |
| CIV | Civilian |
| DECON | DECON Station |
| | Maintanance |
| EPW | Prisoners of War |
| SALV | Salvage |
| S | Stragglers |

## MISCELLANEOUS

| | |
|---|---|
| | Graves Reg. SVC |
| | Hospital |
| MMC | Material MGT CTR |
| | Parking |
| A | Topographic |
| | Traffic Control |
| | Water |

## EXAMPLES

| | |
|---|---|
| 10 — XX — 1/8 | 10th Infantry Division, III Corps, Eighth Army |
| 2 — XX — A/2-15/10 | 2d Platoon, A Company, 2d Battalion, 15th Infantry, 10th Infantry Division |
| 125 — XXX — 3 (US) | 125th Infantry Brigade (Mech), III (US) Corps |

# MILITARY SYMBOLS: UNIT TYPE/INSTALLATION ROLE INDICATOR

| | | |
|---|---|---|
| SAM | (C & E cont.) Dummy Radio | CL V (cont.) Army Air |
| SSM | Commo. CTR | Artillery |
| Survey | TGT Designator | Chemical |
| Topographic | Telephone CTR | Mines |
| Transportation | Teleprinter | Nuclear |
| RPV (unmanned air recon.) | Unknown | Rocket ARTY |
| Veterinary | | Small Arms |

**LOGISTICS INSTALLATIONS**

**COMMUNICATIONS & ELECTRONICS INSTALLATIONS**

| | | |
|---|---|---|
| ADA Radar | Class I Subsistence | Class VI Pers. Demand |
| ARTY Loc. Radar | Class II Clothing/Equip | Class VII Major End |
| Data Proc. CTR. | Class III(POL) Air Force | Class VIII Medical |
| Direction Finding | Army Air | Class IX Repair Parts |
| Elec. Warfare | Ground | Class X Non-Military |
| GND Surv. Radar | Solid Fuel | All Classes |
| Intercept | Class IV Construction | Multiple Classes |
| Jamming | Class V Ammunition All | |
| Radio Relay | Air Defense | |
| Radio | Air Force | |
| | AMMO Transfer Point | |

387

# GLOSSARY

★★★

**AA** – Avenue of approach – where the enemy could come. Typically, two or more adjacent AAs become a Mobility Corridor.

**AO** – Area of operation

**AOR** – Area of Operational Responsibility. Usually Corps or higher

**ADA** – Air Defense Artillery. Now a part of the Fires Branch and Fires Warfighting Functional Area.

**ASL** – Authorized Stockage List. A stockpile of Class IX repair parts usually associated with a Service Support Activity (SSA)

**BFSB** – Battlefield Surveillance Brigade. Now referred to as the Reconnaissance & Surveillance Brigade

**BSA** – Brigade Support Area – A designated area in which sustainment elements of the Brigade Combat Team provide support to a brigade. The Brigade Support Battalion (BSB) manages the terrain and unit locations.

**BSB** – Brigade Support Battalion. BSBs assigned to Brigade Combat Teams (BCTs) have three companies (Distro, Fwd Maint, and Medical). BSBs assigned to Support Brigades (CAB, MEB, Fires) only have two companies (Distro, Maint).

**CCIR** – Commander's Critical Information Requirements – Information required by the commander that directly affects his/her decision and dictates the successful execution of operational or tactical operations. CCIR normally result in the generation of two types of information requirements: priority intelligence requirements (PIR), and friendly force information requirements (FFIR).

**CCL** – Combat Configured Load – A planned package of ammunition or other supplies that are transported as a single load to support a type unit or weapon system. This can be air, rail, or other means of transport. This may also be referred to as "OCL" (Operational Configured Load) or "MCL" (Mission Configured Load)

**CDS** – Container Delivery System

**COA** – Course of Action

**CRSP** – Centralized Receiving & Shipping Point. A CRSP provides a centralized supply distribution operation within an AO where cargo is delivered and backhaul is picked up. This is accomplished using regular sustainment deliveries between FOBs. CRSPs employ the familiar "hub and spoke" concept.

**CSC** – Convoy Support (or Service) Center

**CSSB** – Combat Sustainment Support Battalion

**CSR** – Controlled Supply Rate – The rate of ammunition consumption that can be supported, considering availability, facilities, and transportation. It is expressed in rounds per unit, individual, or vehicle per day. A unit may not draw ammunition in excess of its CSR without authority from its next higher headquarters.

**CSS** – Combat Service Support – The essential capabilities, functions, activities, and tasks necessary to sustain all elements of operating forces in theater at all levels of war. This term is now considered obsolete with the publication of the Feb 08 FM 3-0 *Operations* and FM 4-0 *Sustainment.*

**DS** – Direct Support – A mission requiring a force to support another specific force and authorizing it to answer directly the supported force's request for assistance.

**EEFI** – Essential Elements of Friendly Information – Key questions likely to be asked by adversary officials and intelligence systems about specific friendly intention, capabilities, and activities so they can obtain answers critical to their operational effectiveness. The critical aspects of a friendly operation that, if known by the enemy, would subsequently compromise, lead to failure, or limit success of the operation, and therefore must be protected from enemy detection.

**EN** – Engineers

**EOD** – Explosive Ordnance Disposal – The detection, identification, on-site evaluation, rendering safe, recovery, and final disposal of unexploded explosive ordnance.

**ESC** – Expeditionary Support Command. Also designated as SC(E)

**ESP** – Engineer Supply Point, sometimes also known as a Class IV point.

**FDRP** – Final (or First) Destination Release Point

**FFIR** – Friendly Forces Information Requirement – Information the commander and staff need about the forces available for the operation. This includes personnel, maintenance, supply, ammunition, petroleum, oils, and lubricants status, and experience and leadership capabilities.

**FLE/B** – Forward Logistics Element/Base

**FLS** – Forward Landing Strip

**FMC** – Full Mission Capable, Material condition of an aircraft or training device indicating that it can perform all of its missions.

**FSC** – Forward Support Company

**IPB** – Intelligence Preparation of the Battlefield – A systematic approach to analyzing the enemy, weather, and terrain in a specific geographic area. It integrates enemy doctrine with the weather and terrain as they relate to the mission and the specific battlefield environment. This is done to determine and evaluate enemy capabilities, vulnerabilities, and probable courses of action.

**ISR Plan** – Intelligence, Surveillance, and Reconnaissance Plan. Term is rescinded and now referred to as the Intelligence Collection Plan (see FM 3-55).

**LCOP** – Logistics Common Operating Picture

**LEW** – Logistics Estimate Worksheet

**LOC** – Lines of Communication – All the routes, land, water, and air, which connect operating military force with a base of operations and along which supplies and military forces move.

**LSA – Logistics** Support Area – An area normally located in rear and often positioned near air-landing facilities along the main supply route. An LSA often contains Support Maintenance units and Level III medical assets. Typically, a Maneuver Enhancement Brigade (MEB) might be co-located along with a Rear Area Operations Center (RAOC).

**MCOO** – Modified Combined Obstacles Overlay – The MCOO is a graphic terrain analysis on which all other IPB products are based. A MCOO is produced when a combination or terrain overlays are put together. It should contain at a minimum: NO-Go terrain, SLOW-GO terrain, built-up areas, LOCs, river and water obstacles, obstacles, key terrain, AAs and MCs, objectives, and other critical terrain features for a CSB.

**MC** – Mobility corridor. Usually composed of two or more Avenues of Approach (AA)

**MEB** – Maneuver Enhancement Brigade.

**MDMP** – Military Decision Making Process

**MP** – Military Police

**MSO** – Mission Staging Operation. Mission Staging Operations are initiated by Division order, conducted by the BCT/Spt Bde and enabled by the local Sustainment Brigade at a forward location within the Bde AO. MSO tasks are METT-TC based; may include planning, rehearsals, and limited reorganization ICW sustainment tasks required. The Sustainment Brigade provides replenishment to the BSB/FSC's along with field services and/ or other services as required.

**MSR** – Main Supply Route – The route or routes designated within an area of operations upon which the bulk of traffic flows in support of military operations.

**MST** – Maintenance Support Team – A tailored direct support team that co-locates with a unit maintenance element for a designated period.

**NAI** – Named Area of Interest – A point or area along a particular avenue of approach through which enemy activity is expected to occur. Activity or lack of activity within an NAI will help to confirm or deny a particular enemy course of action.

**OPCON** - Operational Control – Transferable command authority that may be exercised by commanders at any echelon at or below the level of combatant command. Operational Control may be delegated and is the authority to perform those functions of command over subordinate forces involving organizing and employing commands and forces, assigning tasks, designative objectives, and giving authoritative direction necessary to accomplish the mission.

**OPORD** – Operation Order – A directive issues by a commander to subordinate commander for the purpose of effecting the coordinated execution of an operation.

**OPLAN** – Operation Plan – Any plan, except for the Single Integrated Operation Plan for the conduct of military operations. An operation plan is the draft document used to lay out the requirements for an operation. OPLANs become OPORDs.

**PIR** – Priority Intelligence Requirements – Those intelligence requirements for which a commander has an anticipated and stated priority in his/her task of planning and decision-making.

**RFI** - Request for Information

**RO** – Replenishment Operation. Preplanned sustainment operations that allow combat forces to replenish. They may be immediate, but usually routine. They are however, time sensitive, deliberate sustainment operations conducted by the CSSB or BSB to replenish FSCs, or by the FSC to conduct quick, in-stride replenishment of the maneuver or maneuver support battalion.

**ROZ** – Restricted operating zone

**RSR** – Required Supply Rate – The amount of ammunition expressed in terms of rounds per weapon per day for ammunition items fired by weapons, and in terms of other units of measure per day for bulk allotment and other items, estimated to be required to sustain operations of any designated force without restriction for a specified period.

**SEAD** – Suppression of enemy air defense

**SPO** – Support Plans Officer

**TMR** – Transportation Movement Request. A request for movement of personnel, commodities or other items beyond unit capabilities. If reoccurring for same haul mission, it becomes an STMR (Standard Transportation Movement Request)

**TOC** – Tactical Operations Center – A physical group of those elements of an organization concerned with the current tactical operations and tactical support of an operation. Used in conjunction with the term *Command Post* (CP)

**TSC** – Theater Sustainment Command. Also designated as SC(T)

# Acronyms

| | |
|---|---|
| AMC | Army Material Command |
| AO | Area of Operations |
| AOI | Area of Influence |
| APOD | Aerial Port of Debarkation |
| AOR | Area of Responsibility |
| ARFOR | Army Forces |
| AFSB | Army Field Support Brigade |
| AHRS | Army Human Resource System |
| BAS | Battalion Aid Station |
| BCS3 | Battle Command Sustainment Support System |
| BFT | Blue Force Tracker |
| BMO | Battalion Motor Officer |
| BSA | Brigade Support Area |
| BSB | Brigade Support Battalion |
| BTB | Brigade Troops Battalion |

| | |
|---|---|
| C2 | Command and Control |
| CAB | Combined Arms Battalion |
| CABSA | Combined Arms Battalion Support Area |
| CAISI | Combat Service Support Automated Information System Interface |
| -BM | Bridge Module |
| -CL | Client Module |
| CENTCOM | Central Command |
| COCOM | Combatant Commander |
| CROP | Container Roll-in Roll-out Platform |
| CSSB | Combat Sustainment Support Battalion |
| CTASC | Corps Theater Automated Service Center |

| | |
|---|---|
| CTCP | Combat Trains Command Post |
| DCGS-A | Distributed Common Ground System - Army |
| DLA | Defense Logistics Agency |
| ESC | Sustainment Command (Expeditionary) |
| FBCB2 | Force XXI Battle Command, Brigade and Below |
| FLOT | Forward Line of Own Troops |
| FHP | Force Health Protection |
| FLB | Forward Logistical Base |
| FLE | Forward Logistical Element |
| FSC | Forward Support Company |
| HRSC | Human Resources Support Center |
| HSS | Health Systems Support |

| | |
|---|---|
| ILAP | Intragrated Logistics Analysis Program |
| ISB | Intermediate Staging Base |
| IAW | In Accordance With |
| ITV | In transit Visibility |
| JOA | Joint Operational Area |
| JFC | Joint Forces Command |
| LOC | Lines of Communication |
| LOGPAC | Logistics Package |
| LRP | Logistics Release Point |
| MCB | Movement Control Battalion |
| MSO | Mission Staging Operations |
| MTS | Movement Tracking System |
| OPCON | Operational Control |
| PLS | Palletized Load System |

# Acronyms

| | |
|---|---|
| PBUSE | Property Book Unit Supply-Enhanced |
| RO | Replenishment Operations |
| RSOI | Reception Staging Onward Movement and Integration |
| RCC | Regional Combatant Commander |
| RFID | Radio Frequency Identification |
| SAAS-MOD | Standard Army Ammunition System-Modernized |
| SAMS | Standard Army Maintenance System |
| SARSS | Standard Army Retail Supply System |
| SDDC | Surface Deployment and Distribution Command |
| SP | Supply Point |
| SPO | Support Operations Officer |
| SPOD | Sea Port of Debarkation |
| STB | Special Troops Battalion |
| SUS Bde | Sustainment Brigade |
| TACON | Tactical Control |
| TASMG | Theater Aviation Sustainment Maintenance Group |
| TAV | Total Asset Visibility |
| TCAM | TAMMIS Customer Assistance Module |
| TMIP | Theater Medical Information Program |
| TSC | Sustainment Command (Theater) |
| UD | Unit Distribution |
| UMCP | Unit Maintenance Collection Point |
| USFK | United States Forces in Korea |
| USTC | United States Transportation Command |
| VSAT | Very Small Aperture Terminal |

Made in the USA
Middletown, DE
08 February 2015